Surviving Intimate Terrorism

Hedda Nussbaum

Introduction by
Gloria Steinem

Afterword by
Samuel C. Klagsbrun, MD

PublishAmerica
Baltimore

First printing

ISBN: 1-4137-5652-2
PUBLISHED BY PUBLISHAMERICA, LLLP
www.publishamerica.com
Baltimore

Printed in the United States of America

JUN 0 6 2006

This book is dedicated

To the memory of my beloved little girl, Lisa,

To my dear little boy, Mitchell,
Who is now a young man named Travis,

To the memory of those who have died
because of domestic violence,

and

To all the brave survivors of family abuse.

Acknowledgments

I would like to thank the following people for their invaluable help during the 15 years it took me to complete this book:

The staff and editors at PublishAmerica; Archie Gresham and Linda Crawford for their indispensable editorial assistance; my agents, Fifi Oscard and Charlotte Sheedy; Douglas and Aimee for producing graphics and a cover design; Jan Phillips for helping me break through a major block; Gloria Steinem and Jeremy W. Prince for their priceless suggestions; and Dr. Samuel Klagsbrun, Naomi Weiss, Betty Levinson, and my sister, Judy Liebman, for their continued love and support.

Note to Readers:

If you have experienced family abuse,
please use the blank space in this book to jot down
your own thoughts, feelings and experiences.

Introduction

By Gloria Steinem

*"Drop a frog in hot water and it will leap out to
save itself. Heat the water little by little and it will die."*
—Proverb

In the early 1970s when the [*contemporary!*] Women's Movement was just getting under way, I was traveling as a speaker and organizer with Florynce Kennedy. As a pioneer in family law as well as a civil rights activist, she had a much better idea than I of what we would find.

"You'll see," she said, "wherever a dozen or so women are gathered together, there will be at least a couple who've been beaten by the men they live with."

I thought Flo was exaggerating or reflecting her experience as a lawyer, but after a couple of years of listening to random audiences in suburbs and inner cities, union halls and universities, I had to admit that she was right. Wherever discussions lasted long enough, whenever women felt safe enough, there were stories of humiliation and violence at the hands of lovers and husbands.

Indeed, those stories were second in number only to revelations of childhood sexual abuse, yet the violations suffered in adulthood seem to have

9

resulted in even more self-blame. After all, Freud himself, who wrongly accused children of "fantasizing" sex with their parents, didn't blame the children in the few cases he admitted were real. Yet family, friends, and professionals tended to blame grown-up women for having incited or "asked for" male violence, or for "choosing" violent men. Psychologists spoke of "female masochism" as if it were biological and looked for the cause of violence in the victim as much as in the victimizer. Even police complained about having to answer "domestic incident" calls and treated male-on-female violence as if it were inevitable. Indeed, I can think of no other crime in which the goal was to get the victim and the criminal back together again.

Meanwhile, the Women's Movement was not only a place where women's experiences became visible but also a place where they could be named; in this case, by creating new terms like "battered women" and "domestic violence," a big step considering that violence between lovers and spouses had just been called "life." Yet the world behind closed doors remained outside the law because of ideas about "private" versus "public," or "a man's home is his castle", with no parallel that a woman's body was her own, or calling what happens to men "political" but what happens to women "cultural." *Earlier, "wife beating"*

No wonder so many battered women blamed themselves, despite the fact that the estimated one in eight men who are violent toward their partners made the problem hard to avoid. No wonder so many responded with obedience, despair, or more concern for their children than themselves. Some told stories of successful escapes but, as later studies would show, escaping was also the point of maximum danger, the time when men hooked on control were losing their drug of choice and might do anything to get it back. For the most part, women were just existing day to day as broken-spirited inhabitants of private concentration camps. If well-meaning outsiders tried to intervene, they rarely did so with more than the naïve question, "Why don't you just leave?" Few kept on trying after a woman had left and returned, as most women did at least once out of hope or fear.

No wonder so many men stayed locked in their prisons of self-justified violence, prisons that probably felt like the home of their own childhood. If we grow up learning there are only two possible choices, to be the victim or the victimizer, then gender roles come along later to convince us that the first is "feminine," the second is "masculine." The result may look different for women and men, but the root cause is the same. Since "masculine" and "feminine" qualities are simply human traits that are natural within everyone, women then suppress their anger because it's "masculine," and men reject their empathy because it's "feminine," a denial of wholeness that society reinforces in infinite ways. For example, it's probably no exaggeration to say that the woman a man most fears is the woman within himself.

After much listening, I began to sense what Judith Herman would later document in her landmark book, *Trauma and Recovery*. She compared the trauma suffered by (mostly) women and children in domestic wars with that suffered by (mostly) men in military wars and concluded that, though trauma is trauma—there should be no competition of tears—the first is often more spirit-breaking. For one thing, it happens when we are more vulnerable, for longer periods, and with less likelihood of support from others in the same situation. For another, the perpetrator is not a stranger or enemy, but someone we love who may plead with us for forgiveness after each beating, or tell us we brought it on ourselves by our imperfections, or alternate fear and pain with love and support, or turn our homes into places of suffering that are so invisible to the rest of the world that we are returned or accused of desertion if we run away. Like abusive parents, batterers may even convince us that our pain is "for our own good," or that this punishment "hurts me more than you." For all these reasons, it may become the ultimate annihilation of the sense of self.

On the other hand, when kidnappers or terrorists take hostages—usually men as well as women, and for financial or political reasons that are far less intimate—studies show that even those hostages tend to retain feelings of fear and dependency long after they regain freedom. This is so common that it has been given a name: the Stockholm syndrome. How much deeper are the feelings instilled in women who have lived with and loved the enemy? Slept with him and borne his children? Known him in kinder times before pregnancy or child-rearing made him feel displaced as the center of her universe? Heard threats of violence that could follow them anywhere? Even the lethal promise, "If I can't have you, no one will?" If women have any doubt about who has the upper hand, they have only to read the newspapers to see how rarely a batterer goes to jail, how quixotic police procedures and restraining orders still are, and how often a woman is murdered by a husband or lover.

When Flo and I began traveling, it was too early to see shelters. Though we later learned that at least one had started in California in the mid 1960s, we mostly saw individual feminists who were beginning to take women and kids into their own homes or drive them secretly across state lines in search of new identities and safety. Some were lobbying to reform laws, police procedures, and courts so that violence inside the family would be taken as seriously as violence outside it. Others took up the cause of women in prison who had been convicted of murder or manslaughter because a plea of self-defense wasn't even offered.

It wasn't until I went to England that I saw my first shelter: Women's Aid in Chiswick, West London, a pioneering effort that would eventually lead to a Women's Aid movement of hundreds of shelters, plus a national phone hotline. A television documentary had been made about some of the women at Chiswick, and I brought it home to show on public television. Because I introduced it on camera, I became the recipient of questions that I might have asked myself before I had had the luck of listening:

How can there be so many battered women when no one I know has this problem, and I don't see it in my community? It may be hidden in plain sight. If you ask, listen and make truth-telling acceptable. There are probably few groups that are exempt. For example, a survey on Long Island found that the most frequent occupation of battering men was "police officer." In Israel where traditional charities assumed that a lower rate of alcoholism and a higher status for women made domestic violence a non-problem, the first shelter funded by the progressive New Israel Fund brought together so many Israeli and Palestinian women that they co-founded a women's peace movement. They united against violence at home *and* between Israelis and Palestinians, and also explained that the former normalized the latter. Like the Irish peace women who won the Nobel Peace Prize for crossing religious lines to work for peace, they traced violence from the streets to its birthplace in the home.

Doesn't violence happen because men drink or lose their jobs so they can't support their families? True, alcohol weakens inhibitions, but it rarely creates what isn't there in the first place. Gentle men tend to become gentle drunks, and violent men become dangerous ones. Drunk or sober, many men are peaceful, so violence isn't inevitable in a biological sense. In fact, it's often the other way around: men drink in order to excuse their violence. As for job loss, spending money on alcohol and adding physical to economic pain is hardly a logical response to poverty. If it were, women would also be doing this to the same degree, especially since they are far more likely to be poor and jobless. Clearly, the problem is not so much the loss of a job as the loss of "masculine" superiority. For example, a survey of an affluent, white Connecticut precinct and a poor Harlem precinct found about the same incidence of violence per household. What the two had in common was not economics, but a shared idea that "masculinity" required superiority to women.

Have you ever been hit by a man? No. In some ways, I think this is why I can believe survivors. I don't have to find fault with their behavior in order to bury old fears or tell myself that it can't happen to me again. I know my safety has been almost entirely a matter of luck. I had a gentle father, so I didn't grow up believing that male violence was inevitable or excusable, and my work shows me everyday that good judgment is not enough to protect me. For instance, when *Ms. Magazine* did its first major cover story on domestic violence, I called a friend who had the most delicate, flower-like face I could imagine. If contrasted with a realistic black eye and facial cuts created by make-up, her photograph would make a shocking cover image. After I explained this, there was a long silence on the other end of the phone. Then she said, "You know, don't you?" Her ex-husband, the well-educated and respected son of a prominent New York family, had beaten her throughout their marriage. She was one of the lucky ones who got away.

I offer all of the above as a bridge to Hedda Nussbaum's story for several reasons.

For one thing, I needed those experiences before I began to uncover my own growing-up memories of violence—memories that must have been too close for comfort—which says something about the power of denial.

How could I have forgotten the hours I'd spent lying awake in bed, listening to blows and cries coming from the apartment downstairs in our two-family house? I knew the husband as a handsome and swaggering young factory worker, and the wife as a sad woman in her twenties who had confessed to me that she was a few years older than her husband and grateful to him for marrying her. After beatings, he often locked her out of the apartment in her nightgown, even in the snow and ice of a Midwestern winter, until neighbors called the police. They never arrested him, just ushered her back into the house.

How could I have blotted out the memory of my friends' mothers who took refuge in each other's houses on weekends when their husbands were drunk and violent? Or the local Catholic priest who responded only by warning them against disobeying their husbands? (Men can't control their violent or sexual instincts, he explained, so it's women who are responsible.) Why had I forgotten the neighbor who lost her job at the phone company because she was ashamed to go to work until the bruises went away? Or the walking-on-

eggshells feeling I had when entering a girlfriend's house where a violent brother-in-law ruled the roost?

These experiences briefly drew me into a fundamentalist Christian church when I was in junior high school. Religion seemed to be the only force powerful enough to tame violent men, even though I saw no such evidence. (Decades later, Andrea Dworkin would write a brilliant book, *Right-Wing Women*, that explained the appeal of fundamentalism to women for this reason—at best, an exchange of freedom for safety.) In high school, violent scenes from my working class neighborhood added to my determination to go to college. I wrongly thought that education and class would be protection. Later still, I remember the moment of standing with a group of women in a New York street at night, finishing up the discussion after a meeting, and realizing that the street belonged to us, too; we weren't inviting violence by being there. It was an epiphany.

How much of our behavior is motivated by this idea that women are at fault for violence by our very presence?

For another thing, I hope that my memories might provide a context for the blame and disbelief with which Hedda was greeted when she was led out of her concentration camp. She was clinging to life by a thread after years of torture, malnutrition, brainwashing, and drugs, yet some people—perhaps especially women—blamed her as much as or more than Joel Steinberg for the death of Lisa, their six-year-old adopted daughter. Part of this was the death of a child, for which any woman present is likely to be held more responsible, but it was Joel who had beaten Lisa, and Hedda who had pleaded with him until he had allowed her to call 911.

"Even Steinberg could not satisfy Hedda's appetite for self-annihilation." That was the promotional blurb in *Vanity Fair* for an excerpt from Joyce Johnson's Hedda-blaming book, *What Lisa Knew*. I did not know Hedda except for what I had read of her in the newspapers, but I had met Tina Brown, editor of *Vanity Fair*, so I called her to object to the misplacing of blame. What I got was not an apology or an explanation that this was the writer's view, but Tina Brown's own angry attack on Hedda for "choosing" to bring a second adopted child, a day-old infant named Mitch, into a sadistic household.

In fact, Steinberg had asked a physician friend to be on the lookout for an adoptable male infant —without any knowledge or consent from Hedda— and this "son" for Joel had just been brought over one day. Hedda tried to love and care for him, though she was incapable of loving or caring for herself.

Even Susan Brownmiller, the admirable author of *Against Our Will*, a pioneering book on rape, wrote an article about the Steinberg murder trial that took Hedda to task, and followed it with a fictionalized version that did the same. I was angry and discouraged by this and other responses, but I also understood the need to identify some internal fault in Hedda. Then, if only we didn't have that fault, we would be saved from her terrible fate.

In his Afterword to this book, Samuel Klagsbrun, the wise and kind psychiatrist who saw Hedda through years of treatment at his Four Winds Hospital, also admits to assuming that part of his task was to help discover the roots of her pathological masochism. Only after months of examining her family history and communicating with her deepest self did he realize there was no masochism. Hedda had simply fallen in love with and become the prisoner of a charismatic man who happened to be exactly the right person to annihilate her sense of self. It was Dr. Klagsbrun's own training that had led him to look for the cause of suffering in the sufferer.

Probably, under exactly the right circumstances, each of us could suffer some parallel fate. That is part of our shared humanity. Yes, we are all responsible for our actions if they are within our power. If feminism stands for anything, it's for taking responsibility for our lives. But the question is still, where does the power lie?

Now, more people would recognize the signs of danger. There are more shelters and more education programs. Men, too, are involved in ending this "domestic violence" that might better be called "original violence," so much is it the wellspring of violence outside the home. Groups like the Family Violence Prevention Fund have involved male athletes and sports coaches in its national effort. Also now the agenda is forcing the criminal to leave home instead of the victim, and jailing the criminals who have previously only been given a restraining order.

This brave book is an important part of that education and change. It shows us how an intelligent woman with a nonviolent childhood, who was a middle-class professional with a way to express herself and had a family that loved her, could be turned into an automaton without anger or will. It happened inch by inch, day by day, with control turned up as gradually as the heating of the frog in water.

By helping us to understand how this can happen, Hedda Nussbaum's words will help us to keep it from happening.

But many more books will be necessary to explain Joel Steinberg.

Prologue

My muse speaks to me: Listen to me, Hedda. Don't fear Joel's power. It's gone. You have the power now—power over your own thoughts, memories, and words. He can't hurt you. His words won't misguide you anymore. Let your own words come, let them flow. It's okay. You have the strength, the energy, the inspiration, the dedication. It's there. Fear it not. Fear him not. You are *you*—only *you*. He is gone. He is no more. Now his words can teach others—in a very different way. *You* can see through them, so don't be afraid of them. You are in control. You have the power. You are made of strong fibers, tough meat, intense heart, love, goodness, truth—and yes, beauty. Fear not evil. That evil can be used to do good now. Its power is in *your* hands—your goddess hands that will do no harm, only blessed good. You, Hedda, will continue to save lives of women and children. Just trust in yourself and in me. I'm here. Surprise! Hello! We meet at last. Yes, I've replaced *him*—Boo to his evil. *We*—you and I—will use our power to do good for all women and children. We are blessed. You are blessed. Smile.

My muse, of course, is really me. Her words are my words; her insights, mine. Finally, after struggling for years with this manuscript, unable to allow Joel Steinberg more than a phrase or a sentence, I fathomed the reason. His powerful hour-long monologues, which had fascinated me while I was under his power, terrified me after I understood the evil they held. But my muse's words have freed me, and so this book has emerged with the hope of bringing insights and enlightenment to other women—of saving other children even though my understanding came too late to save my own.

Mine is a story of transformations, of metamorphoses, first from a normal, shy, young woman in love into a battered, bruised, and numbed robot. The source of my transition was a manipulative, controlling, depraved man who tortured and brainwashed me repeatedly, year after year, causing me to become psychologically damaged and trapped in his evil web. Because his abuse began slowly and subtly, I continued to love the man until escape became impossible. And finally, by the time disaster struck, I'd been brought down about as far as anyone can go. Joel Steinberg's actions, together with the protective numbing my brain offered, caused me to stop functioning almost totally, hastening the end for my daughter. But did that mean the end for me? No, I got back on my feet and used the power within me to turn this tragedy on its head.

And that, of course, is the second metamorphosis: from the numbed automaton I describe above to one who experienced an epiphany, which I call "The Day My Eyes Opened," enabling me to stop loving Joel and be a convincing witness at his trial. Over time and with the support of good friends, loving family, and a marvelous psychiatrist, I was transformed a third time into the woman I am today: strong-minded, healthy, outspoken, and committed to helping other victims of domestic violence.

I pray that my story will be an inspiration to women to see the truth before it's too late and to use their inner strength to save their own lives and those of their children. If this book saves just one child or one mother, I will be content. If it saves even more, I will be fulfilled.

Safe

November 3, 1987. Safe. Now I'm safe in this hospital and I can rest. For once I can close my eyes, cuddle into a blanket, and fall asleep in a real bed. So what if I'm handcuffed to it? Joel will have both of us out on bail in a few hours, Lisa will be fine, and we'll get Mitchell back. Everything'll be okay. I can always rely on Joel to make things all right again.

The past two days have been pure hell. I find it hard to even think about it all—so much horror. And amazingly, sweet little Mitch seemed to understand that things weren't right. When I kept telling him to go back to sleep, he did—no matter how many hours he'd just slept and no matter how wet his diaper may have been. He knew. Somehow, he knew I had more than enough to deal with.

He was still sleeping when the EMS workers arrived and took Lisa off to St. Vincent's. Joel went along too, and I stayed home because I looked such a mess. With two new black eyes added to my split lip, broken nose, and right leg oozing bright yellow pus, Joel obviously didn't want any medical people observing me.

Lisa'd been unconscious all night. I'd tried—oh, how I'd tried for hours—to revive her, but I failed. Thank heavens she's in good, professional hands now, especially since Joel and I gave them permission to drill a hole in her skull and relieve the pressure. I'll bet by now she's up and alert. I can't wait to see my little girl again.

When the two detectives arrived, Joel was already back from the hospital. After they questioned the two of us for a while, they asked us if we'd like to go to the precinct with them.

"Are we under arrest?" Joel had inquired.

"No, it'll just be more convenient for us to question you there," the cop told us. And he wasn't lying. It was more convenient for them to have us in custody—since they obviously intended to arrest one or both of us.

And they did end up arresting us both because I wasn't about to tell them what had happened or where my bruises came from. Why would I hurt Joel like that? After all, I knew Lisa'd be fine very soon, and then we'd all go home. But every time I asked that nice police woman to call the hospital to check on Lisa's status, she said there was no change. *Strange*, I thought. *Well, it may take a little longer than I'd imagined, but she'll be fine in no time.* And by now I'm sure she is. I'm sure she is.

So after leaving the precinct, in shock from all those reporters crowding around us with flashbulbs popping—*What's with them? Why all the fuss because my daughter's in the hospital?* That's what I kept thinking. It was all so strange. And worse, later, when I went to Bellevue to the ER, someone had a newspaper—a *Daily News*—with a headline that read, "House of Horror," about OUR house. I was aghast.

They'd gotten it all wrong. Lisa was such a happy child. This was all so weird. So very weird.

Just sitting and waiting for hours in the special emergency room for prisoners was an ordeal. There I was with my hands cuffed behind me, very hungry because all I'd eaten all day was the sandwich the police had brought in for me at the precinct hours before, and it was probably about 2:00 a.m. by then, I think. I was so happy to see a man coming around with sandwiches. He tossed one to me, but how was I supposed to eat it without hands? Fortunately, the guy sitting next to me had his hands cuffed in front, so he held the sandwich for me while I ate it.

The only reason I even went to Bellevue was this: As I sat in the big cell at Central Booking where Joel and I had been taken at first, I was among maybe six or seven women. We sat on the benches or the floor for hours, and everyone talked—except me. I refused to tell them my story.

"It's too sad to talk about," I told them. I wasn't going to start telling tales. I knew what prisoners think about someone jailed for hurting a child; Joel had told me about that many times. So even though I hadn't hurt Lisa, I decided to keep my mouth shut. It's what Joel would have told me to do, I'm sure.

But the others had all been exchanging anecdotes while I sat quietly, and I heard it all.

"You don't get any food til morning if you stay here," one of them said. "But if you go to the hospital, you can get lots of food."

Okay, I had thought, *my bandages need to be changed, so I'll tell them I have to go to the hospital.* That's how I got to Bellevue where I learned that my right leg—the one Joel had beaten into a dreadful state that he never healed for me as he'd promised—was in worse condition than I'd realized. I might have died, a doctor told me, if I hadn't gotten help soon.

So that's why they sent me here, to Elmhurst
Hospital in Queens, where women prisoners are kept.
But, no more thinking. For now, I'll just sleep.

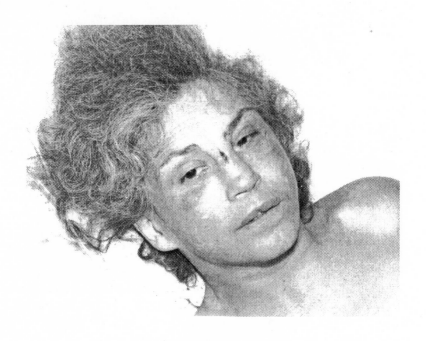

In Elmhurst Hospital, November 1987.

Mr. Right?

The first time I saw him was at a single's party in the Spring of 1975. He was sitting across from me on a plush blue couch, flanked by two others, but I scarcely noticed them at all. Although I was aware of my friend Risa's presence beside me, my attention was focused on the shining hazel eyes and equally dazzling words of Joel Steinberg. Since those eyes were meeting mine the whole time, his words seemed to be directed to me alone.

"That day the wind was blowing at fifty miles an hour, and we were flying—literally flying—across the water. Ah, it was so invigorating! But sometimes, when the breeze is gentle, the boat glides softly and peacefully, and the sail is a dreamy experience." Joel's words entranced me.

I could feel the wind in my hair, the ocean spray on my face. His words brought the sailing experience alive for me, though my one encounter with the sport, that summer I'd attended Harvard Summer School, had been a near disaster with me ending up in the polluted Charles River. Suddenly, however, sailing seemed like heaven and the man taking me on that rapturous trip nothing short of sublime.

Risa and I were at a party given for prospective members of a summer house in the Hamptons, a seaside resort on the south shore of eastern Long Island known for its attraction to singles. You rented a share or a half share for a summer, and there you hoped to meet your soul mate—if you were a woman, that is. For most of the men, the desire was rather less romantic.

Risa was a former roommate and friend since college. We'd been through much together, including a car crash in Puerto Rico, and two trips to Europe made back in the days when "Europe on Five Dollars a Day" made seeing the world possible on salaries far under $10,000 a year. During our six-plus years as roommates in a one-bedroom apartment on the upper West Side of Manhattan, we'd each gotten extremely familiar with the other's string of boyfriends.

I'd had three significant relationships during those years and another more recently—after I'd moved into my own apartment on West 76th Street across the street from Risa. She and I had become roommates during the tail-end of my year-and-a-half relationship with Bob, the bio-chemistry professor with a Cancer Society research grant. It had been a good thing he hadn't wanted to marry me because, although he had been great company on an intellectual level, there had been no way I could get him to express his feelings. Still, I'd foolishly hoped for a proposal. After all, raised in the pre-women's liberation 1940's and 50's, my main goal in life—education and career be damned—was to find a husband.

"Richie" was next. That had lasted for five long years even though I hadn't been very happy with him after the first few months. He'd put me down so much, I felt I'd never find anyone else. We had what these days would be called an abusive relationship—emotionally abusive, never physically. But I surely couldn't have put a word like "abusive" to it back then.

I met Steve when I worked at the publishing house, Appleton Century Crofts. Just out of college and eight years my junior, the man had opened the then uptight me to the joys of sex. But a relationship like that couldn't have lasted, so I'd ended up feeling hurt and rejected by him—an already familiar feeling when it came to dating.

Bill, an artist, had been in publishing, too. Although our courtship had been fairly casual, it had meant as much to me as any committed relationship. You see, when I give my heart, I give it all the way. And as corny as that may sound, it's one hundred percent true and always has been. Therefore, because Bill chose to end our relationship with one quick telephone call, I'd been left feeling totally devastated. The therapist I'd been seeing for two years convinced me that I had a right to a heart-to-heart with Bill, which conversation I'd just had two weeks prior to this party. The talk had freed me up, and now I was ready to meet Mr. Right.

So there I was, looking for HIM and all the myths of my times; the fairytales of childhood, popular songs, movies, and TV shows indicated that

HE existed. Although I was already 32 years old, I found the fantasy appealing; all I had to do was find him, and we'd live happily ever after.

My ideas were romantic for a 30-something and continued to be somewhat unrealistic. Having emerged from a decidedly over-protected childhood, I was a rather shy woman, insecure about my own abilities and uneasy with competition. I believed my face was pretty, but I disliked my body and felt overweight—though I hadn't been even chubby for nearly twenty years. Despite several years of therapy, I'd not overcome self-doubt and a tendency to social discomfort. I didn't realize that the quieter qualities I possessed—such as honesty and caring—were worth more than a gorgeous body. And looking back, I must say that I certainly approached that superlative, too, though there would have been no way to convince me of it then.

How I looked in 1975.

By this time my self esteem was definitely better than it had been in my youth when my self-confidence was at its lowest. In high school, I'd developed intense crushes on boys who scarcely knew I existed, and then I had felt unwanted, even though I had dated others. By college, my record had improved somewhat, but my dream man still hadn't appeared.

I'd participated in many singles functions during those pre-Internet dating years: dances, parties, weekends, and even, from time to occasional time, bars in the scary New York City bar scene, but this was my first shot at a share in a summer house. And now, even before I'd signed up, there before me was a prospective candidate for *the* title: Mr. Right. Yes, I believed someday my prince *would* come. Could this man with the dark curly hair, thick mustache, and fire eyes be the one?

Arthur, one of the two men renting the house shares, had pointed Joel out to me not five minutes earlier.

"See that guy? He's one of the top attorneys in New York." Arthur, also a lawyer, ought to know. I was impressed.

I studied Joel. He was dressed in jeans and a weathered, pale blue denim shirt with the sleeves partway rolled up. Rugged. I was also in jeans, and a polyester print blouse. Unsophisticated.

"I'm not here to rent a share in the house," Joel confessed. "My sailboat is docked in South Hampton, so I'll be visiting." Arthur's house was in East Hampton, just a short drive away from Joel's boat.

Joel smiled, his gaze still meeting mine. I smiled back.

Hmmmm, I thought, *that would certainly make joining this house worthwhile.* I liked the idea that he wouldn't be living in the house, just visiting. If our date didn't work out, it might get awkward if he were sharing the same space. I was already pretty sure that a date was certain.

As Risa and I took the elevator to the street and walked out into the New York spring day, she turned to me and proclaimed, "I'm in love with Joel!"

"So am I," I responded quickly with a laugh like a giddy teenager.

Apparently, we'd both been charmed by the man's sparkling eyes and captivating personality, so full of life. The vivacity I saw in Joel was exactly what I was looking for in a man. My continued shyness made for a lack of zing in my life. With a man like Joel, there'd be plenty of excitement.

Like eight or nine other women—it turned out that the two men renting the summer shares preferred being the only men in the house—Risa and I decided to take half shares, meaning that we'd be there on alternate weekends.

All the members, new and old, met for dinner one Sunday night at an Indian restaurant in mid-town Manhattan. While I chatted with Arthur, who I'd learned rented an office within the suite Joel had leased, I deliberately mentioned that I found Joel intriguing; I hoped Arthur would tell him. He did, and the very next evening, I got a call from Joel.

My heart beating fast, I told him when he asked me to have dinner with him that night, that I was already preparing mine—which I was. But I gladly let him persuade me to supplant my canned stuffed-cabbage-for-one with veal-and-pasta-for-two in Little Italy.

First Date

I met him at his office, which was near the courts in lower Manhattan. Very impressive: large, with a private bathroom, and two picture windows overlooking New York City's Hudson River.

"I need water around me all the time," he declared as we looked out the window, "even when I'm not sailing."

Joel was wearing a well-tailored, conservative blue suit, a pale blue shirt, and a not-so-conservative silk print tie. He definitely looked the part—of an attorney, that is. I was concentrating so much on him that I didn't even think about my own outfit—a straight navy blue skirt and plain white blouse—conservative, and inexpensive; I assumed that Joel's outfit had cost him a bundle. He looked quite prosperous.

He showed me around the office. I followed as he walked and narrated a story about the occupant, now gone home, of each office in the suite. There was Dan, who, Joel said, was not doing so well; and Arthur, whom I'd met; and, of course, Kreiger, the man Joel called his partner.

The highlight of the tour was the file room where Joel quickly opened and shut the file drawers and reeled off clients' names I supposed I ought to recognize. I didn't, but Joel had succeeded in impressing me nonetheless. I was even more dazzled when he told me all about Joe "Bananas" Bonano, the big-time Mafioso—whom "we represent," he said.

Dinner was at the restaurant of one of his clients. The owner's petite, middle-aged wife, whom I'll call Angie, greeted Joel warmly and sat down with us. A gregarious woman, she babbled on about life with her husband, "Sal." Sal, she told us, regularly went out with other women.

"But what can I do?" she said resignedly. "I iron a clean shirt for him whenever he's going out, and this means before each date, too, naturally. I don't think he realizes that I know." She sighed.

I was quite shocked. Aiding and abetting a husband's philandering was not, in my estimation, a wife's role.

Angie also talked about Joel.

"Every time I see you, you're with a different woman," she noted. "Whatever happened to Rona?"

It didn't surprise me to hear that Joel was a ladies' man. I was enjoying the fantasy image of Joel being unattached and free-floating, and finally meeting me—the woman who would capture his heart.

When Angie stepped away from our table, I couldn't resist but to ask Joel how he could represent "such people," meaning Mafia. He explained, very persuasively, that, "these aren't types, but real people, often likable ones, ones who deserve representation, just as all humans do." How could I, a sixties-bred liberal, resist that argument? And more, I admired him for it, especially when he said that he, unlike the stereotype of the Mafia lawyer, had never been bought by them. He'd retained his independence and dignity.

Hmmmm, I thought, *this man gets better and better.*

When we left the restaurant, we began to walk and talk. I felt relaxed, enjoying myself. Joel seemed to have a talent for making me put aside my usual awkwardness with a new man. His talk was humorous, exciting, thoughtful, engrossing, and what I had to say seemed to truly interest him too because Joel really listened. Our hands joined as we walked.

"We've really covered a lot of territory," I noted, suddenly realizing that we'd walked quite a few blocks.

"I have to go home to walk the dog," he told me.

Now, I was generally quite trusting of people, probably too trusting, but I'd had enough experience with men to know a line when I heard one. And this had all the earmarks. But feeling so very charmed by Joel, I really didn't care. I knew I was being seduced, and although remnants of my over-protective upbringing caused my conscience to nudge me a bit, I decided not to pay any attention to it. I was having too good a time.

When we arrived at his street, lined with trees and 19th century brownstones, he pointed out the plaque on his building:

In this House Once Lived Mark Twain (Samuel Langhorne Clemens) Author of the Beloved American Classic "The Adventures of Tom Sawyer."

As a former English Lit major, I was impressed.

Riding up the elevator (the first time I'd ever seen one in a brownstone), Joel warned me not to be frightened by his dog, Sasha.

"He's a Dane," Joel told me, "the largest Great Dane you'll ever see, but he's just as gentle."

Joel was certainly right about Sasha's size; he was HUGE! And definitely the largest dog I'd ever seen.

While Joel walked Sasha, I waited in the apartment, scrutinizing the living room. Set into one wall was an elegant marble fireplace. On either side of it were bookshelves that stretched from the Persian rug-covered floor to the 12-foot-high ceiling, one side filled entirely with law books. There were a number of fine-looking pieces of antique furniture. A gigantic window box filled with plants, and still more plants hanging above it, made the room even more warm and inviting. They were flourishing, and as a member of the Horticulture Society, I took note of that.

Aha, I thought, *four new marks in the plus column: Mark Twain's house, great dog, outstanding apartment, and healthy plants.*

When Joel returned, we picked up where we had left off, talking, chatting easily and comfortably. I was simply enthralled by what he had to say and the spirited way in which he said it; I was excited by the energy that emanated from his fiery eyes. Spirit and energy—ah, irresistible to me. After several hours of talking and eventually kissing, I was the one who suggested that we go to bed.

Never before in my life had I been so bold; it was definitely unlike me to have sex on a first date. Quite the opposite, in fact. A virgin until I was twenty-three, in the decade since, I hadn't let go entirely of some attitudes that seemed almost prudish in the liberated atmosphere of the seventies when everyone was jumping into bed with everyone else. But this time, two factors—two possibly conflicting ones—caused me to make my proposition.

Being somewhat intuitive, I sensed that Joel was orchestrating the situation to get me into bed (*Just like so many men*, I thought). And since this behavior was typical of men of the 1950's, 60's, and now 70's, I didn't take his actions as a warning signal that he was especially controlling. So instead of simply saying goodnight and missing the opportunity I wanted of spending the night with him, I chose a different tack: I would be the one to control the situation; I would take the power away from him. Ergo, I said, "Let's move into the bedroom," and we did.

Had Joel been controlling or selfish in bed, I'm pretty sure I'd have ended it right there. But he wasn't like that at all. He seemed caring and thoughtful, as much concerned with my pleasure as with his own. So I ignored his manipulation and kept the "special" feelings I'd been amassing about him— my first step on the road to ruin.

Conversations

During the next few weeks, I saw a lot of Joel, and what I remember most about that time is our conversations, those enthralling, mesmerizing words of his. No matter what he talked about, he made it attractive—in fact, fascinating.

His law practice had an allure all its own, whether the story was about the guy who'd killed his girlfriend and wanted to go to prison to atone or about one of Joel's Mafia clients, and his language changed appropriately with the tale's atmosphere.

"This guy's just a strong-arm man, ya know—no real position. But seems real nice when you meet him—very protective of women and children. If anyone ever hurt a woman or child, he'd kill the guy.

"So, he's telling me this story, real proud-like of what he accomplished. He'd been told to break some poor shmuck's legs," Joel said with a giggle. "So he describes how he knocks the guy down with the car. And then, to make sure he gets the assignment right, he backs up the car over the guy's legs! Can you imagine?"

Joel's childhood and high school friends came alive, as did his parents, in his tales of growing up in the Bronx and Yonkers. He portrayed his lawyer father as a uncommunicative man who was always reading a newspaper, while his mother ran the show. He told me how, as an only child, he had wanted more than anything to have a sibling.

"But my mother kept telling me my father didn't want more children. What a liar she was—and is. I can never trust what she says. *She* was the one who didn't want more children because kids would tie her down. She wanted to be free to play golf, to swim, to do whatever she wanted. What a liar, putting the blame on my father. And of course, *he* never said a word about it one way or the other. But I knew. So, no matter how sweet she seems, never believe a word she says."

Other favorite topics were his years in the Air Force and the Defense Intelligence Agency. And he told me tales of his college career as "the token Jew" at Fordham University where he grew to respect and admire the Jesuits who ran the school and about New York University Law School where he'd gotten his LL.D.

But he also listened with interest to me. And I felt totally comfortable talking about anything and everything with him. I described my job as an associate editor of children's non-fiction books at Random House—a job I loved. I told him all about my childhood in Washington Heights where, as the baby of the family, I was coddled and overprotected. I recounted tales of summers in the Catskill Mountains where I had been allowed to run free—as opposed to life in the city where I had had to stay indoors and play quietly with my dolls because of my mother's fear that one of her kids would get hit by a car. I even gave Joel reports on the discussions I had with my Freudian-oriented therapist, Dr. James Bradley Norton. (In those days, just about every normal human being who could afford a therapist was seeing one, even if it had to be on a sliding-scale basis—the way I paid Dr. Norton.) And, of course, I told Joel all about my friends and my former boyfriends, from my first "love" at age 12, whose name was coincidentally Steinberg, to Bill, the man I'd last dated before Joel.

On the flip side were Joel's frequent stories about his ex-girlfriends and the lovely little girl named Dawn he'd raised for several years with a woman named Anne.

"Anne recently remarried, so I've deliberately slipped into the background. I call Dawn once in a while, but I want her to get close to the man who'll now be her father. I think it's better for her that way."

Rona, Joel's last lover, was portrayed as a nut who was, however, great in bed.

"She was a prima ballerina as a kid, and, boy, could she move!"

Listening to that surely didn't help my confidence. But I said nothing and quietly felt I'd never live up despite my experiences with Steve—the guy who'd shown me the light regarding sex. I knew for certain *he'd* found me a lot more than adequate in bed. Likewise, I considered Steve my finest lover— until Joel, that is.

Too Much

Joel was everything I wanted in a man—he was intelligent, energetic, witty, charming, and an excellent lover. He also had a successful career, and he was Jewish and felt as I did about Judaism: It was a meaningful culture to us, but we weren't very observant of the religious rituals. And he was good looking—in later years when Tom Sellick became the star of the TV show *Magnum PI*, everyone would tell me that the two were look-alikes.

Joel was often the subject of one of my therapy sessions.

"I'm really crazy about him, but he just won't take no for an answer," I complained to Dr. Norton one day. "For example, you know why I canceled our appointment on Tuesday? That morning, Joel called me at the office and asked me out for dinner right after work. I told him I had a session with you.

"He tells me, 'Well, so what? If you miss one session, what difference will it make? You see Norton a couple of times a week anyway—not to mention group. You don't need all that therapy. And, I was planning to take you to a really special Greek restaurant in midtown; you won't even have far to travel. I know you'll love the food at this place.' And he describes this great-sounding restaurant.

"Then he says, 'So please say yes. We'll have such a good time.'

"And I felt yeah, it really wouldn't matter if I missed one therapy session, so I canceled with you. But that's really *not* what I wanted to do. I let Joel talk me into doing something that I didn't want. In fact, he wants to see me nearly every evening, and for me, that's too much too soon.

"You know how at first I felt so complimented by all Joel's attention; his eagerness made me feel *so* very desirable. But I'm starting to feel pushed. He's too insistent, unwilling to take no for an answer, and whenever I refuse him, he seems to persuade me to change my plans. That, in fact, is really what's bothering me most about all this. I feel like a patsy in the face of his powerful words of persuasion.

"It's my malleable mind that's the real problem, not Joel. Remember when I had that political conversation with my neighbor, Gary, and he actually persuaded me that Richard Nixon isn't such a terrible guy? Well, I know the facts, and I know exactly why I hated him as president and why I was thrilled when he resigned. But at that moment, Gary had me persuaded of *his* point of view—that is, until I had time to think it all through. And then I realized that I'd been mentally waylaid and wondered how I could have been such a jerk to be pushed into agreeing with something I knew was totally wrong! I'm just too impressionable; it's like a curse! And in the face of Joel's powerful words and ideas, I'm just a dupe, and I hate it.

"And yet, I really love so many things about him. I'm tempted to break it off, but I'm afraid I'll regret it."

"Well, Joel certainly is a complex man," Dr. Norton responded. "I think you've got to weigh the positives against the negatives and make a decision."

So that's what I did, and the negatives won. I told myself I didn't want to be pushed into doing things I really preferred not to do. So I told Joel I wouldn't see him anymore. Period. That time I didn't give him a chance to persuade me. Good-bye, Joel Steinberg. Hooray, Hedda, for being assertive.

Serendipity

Generally, I kept to myself as much as possible at the East Hampton summerhouse where Risa and I had rented half shares. I trekked to the beach when the weather was good, and I stayed inside reading and knitting when it wasn't. The group house had turned out to be a quarrelsome place, filled with petty squabbles over who would use the washing machine or how much to chip in for food.

On one sunny weekend, both Risa and I were restless and bored, wanting to get out of the group house, but we had no car since we'd gotten a ride that Friday evening with someone else. I was feeling stranded in that unpleasant environment when suddenly, a chance for escape appeared. Joel Steinberg showed up.

He said he was there to visit Arthur, the other lawyer from his office. But I was absolutely certain he was there to see me. I felt flattered and glad to see him even though Joel hadn't been on my mind very much for the past few months. I'd been far too busy with my work at Random House. Not only that, but I'd been concentrating on developing ideas for the juvenile book I'd recently contracted to write; it would be the fulfillment of a long-time dream.

So although I was delighted when Joel appeared that Saturday morning, a conversation Risa and I had shared one quiet night not so long ago kept popping into my mind. We'd been sitting behind the house under the stars, listening to the crickets, slapping at mosquitoes and discussing old boyfriends.

"I sure am glad I got rid of that guy, Joel," I had confessed to her. "I hate being pushed around, and that's exactly what he was doing."

"But he *is* kind of cute," had been her reply.

"Yeah, I know. He *really* turned me on...so he was hard to resist. Too hard. That's exactly why I needed to end it with him."

With that conversation in mind, I felt a definite conflict about the man's arrival. I could still feel the old attraction, but I knew better. Finally, I decided to be cautious and keep my distance. However, my eyes were secretly on Joel Steinberg throughout the day.

I recall peeping out the screen door in the kitchen, watching him frolicking with Sasha on the huge lawn outside the group house. I observed him and his friend, Bernie, who'd accompanied him, concentrating very hard on a game of checkers. Then there was a softball game with other house members; Joel had no trouble joining in. At one point the object of my spying apparently drove to the ocean and gathered clams because he disappeared for a while, returning with a bucketful of those mollusks. Then he tore open one after another, tilted his head back, and swallowed each with relish while sea water dripped down his chin. One of the women in the house stood on the lawn beside him, fixing him with an erotic gaze, intently watching this display of appetite. I resented the feelings of jealousy welling up inside me and continued to keep my distance.

However, when Joel popped into the kitchen and asked if Risa and I would have dinner with him and Bernie, it seemed like a godsend. We'd be getting out of the house after all. Not only that, but I was incredibly pleased that Joel wanted to be with me and not Ms. Drooler.

With one statement, I made sure Risa would agree to go: "We have a way out of this dreadful house tonight!"

We ate at a nearby restaurant and went dancing afterward at a popular local club. When the music had a rock beat and we danced apart, Joel never took his eyes off mine. I felt that we were connected even when we didn't touch. During slow dances, he held me close, and I liked feeling his arms around me and his face touching mine. Once again, I was having an exhilarating time, delighting in being with Joel in spite of myself.

Back in the car with Joel (Bernie and Risa had traveled in a separate car), when he asked me to spend the night with him at his motel, I really wanted to say yes. But what would Risa think if I didn't make it back to the group house, especially after all I'd said about needing to end it with Joel Steinberg? I'd be horribly embarrassed. So I told Joel no.

However, after driving a ways, he pulled up in front of his motel. Although thoroughly surprised, I was actually glad he'd made this move and chose not to point out that I'd refused his offer. So I'd suffer embarrassment when I got home the next day. What the heck; this night would be worth it.

And so I spent that night making love with Joel, and I found him to be as exciting as ever. Waking up the next morning to sunlight streaming in the window, Sasha on the floor by the bed, and Joel beside me felt wonderful. We made love again. And, of course, we talked. From the beginning, it was as though we were spinning a web of words that tied us to each other.

So, even though I'd have preferred to linger in bed all day with Joel, I did have to return to the group house. When we finally got back, not one of the house members was around. I breathed a sigh of relief. At least I wouldn't have to suffer Risa's probing, not just yet anyway.

It was past lunchtime, so Joel and I made salad and sandwiches for ourselves. Even this simple act became an adventure, both instructive and fun. Spotting some lettuce leaves in the kitchen trash can that were just slightly brown around the edges, he pulled them out, removed the wilted parts, and washed them for our salad, saying, "People are so wasteful; this lettuce is still good."

That afternoon, the two of us and another house member went to the bay where we took out a rowboat and began to gather clams. The three of us roared with laughter and made slightly off-color jokes as we stuffed the mollusks inside our bathing suits because we'd not come prepared for harvesting.

Joel also displayed both his knowledge about and his utter comfort with the water, and I thought of the day I'd met him, how he had made me feel as though I were sailing aboard his boat. The sea seemed like his natural habitat, and this only added to his appeal.

On Sunday night, Joel drove me home to the city. Of course, Risa came along too, and she sat quietly in the backseat beside Sasha. She'd had her say that afternoon, pointing out angrily that Joel had ordered wine at dinner without consulting anyone else.

"Big deal!" I'd replied, dismissing Risa's complaint as petty and insignificant. I was still feeling the glow of my glorious night with him.

Now, while Joel told a series of hilarious Hamptons stories, I was sure Risa wasn't listening. And then Joel also grew quiet, uncharacteristically so, and I had time to think about all that had occurred that weekend.

Wow! It's so amazing. Two days ago, Joel was part of my past, and now, here we are again. I'd been so sure he wasn't right for me, but I guess I was wrong. I'd simply jumped to a conclusion before really knowing the guy. He's certainly a lot of fun—and in bed, too. And I giggled out loud, causing Risa to say to me, "What?"

"Nothing," I replied with a smile and went on thinking.

Yeah, I was just plain wrong about him, I said to myself, glancing over at Joel who was seriously concentrating on the road. *At one time I thought he was pushy, but I've realized that's only because he reads people quite well and merely convinces them to do what they actually want.*

And then I thought about Saturday night. *I'm sure he knew that I really meant "yes" when I said "no."*

That seemed to be proof enough. I was certain I should give Joel Steinberg a second chance. In fact, I was once again positive that my prince had come.

Special

There's no doubt that, to me, Joel Steinberg was special. Life was always exciting, and in fact, exhilarating, with Joel around, a condition that was now quite frequent and mutually desired. Never, and I mean *never*, was I bored with Joel, not for even one second. And I'd certainly felt a lot of boredom over the years, not only when alone, but even when with some of the men I'd dated.

People were always coming in and out of Joel's house—clients, friends, acquaintances, Mafia types, drug dealers, actors, lawyers, police officers, physicians, workers from his office—and they'd always stay a while to chat, to invite us for dinner, or to join us for pot luck at home. And to a rather shy woman who'd lived a quiet life but was bursting to socialize, to mingle, to be surrounded with interesting people, this was a dream come true.

As a child, I'd been terribly fearful of new experiences and new people, petrified of doing things on my own, dependent on others and inept at making friends. The first time I went anywhere alone—the public library—I was 12 years old. (Normally I went with my sister.) My fear, in that instance, had been that if people saw me by myself, they would know the terrible truth: I had had no friends to go with. When I was 14, I had cried for an hour before screwing up the courage to telephone a stranger on behalf of B'nai B'rith Girls, a club to which I belonged and through which I'd made a few acquaintances but no real friends.

During the summer I turned 17, I'd written in my diary after a school acquaintance had asked me to meet a group of her friends:

> To meet a whole crowd that is all cliqued off is just not for me. I can't fit in. My personality isn't very apparent. I'm quiet. No one would pay any attention to me...It's terrible. I have nothing to say to people unless they start a conversation and are good conversationalists. I can't do it first...Isn't that ridiculous? But that's Hedda

As I passed from my teens into my twenties, I not only learned to make friends—and had a few close ones—but I became bolder and occasionally even assertive. Still, I felt I lacked the wherewithal to have the kind of social life I longed for: the kind Joel Steinberg had. Maybe if I hung around with him enough, I felt, I'd become part of it.

But it was more than the social whirl that made Joel special to me. He seemed able to do things that others couldn't. He could win a tough criminal case. He could receive cheery notes and Christmas cards from a former client in prison very happy with the sentence Joel had gotten for him. He could hold spellbound a roomful of people at a party as he told a tale of...of anything, quite frankly. The subject didn't matter. It was Joel's choice of words and his mannerisms that were a magnet to so many. I felt so proud. No matter where we were, in my eyes Joel Steinberg was the best-looking, liveliest, most interesting man in the room.

He'd take me to dinner at one or another expensive restaurant several times a week, having no trouble parting with what seemed like an abundant cash supply to treat me. Since I'd grown up in a family where there weren't enough funds around for restaurants more than a few times a year, nor was there enough in those days from my modest salary as an associate editor, Joel's seeming generosity impressed me greatly.

One evening, for example, we were dining at an elegant restaurant in mid-town Manhattan. Sitting directly across from my handsome escort, I studied the menu, looking at the prices before the dishes—as was my wont.

Hmm, let's see, $19.95, $17.50—no, I can't order either of those main courses. What's this at $12.95? Oh, chicken cacciatore; that's always good. I think I'll order that.

I guess Joel must have noticed what I was doing, because he said, "Order whatever you want. Don't worry about the prices. Just see what it is you'd like, and order it."

And then he ordered a bottle of fine Pinot Grigio at $21.00.

"You'll like this wine," he smiled. "It's smooth."

Gosh, $21.00. That's more than I spend on groceries for an entire week!

Joel also took me with him to business dinners where the client picked up the tab. Since I was too shy to have much to say on those occasions, I felt very flattered that Joel still wanted to take me. In fact, early on he started building my confidence to say more.

I was especially delighted one Sunday when we were dining on a boardwalk-like terrace with Joey, a Mafia-related client, at a seafood restaurant located right on the water of Long Island Sound about an hour from the city. As usual, I sat and listened to Joel's talk about Joey's upcoming court date as I watched the boats docking below us.

"You don't mind if Hedda sits in on this discussion, do you?" he'd asked Joey when they'd made the dinner date. "She's someone who can be trusted completely." Getting Joey's permission was the ethical thing to do.

How like Joel, to do that, I'd thought after he'd told me about their phone conversation.

As the two men talked, I wished I had more to say, but I just didn't. Then, finally, when the talk turned to Joey's tenuous relationship with his son, I commented,

"I think it's important to try your best to keep close to your family."

Joel smiled then, turning to Joey and saying, "Hedda doesn't say much, but when she does, you can be certain it's significant."

What a man!

An experience that summed up Joel's essence for me happened at the tail end of 1975, after I'd been dating him steadily for more than four months.

We'd gone to Puerto Rico on a gambling junket. Joel loved to gamble and seemed to have an extraordinary amount of luck when he did.

One evening, in the casino, after losing my $10 limit at the blackjack table, I headed for the table were Joel was shooting craps. There was quite a crowd there, so I had to squeeze my way in to see what was happening. Joel was rolling the dice, and dozens of people were betting on him—big piles of chips, amounting to thousands of dollars each, I later learned.

Over and over I watched Joel toss the dice without rolling a seven or eleven. And each time he did so, the excitement mounted and the bets got higher. As I stood there amazed, the stakes kept on rising, and he kept throwing: 40 passes, 45, 50, 52.

At that point, the manager, who'd been standing there for a while, took his arm and with a grand gesture, wiped the craps table clean. The casino, it turned out, under new management would have gone broke with another similar round.

Everyone at the table got paid off, but the incensed management refused to pay Joel. The next day, after thoroughly discussing with me what he should do about this, both Joel and our traveling companion, whom I'll call Frank, a New York City policeman, sweet talked the casino director into paying Joel all the money owed to him. Ironically, of everyone betting, Joel had apparently bet the least since, I assume, the thrill of the win had been his main goal. Of course, he *did* come home a few thousand dollars richer.

After the casino incident in Puerto Rico, I was feeling particularly happy being with my very special man. Parting from Frank who stayed on in Puerto Rico to visit relatives, Joel and I stopped in Miami to stay with a client from New York who was in Florida for his Christmas vacation. The client had been arrested for selling Quaaludes in great quantities, but he didn't look the part. In fact, he appeared to be a nice, intelligent young man; I had no objections to his putting us up. And he had friends who were members of the Jets football team, then in Miami. So we spent New Year's Eve at a party with several of the Jets. How much more glamorous could it get? *And*, I sighed to myself, *I had Joel Steinberg to thank for it all.*

On the beach at Fire Island.

No Boundaries

Another thing that seemed so special about Joel was his insistence that we keep nothing hidden from each other; everything should be totally in the open. I liked the idea of concealing nothing, no secrets, a special closeness beyond what even my sister Judy and I used to have, and we'd been each other's best friend. In fact, we were so close that until she got married when I was 19, she and I never even had a dream that the other wasn't in. And now Joel and I were a team, a unit, Plato's two halves finally joined as one. Ever since I'd read some Plato in college, I'd thought that yes, my other half was out there somewhere. I'd been searching for him for a very long time, and now here he was at last.

There was, however, one aspect of Joel's openness that shocked me—at least, at first. It happened during one of our first weekends together. I was carrying two cups of hot coffee from the kitchen to the bedroom where I'd left Joel just waking up. En route, I passed the bathroom. The door was open, and there sat Joel, directly across from the door on the toilet and in full view as I walked by.

"Oh, thanks," he said, motioning with his head to the coffee, which I nearly dropped, I was so dumfounded by the sight.

Never in all my years had I experienced someone not closing the door during his or her most private moments on the john. At home, my parents certainly kept the door shut, and so, of course, did Judy and I. In fact even after the "famous" family incident when my father had fainted while on the toilet, he had continued to keep his privacy. This, of course, had caused my mother, a compulsive worrier, to become particularly anxious whenever he had been behind the closed bathroom door for more than a few minutes. In fact, we had teased Mommy for years because she'd invariably knock and query from the hall side.

"Willie, you all right?"

But walk in on him to check? That was beyond her idea of decency.

Eventually, I got used to Joel's open door policy and complied when he urged me to follow suit. So it soon became standard practice for us.

It shouldn't come as any surprise, then, that Joel also walked around the house nude. His windows weren't close enough to those of the neighbors for peeping or indecent exposure charges to be of any consideration. I, however, had always been shy about exposing my body, so I didn't emulate *that* behavior.

But sitting in the bathtub was a different story. Joel and I always took baths together—long, leisurely baths. Although I'd never been a bath person and had always preferred showers, Joel loved to sit in the tub for hours. And now I did too because there, he and I would share intimate stories and ideas, sing, laugh, and wash each other's backs. Very occasionally we'd become sexually aroused, and the diversion would turn into an entirely different sort. However, in general, these baths were simply a fun-filled aspect of our openness.

It seemed to me that confiding absolutely everything to each other would be completely in line with what was now our philosophy of mutual accessibility. I most certainly divulged to Joel essentially all my thoughts and experiences. Everything, really. For me, doing so was Elysium found. Here was half of me, my mate, my lover, now also my confidante. And, of course, I assumed that Joel also shared all things with me.

Warts and All

Although Joel seemed positively wonderful to me, I didn't find him totally perfect. And no, that wasn't because I recognized any of his manipulative qualities. It would be years and years before I became aware of any of those. My judgment came from some habits the man had that were, quite frankly, odd. And so were some his beloved dog's, Sasha.

For example, Joel kept his shoes piled up in a ceramic barrel in the living room. However, because our policy of openness helped me feel free enough to mention it, one day I said to him, "Joel, are you aware that's a very weird place to keep shoes? With clients sometimes coming here, I think it would be a good idea to find another spot that's both less public and that'll make finding the pair you want a lot easier."

So although he said nothing in reply, the very next time I visited his apartment, the shoes had been neatly transferred to a newly-cleared shelf in one of Joel's closets.

Wow! I thought. *He's not only open to change but apparently eager to please me.*

And, of course, Sasha could sometimes be a problem. I adored the dog, but since Joel didn't have a real bed, only two mattresses on the floor, they were very easy for the Great Dane to climb onto when no one was home. Did I say climb? There was no climbing involved, of course. So it was difficult to keep him out of them. But Joel didn't mind that—except when Sasha tried to come

47

between us in bed. The dog didn't like to be excluded when there was petting going on, I guess.

It was a lot more upsetting to Joel when he found Sasha on the living room couch, which was beige corduroy—and Sasha was a drooler. The dog didn't dare climb up there when people were in the house, but frequently when Joel would come home from work, there would be Sasha on the sofa. But before Joel could call out, "Sasha, get off that couch," he'd be down on the floor sporting an innocent look.

"He does that every time," Joel complained to me. "As soon as the house is empty, Sasha makes himself at home."

"So I've seen," I laughed. "You're so bright, Joel. Surely you can think of a way to outsmart a dog!"

However, he never did; it was I who eventually found a way to keep the big drooler off the furniture. If there was anyone or anything sitting on it, Sasha would stay off the couch. So before leaving the house, I'd strew a few books across the sofa cushions, and that did the trick.

But the most disturbing of all happened during our very early weeks together. Joel had invited me to accompany him to dinner at the home of a lawyer acquaintance and his wife. For some reason, Joel seemed extremely uncomfortable all evening. And I remember feeling totally appalled when he sat at the dinner table contorting his face in strange ways. Up went his cheeks, lips stretched tightly across his open mouth with teeth showing. Then the mouth formed a circle, then spread wide again, jaw and cheeks moving up and down. Up, down, wiggle all around.

Egads! I thought. *Is this man crazy?*

And I'm sure this incident contributed to my original breakup with him. But after we were reunited, I quickly learned that the bizarre routine was a method of self-focusing, centering, which Joel had learned from his therapist, Ed Eichel. I later understood, after eventually becoming a part of Ed's couple's group with Joel, that squeezing up your cheeks and wiggling them around really helps you feel your face and center yourself when under stress. But this is normally done when no one is looking. Maybe the fact that Joel let me witness his very personal performance actually meant that when he felt uncomfortable with others, my new lover felt just the opposite with me.

Introduction to Ed's

When I met Joel, he was attending weekly group therapy sessions at Ed's and had done so for maybe a year with his previous live-in girlfriend, Rona. Ed, Joel told me, had been the first therapist whom he felt could do a person any good, and so he'd broken his past tradition of avoiding any and every sort of therapy.

Ed Eichel did mostly couples groups with a behavioral approach. Having been trained as a Reichian, he'd come up with his own techniques, one of which was the feeling-your-face routine.

Joel was forever talking about Ed: how wonderful his group was, and how Ed was an infinitely better therapist than Dr. Norton.

"Ed's work doesn't deal with your mother or your kindergarten teacher; it deals with now, the way you behave and how to be focused about it. I've grown to trust Ed and can't praise him enough. Once you try Ed, you'll see how much more he can do for you than Norton ever could."

But since I was quite attached to Dr. Norton, I was resistant to Joel's repeated suggestion to switch.

One day, Joel told me the following: "Ed's having a video demonstration of the sexual technique he's developed. Everyone from the group'll be there, but outsiders are welcome too. This'll be a perfect time for you to see what I've been talking about. You've got to come with me, Hedda."

"Okay," I said, my curiosity having been roused. "I'll go."

We walked from Joel's place to the studio in Soho, an artist's community, where Ed's groups were run—a good 30 or 40 minutes on foot. Joel and I enjoyed long walks and talks, but this night I was a little distracted as we passed through Green Street. That's where Bill, the man I'd last dated, lived.

Bill was the artist I mentioned briefly before, the man who'd told me goodbye in a single phone call. He'd taken his ex-girlfriend's challenge to move in with her and give the relationship a full try, once and for all.

"It's not you," he'd told me. "You're wonderful."

But that wasn't enough to mend my broken heart; I felt devastated. And it wasn't until Dr. Norton had encouraged me to have a face-to-face conversation about the incident with Bill that I'd gone ahead and done it—just a few weeks before meeting Joel. At that time, I'd felt ready for a new love, but passing so close to an old ache caused me to feel preoccupied and sad. As a result, I was feeling rather estranged from Joel and preferred to remain alone with my thoughts. Joel, however, very attuned to moods and subtleties of emotion, noticed and pried the story out of me.

"What's going on, Hedda? Why so quiet? Is there something bothering you?"

"Well, kind of."

"So? Tell me about it. You'll feel better if you do."

"Well, it's hard to. You see, it relates to another man...and I'm not comfortable talking about it."

"The only way to feel better, Hedda, is to discuss it with me. You know that. It's us now that's important."

So I did, and talking about it to Joel made me feel closer to him. Ergo, I ended up feeling very glad he'd convinced me to open up.

When we got to our destination, the large loft was crowded with strangers. Joel seemed to know most of them, but I felt alienated and overwhelmed by shyness—my typical reaction to a roomful of people I'd never met. Joel introduced me to a host of faces, but I can now recall only three: Ed, of course—a small, slender man about 40 with well-defined features—and Chad and his wife Karen, who were also the subjects of the videotape. In it, Chad, a handsome man in his late thirties, and Karen, an attractive woman with casually styled long hair, were demonstrating what Ed called "The Movement," a sexual technique he was teaching to the couples in his group. Chad and Karen were fully clothed in the tape, but they were performing the basics. I watched this tape, totally at a loss to understand what it was really all about. But those in the group seemed captivated by it. This added to my

50

feeling of estrangement.

After the demonstration, a group of us went out to a Soho restaurant for dinner. Although I didn't say much, I was glad I was there, being fascinated by Chad, a celebrity—the Chad Mitchell of the Trio, popular throughout the 1960's. He was also Joel's client.

Maybe someday I can feel a part of an event such as this, I thought. *With Joel around, I'll get used to meeting exciting people. Joel'll help pull me through. He's that kind of man.* I was sure of it.

January 1976

Joel and I were home from our trip to Puerto Rico and Florida just a few days when, coming back to his house after work, I found my typically energetic man unusually silent and depressed.

"You know the little girl Dawn I helped raise?" he said.

I certainly did know who she was. Joel had spent much time talking about her. Dawn was just a baby when he'd become involved with her mother, Anne, about ten years earlier. They'd lived together for a few years, and Dawn had felt like his own. When Anne and Joel had split, he'd continued to see Dawn often, stopping only when Anne had remarried so that Dawn could become close to her new father, he'd told me. After that, they'd had only phone contact.

"She's dead," he said, staring off into space.

On New Year's Eve, Dawn had died in a house fire. Having cared so intensely for this little girl, I knew that Joel had to be feeling profound pain.

He told me that now, even more than ever, he wanted to have children of his own. But since it was too soon for us to talk about starting a family, I held my tongue about it. As special as Joel was to me, it was too soon to make a commitment.

However, Joel and I were about to start living together, or you could say that we already were living together, though quite unofficially. Once we returned to 10th Street from our Christmas trip, I had just stayed there.

52

Previously, I'd been spending some nights there and some on West 76th Street, gradually moving my clothes downtown. The move was completely without structure. We didn't plan it outwardly. I wanted to be with Joel, and it sure seemed that he wanted to be with me because there we were, living together, but with no actual commitment.

Since I'd never before lived with a man, even Richie whom I'd dated for five whole years, and because I had doubts about doing so without the benefit of marriage, I don't think I could have made a conscious decision to move in with Joel. But by mid-January, both Joel and I accepted the fact that we now lived together—although I kept my apartment as a security blanket, just in case...

Just in case what? For Joel, I guessed it was...just in case things didn't work out between us, since his previous major relationships—with Rona, Anne, and an artist named Susan—had eventually failed.

For me, the just in case meant...just in case he wouldn't want to make it permanent, meaning get married. I wanted marriage and kids, period. The intensity of this feeling probably had a lot to do with my mother's sister Bertha, whom Judy and I called "Beppy."

Beppy had no husband and/or children, no friends, and nobody close except her sister Emma (my mother) and two nieces (Judy and me). Employment? She worked in a bookbindery on an assembly line pushing papers together. Interests? None except seeing movies and reading movie magazines. Beppy smelled from face powder mixed with her own unpleasant body odor. I hated it when she hugged me.

After her dinner each night and each Saturday and Sunday morning, Beppy'd walk the half block from her house to ours and sit on our couch in the living room with her arms and legs folded—for protection against the world? There she'd sit and doze for hours. The most exciting thing she'd ever do was walk into our kitchen and complain to my mother about a rude co-rider on the subway or about her kitchen sink leaking. She never added anything to our lives. Nothing. She'd been a blob.

Daddy had apparently loathed her. Whenever we'd go visiting or out to dinner or on a picnic in the summertime, Mommy had insisted that Beppy go with us.

"She has no one else," my mother would maintain, "so please let her come along." Daddy didn't want her around. She produced bad energy, and I guess he had felt it, as I had. But Mommy always won the argument.

"Okay, okay," Daddy would concede. After all, he was a good guy at heart.

But, as Judy and I noted in our little heads, Beppy was the only thing my parents ever fought over. Not money, not any other relative, just Beppy. So, naturally, we grew to resent her.

My worst fear was that I would grow up to be like Beppy, and I'd had a good start at it. She was timid. I was timid. I'd always had difficulty making friends. Beppy had no friends. I didn't want to end up dependent on my sister and resented by her husband and children. I'd made headway in the friends and career departments, and I was working on being more outgoing. But I still wasn't married with my own family. No matter how different from Beppy I'd become, I simply refused to give up my dream of having a loving husband, like my own father, and, of course, children. So now that I'd finally found "Mr. Right," my passion was to marry Joel Steinberg and bear his children.

But in the meantime, there I was, living in his apartment. To help me feel at home since it was now *our* apartment, Joel offered me a room to do with as I pleased. There were four rooms in the apartment: living room, bedroom, kitchen, and bathroom.

The living room was where Joel had his desk and law books left over from the days when he'd practiced law out of the apartment. I think he identified with that room.

The bedroom needed a ton of work, including a woodworking project Joel had had in mind for years—a captain's bed, the kind with large drawers under it for storage, perfect for a small city apartment. Joel had all the tools in his closet for building it—table saw, planes, chisels, you name it. The captain's bed certainly had to be Joel's endeavor.

The bathroom was a possibility, I thought, but Joel had plans for that too—take down the plaster and expose the brick walls, put silvery Mylar on the walls around the bathtub.

So the room left was the kitchen. It would be *my* room.

However, Joel had a suggestion—*my* room or not.

"Why don't you redo all the cabinets?"

He showed me how to strip the wood with a blowtorch, sand and stain the cupboard doors. I was thrilled with this. Joel, I felt, was teaching me man's work, moving me to a new plane.

"Hedda," he told me repeatedly, "you're really moving. Just think, you've learned how to do a difficult job like this, something entirely new to you. With my help, you're advancing, really advancing. I'm so proud of you."

I felt proud too. I never thought about the fact that I'd pulled up tiles in my last apartment all by myself and had used a blowtorch to do it. Staining the cabinets was a unique experience for me; Joel had me convinced of it.

So I worked long and hard on the project. (We had about eight large wooden cupboards and storage areas in the kitchen.) In truth, they didn't come out bad, though the job looked far from professional—especially with some scorch marks here and there. Joel, however, was uncritical. I was my own harshest judge, forever after feeling inept whenever my gaze hit those ugly, dark blemishes.

Not long afterward, with Joel's okay, I added a woman's touch to the totally nondescript bathroom. Out went the ugly, old black shower curtain and the array of faded, unmatched towels, and in came brand new ones, all in Joel's favorite color: blue. I was happy to spend my own money on the project.

I'm Converted

Although I'd been introduced to Ed's group a few months earlier, now that Joel and I were living together, he *really* wanted me to become a member. He still attended weekly sessions with Ed, and I still saw Dr. Norton and also went to his therapy group.

Besides pleading with me to call my therapist simply "Norton" and stop "aggrandizing" him by using "Dr.," Joel also spent hours detailing to me why Ed's kind of therapy was better.

"Why spend time on what *was*? Ed deals with what's happening *now*. That's what's important—today, not yesterday."

Joel kept pointing out how Norton's Freudian-oriented techniques missed the mark, and Ed's behavioral ones hit it. For example, Dr. Norton suggested that Joel massage my neck and shoulders, which had suffered from chronic pains for years.

"Massages deal only with the surface," Joel told me while actually giving me such a massage in the bathtub. "Ed can get to the core and really get rid of those pains."

Finally, I agreed to go to a session. But because Joel's ex-girlfriend Rona was still in the same group with Joel, my sensitivities were piqued. Something, I felt, was not right about that. She needed to be out of the picture.

So I told him, "I'll go, but only if Rona's no longer in that group. Let Ed put her into one of his other sessions."

I had no trouble asserting this demand, and Joel seemed to have no trouble meeting it.

He talked to Ed, Ed talked to Rona, Rona was transferred to another group, and I went with Joel to my first session.

In the groups, Ed worked individually with each member, and the others gave support in one way or another—sometimes verbal, sometimes physical, and sometimes just spiritual. On this, my first, session, Ed chose to work with me on those chronic neck and shoulder pains I had. Although I'd not told him they existed, he must have sensed the tension I held in those areas.

He asked me to grab with my teeth the end of a towel he was holding. And we both pulled at it. That's it. And, lo and behold, like a miracle, those persistent neck and shoulder pains disappeared, instantly, and even more wondrously, they stayed away.

I was convinced by Ed's grand success that Joel's opinion of his therapist was correct, and not long thereafter, I told Dr. Norton that I was leaving his care. So, although he strongly felt I had separation anxiety and that he and I should go through a careful and deliberate process of separation when the time was right, I left abruptly.

The separation anxiety, I'd learned as I worked with Dr. Norton, came from my relationship with Baba—Daddy's mother. At the time of my birth, Judy had been two and needed Mommy's attention badly. So Baba, who had lived with us, fed me, often changed my diapers, and played with me. To me she became "Mother."

However, when I was two years old, in 1944, Baba suffered a nervous breakdown supposedly because her youngest son had been drafted to fight the war in the Pacific. So Baba, who had been a mother to me, now disappeared into a hospital. When she did finally return some six weeks later, I'm told I grabbed hold of her legs and wouldn't let go.

But she was utterly changed, a shadowy recluse now who ventured out of her room only to shop for food or occasionally argue with Mommy. She rarely showed me affection or appeared even to notice me. It wasn't until I worked through the material raised by a dream about Baba (a dream I had immediately after Bill and I split), that I recognized how abandoned I'd felt in her absence when I was only two, and how responsible I'd felt for her disappearance.

My way of guarding against the repetition of such an event, my therapy taught me, was to be the "good girl." I tried always to please my parents, my teachers, friends, boyfriends. What they wanted from me took precedence over what I wanted for myself.

But now I was starting a new life with a new man, and I wasn't worried about needing to deal with separation anxiety again. Besides, I'd had enough of rehashing the past. Ed's techniques seemed to work so much faster. What difference did it make today if my grandmother had made me feel abandoned some thirty years ago? I didn't need Dr. Norton. I had Joel's wisdom, and that wisdom had led me to Ed's. What more could I ask for?

Advice and Counsel

Before living with Joel, I'd always been asleep by midnight. With him, the lights never went out before 2:00 a.m. We spent our evenings watching television together and/or talking. Those talks usually focused on what I've come to think of as our "therapy" sessions: Joel would offer advice, guidance, "suggestions," and I'd try to absorb as much as I could.

Most of a typical "session" consisted of Joel speaking, usually while pacing back and forth beside the captain's bed I had "inspired" him to start building—but never to complete. However, eventually it had a queen-size mattress, and the bed part functioned just fine, even though the plywood drawers had no handles so you had to squeeze your hands around the top of the drawer to open one, and the "sliding doors" didn't slide; you had to push and pull one off the frame to get something from inside.

Picture this scene, the same one that would be repeated day after day, year after year, but with different dialogue—or, perhaps I should say "monologue," because Joel did all the talking and I the listening. I'd be sitting on the bed intent on Joel while he spouted his lectures:

"You've lived a quiet and colorless life, while mine's been exciting. And you know one of the things that made it so stimulating? Building and fixing things. Like this bed. It's more than just a bed. It's a way I've learned the universal principles connected with it. The measuring, the balancing, the sawing—each part contains its own infinite laws. And then you take those precepts that you learn and you apply them to the next thing you do, or see. And the lightbulb goes on. 'Oh, now I know!' you say. 'It's like sawing the wood for the bed!' And then you grow and life is exciting. That's why I taught you to strip and sand wood. You have the potential to come alive. You can be as exciting as you'd like to be..."

That's just a small example of what I might have heard from Joel in an evening. For me, his words were magical. They sparkled; they fascinated me. They made me love him even more. And, of course, he was always teaching me something; and to me that meant he cared.

And speaking of caring advice, Joel's counsel resolved a problem regarding my first children's book, *Plants Do Amazing Things*. Well before our first date a year earlier, I'd already begun working on writing the book. During the year that had just passed, I'd spent a lot of time doing both the research and the writing. Joel had been patient and encouraging about the time I spent away from him because of the book.

For that reason, and a hundred more, I considered myself very lucky to love such a remarkable man, and I wanted to dedicate the book to him. But I had a problem. I also wanted to dedicate it to my only nephew, Judy's 12-year-old son, David, and to the person who had first given me the idea for writing the book, an artist named Murray.

Murray occupied the office next to mine at Random House. Daily he saw the roughly two dozen plants I had near my large picture window—hanging plants, large standing plants, and small potted ones. And one day, he said casually, "You know, you ought to write a book for children about plants."

I did exactly that, and now that the time had come to write a dedication, I was in a quandary. I finally talked to Joel about it.

"You may be able to come up with a dedication that will include all three," he suggested. And why didn't I play with the word "inspire," maybe using it in a different way for each of them?

The book was published with the dedication exactly as Joel had helped me compose it:

> To Murray, who inspired this book,
> To my nephew David, whom I hope this book inspires,
> And to Joel, my everyday inspiration.

Once again, Joel was the one with the solution to my problem.
He also began helping me with the clothes I wore. My parents didn't know

the difference between polyester and silk, and so neither did I. But since Joel was extremely knowledgeable about wearing what's right, I started learning to dress in a much more sophisticated and elegant way than ever before. I began learning about the quality of silk and other natural fabrics, to study the seams of a garment—do the patterns match up? Oh, but I learned that there shouldn't really be much of a pattern. Maybe a simple tweed or tattersall, but other than those, solids were best.

Yes, I was learning, but I still had a ways to go. Around that time I bought a fake suede jumpsuit in dusty pink, and Joel, very patiently, showed me where the quality wasn't right for me, and the color. He explained why I should wear black, white, navy, tan and brown—muted colors—and to forget the pinks and other bright colors. I knew he was right, but since I really liked that jumpsuit, I kept it and wore it. However, each time I did, I felt that I looked all wrong and should have listened to Joel.

No Sportswoman

I was and am a lousy athlete, although I used to be a lot worse. Joel's tutoring *really* helped me in that department and stuck.

He figured if I lost my ingrained inhibitions about sports that would help me come alive, and to come alive was what I wanted most for myself. I was so glad that Joel recognized it and desired the same for me as I did for myself. So, of course, I worked as hard as I could to achieve that goal.

Most of my associations with physical activity had been humiliating ones. My parents neither participated in nor had any interest in sports of any sort, and because I'd been born with a heart murmur, Mommy had been scared to let me exert myself (even though the doctor had put no restrictions on my activities). So I never learned to throw or catch a ball, roller skate, jump rope, etc.

So there I was in third grade, and I'd neither seen nor played a baseball game. Believe it or not, I didn't even know you had to bat before you ran the bases.

One day my class was playing softball in the schoolyard during recess. When I saw other kids running (after they'd batted the ball, of course), I ran too; but I'd never been up to bat. As you can imagine, the other kids thought my action something to ridicule. This did not encourage my ball playing.

In seventh grade, we girls had been given skill tests in gym class, and I could never get past the first one: pitching a ball into a square drawn on a wall.

My ego surely suffered while I watched all the other girls pass one test after another while I still struggled with the first.

But volleyball had been the worst of all. When it was my turn to serve, and all eyes were on me, I'd swing my arm, carefully aiming my hand at that not-very-tiny ball, and invariably I'd miss making contact. Oops—how humiliating.

But now with Joel, I began to learn all those skills I'd been deprived of. Together, he and I played Hit-the-Penny on the sidewalk, tossing a ball back and forth, trying to bounce it on a penny on the ground between us. He was patient and encouraging. He showed me how to reach out to catch a football and pull it in toward my body. And learning basketball was accomplished in the following manner: when Joel read a magazine, he'd complete a page, tear it out, crumple it into a ball, and toss it into the wastebasket. I followed suit, and each of my on-target baskets received a cheer. With Joel, sports had become fun, almost a treat. And he never made me feel inadequate; rather, I began to think I could do it.

Joel, I felt, was simply amazing regarding me and sports; he was patient and caring and spent more time and energy on little ole me than most men did on their wives or girlfriends. Of course I had no idea that this untiring coaching was part of Joel's long-term plan to gain control over me. And please have no doubt about that: Joel Steinberg had such a plan somewhere in the back of his mind starting the day he'd met me. But of course, I had no concept of that back in 1976; instead, I was led to believe he was the best—better than all the rest, as the song goes. So my love for him grew stronger and stronger.

Rona

Although Joel was forever talking, and he covered all sorts of topics from the Supreme Court to his teenage summers in Mahopac, New York, and from Lyndon Johnson (one of his heroes) to the trouble he had collecting the rent from his law office tenants, he did an awful lot of chattering about Rona. Most of what he said about her was negative, but she was definitely still on his mind.

Then I started getting the uneasy feeling that he'd been seeing her again. And one day after he'd been gone with Sasha for a very long "walk," I confronted him.

"You've been seeing Rona, haven't you?" I said quietly.

And he answered me honestly, "Yeah. You see, I haven't yet resolved my feelings about her. I still need to work it through. Yes, I'm the one who ended it, and yes, I'm the one who packed up all her stuff, put it outside the door, and then I changed all the locks so she couldn't get back in. But I need one definite act, something to prove that she's really a part of my past now."

Although I was pleased that Joel felt he could talk to me about this, I was also worried. What if he couldn't resolve it? And in the meantime, I had to share my man with this woman whom he'd been telling me was so great in bed. This I *definitely* did not like, and I was pretty sure sex was part of what had been going on between them. Fortunately, in those days, we didn't have to worry about AIDS. But I worried anyway: What if he decided that the great sex was what he really wanted? I felt somehow inadequate because she'd been a ballet dancer and could, according to Joel, move in ways that I couldn't.

Fortunately, soon thereafter, Joel found the definite act he'd been after to resolve things about Rona. One night, Joel came home thoroughly incensed.

"I can't believe it!" he fumed. "Do you know what I saw tonight? Rona getting out of a car with Charlie [the pseudonym I'm using for a former client of his] and going into a restaurant on 9th Street. You can't believe the horrible things she used to say about him! What a hypocrite!"

And on and on he ranted.

"Now I know that this is definitely over for me," he announced.

"But do you still love her?" I asked.

"What's love, anyway?" was Joel's reply. "We think we love someone, but it's really a physiological reaction. And then after it's over, we manage to go on to the next person and put our former "love" out of mind. It's all a joke. Oh, I was devoted to Rona, before I saw the light. Now you're all that matters to me."

So I never got an answer to the question, but his words left me satisfied.

Happily for me, the relationship between Joel and Rona was definitely over, but still he continued to talk about her incessantly. I kept silent about the subject, trying to be supportive and understanding—until one night at Ed's group, at which I was now a regular.

Ed must have sensed that a confrontation was needed because he asked Joel to look each group member in the eye and tell him or her something he liked about Rona. Joel complied, while I sat there, quietly freaking out, hearing how he respected her being a dedicated school teacher, how she was such a terrific lover, and so on, things I had by this time definitely and gratefully forgotten.

By the time Joel got around to telling me something about Rona, I exploded with, "I've heard enough about Rona! I don't ever want to hear another word about her—ever!"

And amazingly to me, Joel curtailed his incessant talk about her. Once in a while he mentioned her the way he mentioned anyone from his past, but I'd managed to really make an impact on his behavior.

Houses

April 1976. We're looking at houses today! I've never lived in a whole house—always an apartment. Even in Berkeley, CA, where I lived about ten years ago, the house was divided into four apartments, and I shared mine with roommates to boot. But Joel really wants to buy a house. He hates living in the city as much as I do. There's only one difference: I want to live in "the country," and he wants to live at the seashore. As a child, I spent my summers in the Catskill Mountains, which I always called "the country."

I *loved* being in the country. In the city, I had to stay in the house most of the time when not at school, I had few friends, and life was dull. But in the country, I was allowed to run around and play, and there were lots of kids to play with.

With the perils of city traffic gone, Mommy and Daddy allowed Judy and me to play outdoors—not only during the day, but until bedtime in the evening. When I was thrown together with other kids there, the timid Hedda disappeared, and I did fine. In the country, I felt alive and free.

In fact, since that time, I've wanted to live where I could see green and not gray when looking out my window. But, as a matter of fact, Joel's love, the seashore, will do me very nicely, thank you, since modern houses on the shore have plenty of grass and trees surrounding them.

We've borrowed Joel's mother's car for the day. Actually, Joel says it's really *his* car, but since his mother lives in Yonkers, she needs it more than he does in the city, what with alternate-side-of-the-street parking and ridiculously priced garages.

Joel has developed relationships over the years with a couple of real estate agents. Obviously this is not his first time looking at houses. But when he was with Rona, he's told me, a house would have been too large a commitment for him. Gosh, does that mean he's ready to make a commitment with me? I don't think so, but this is a step in the right direction.

The agent we're going to see today is Audrey Ellis in Mamaroneck. She's shown Joel houses before in that town and in nearby Larchmont—on Long Island Sound, of course. Joel's dream is a house on the sound, and a sailboat to go with it. During our hiatus, he sold the boat he'd told me about when I met him. But with a house on the sound, he'll get another bigger one. That old one was only a 21 footer. I see its photo daily on the wall in the hall opposite the kitchen and bathroom where Joel's hung an array of black and white pictures from his recent and not-so-recent past.

There's Joel, about 17, slim but quite muscular in chinos and a tee shirt, leaning on the beloved little MG he owned then. And there's a shot Joel's so proud of, showing him in the plane he flew in the air force, unshaven and looking *very* tired. There's also Joel cutting into a large mango-like tropical fruit from a vacation a year or two ago—mustachioed like now, a bit of a paunch sticking out from a dark, striped tee shirt that's still in his closet. (Gotta keep him exercising.) And there's the boat. On it with a young-looking, handsome Joel is a tiny blond Miss of about two: Dawn, the little girl he'd begun raising, the one who was killed in the Christmas tree fire this past New Year's Eve. There'd been a picture on that wall of Rona, too, but Joel's finally taken it down. Thank goodness.

LATER: We looked at a magnificent house on the sound. It was so large! I've never dreamed of living in a house that's huge like that. Wow! It had two stories, three bedrooms, a huge living room and dining room and it's own waterfront and dock. Gosh! Imagine if we lived in a place like that!

Audrey seems to enjoy Joel so much. I guess that's why she keeps showing him houses, even though he's never come close to buying one. I think just about everyone appreciates Joel's charm. He's like a magnet, attracting people to him all the time. I wish I could be like that. But I'm quiet, shy. However, Joel's been working with me to get me to be more outgoing. Just being with all the people that constantly surround him has already made a difference.

Oh, and we had dinner at a lovely restaurant right on the sound. Gosh, Joel makes life so wonderful.

Paris

It was May 1976, and Joel had something new to be animated about. He was going to Iran! (At this time, the Shah was still alive, and the US was on good terms with that country.) A former client who'd fled to his native Teheran to escape criminal charges here had now decided he wanted to return to the USA, and he needed Joel over there. That was the message Joel received, along with a ticket to Paris. The instructions: wait in Paris for further word and a plane ticket to Iran.

Ooh, I felt, this had the aura of Joel's stories about his days in the Defense Intelligence Agency. Adventure. Romance. It seemed to surround Joel all the time.

I was probably as excited as Joel. He'd be going to Paris for a few days with his buddy, whom I'll call Tim—a fellow member of Ed's group—and then moving on to Iran alone for a total of two weeks. I helped him make all the arrangements for this, his first trip to Europe and the Middle East, eagerly studied his Iranian visa, and packed for him at his request. Like a child, he seemed to need me to select his clothes and put them in the suitcase.

"Aw, please, do it for me."

Being needed felt good to me, so I didn't insist that he pack for himself like an adult.

And when he was finally gone, I took Sasha with me and slept once more in my own bed on 76th Street where I stayed until Joel returned to the USA.

But there was one day during that trip that I spent not on 76th Street but on 10th Street, and that was the occasion of a big step for me. I'd never told my parents that I'd moved out of my own apartment and into Joel's. Since I always telephoned them, they didn't have much need to call me, and when they did, Mommy would call me at my office during the day. So there was no real way for them to know I wasn't living at home.

Being virtual dinosaurs, they'd be horrified at the news, I was sure, even though they were both crazy about Joel, a Jewish lawyer who had taken a strong interest in their daughter, was attractive, had a great sense of humor, and treated her well. (That's what I'd told them because I believed it was true.) Anyway, according to Mommy at least, living with a man out of wedlock would wreck a woman's reputation totally and ruin her chances for marriage.

As you can see, Mommy was quite old fashioned in ways typical of the days before women's liberation. She had spent her married years at home, cooking, cleaning, doing laundry, and taking care of the kids, but never writing a check. Financial affairs were in the man's domain, not the woman's. This was traditional thinking, and Mommy had continued to look at all aspects of male-female relationships in a similar, antiquated fashion. So living with a man out of wedlock would shake the foundations of her reasoning.

However, I'd decided that the time had finally come to inform her, as well as Daddy who, I believed, was a little more modern in his beliefs, but not a whole lot. So I called them and said that while Joel was away, I was dog sitting at his place, and why didn't they come down there to visit? They did, and for that day, so did Sasha and I—making for delicious irony because we had to trek down from my apartment on West 76th Street.

That's when I broke the news: I was living with Joel. Mommy was silent and grim faced. Daddy smiled and said, "That's what I thought." My thinking had been right: he kept more in tune with the times than she did.

The relief I felt because they now knew about my "indiscretion" left my mind free to dwell on a more pleasant topic. Joel's birthday was coming up on May 25th, and I wanted to make a birthday party for him. After much thought, I decided on a large, catered surprise party the day after his return. I made a list of all his friends and business associates. Wow! It was long. I'd hardly fit them all into his apartment. But I'd invite every one. Maybe a few wouldn't be able to make it, I hoped.

One of my 76th Street neighbors, Evelyn, gave me excellent ideas for menus and caterers. But there'd be no room for Evelyn, or any other of my own friends, so I didn't invite any of them. But did I use my brain and explain the circumstances to Evelyn or to Barbara, another of my close friends who'd heard about the big party? No. I was totally focused on Joel. It never even occurred to me that either of them might feel offended. Of course, when my head cleared years later, I felt pretty terrible about treating them in this way. I guess this statement is my belated apology.

About two days before the party, I got a phone call from Joel. I felt thrilled to hear from him. I could tell he'd been drinking. He was always more glib and even more verbally expressive with a little alcohol in him.

To my surprise, he was still in France—at a woman's house on the outskirts of Paris, he said—and he enthusiastically described to me some of his marvelous French experiences. He'd never heard from his client, he reported, so he'd never gotten to Iran, but, hell, he was having such a fantastic time in France that he was going to stay on for another week or two. So much for my party.

The Teapot

My prized English china teapot was the first victim in my saga of intimate terrorism, otherwise known as domestic violence. And I was the one who smashed that teapot, but Joel's "game" was the cause.

Maybe he was testing me, seeing how far he could push. If he got angry with me for something insignificant and then demanded that I leave the house for the night, what would I do? Would the insights he'd gleaned about me from my openness with him be correct? Would my separation anxiety and fear of loss ensure my compliance, or might I resist?

Here's how Joel's experiment played out. One night during one of our long conversations, he became angry with me, though I have no idea what it was all about. When the demand came, "Pack your bag and go to a hotel for the night!" I was in shock. I was in a panic. My old separation anxiety popped up, just as he had probably assumed it would. *I can't lose Joel, not now that he's come to mean so much to me*. So I complied and packed a small bag with a nightgown, toothpaste and toothbrush, my hairbrush, and clean underwear for the morning.

As I was reluctantly about to leave for the hotel, Joel called me into the kitchen and handed me the exquisite Royal Dalton china teapot I'd purchased when Risa and I had visited England in 1966. Designed to be simple—pure white interrupted only by silver trim around the edges—Joel knew that I loved it dearly. In fact, except for the piano that still sat in my unoccupied apartment on 76th Street, this teapot was my only treasured possession.

"You'd better take this with you," Joel directed as he handed the teapot to me.

I stared at this piece of china now in my hands. I loved it, true. But I didn't love it nearly as much as I loved Joel. I wanted to have it with me, true. But I didn't want to be near it as much as I wanted to be near Joel. And to take it implied some sort of permanent separation from him. Without even actually forming these thoughts, I reacted to them. And as if to demonstrate them, I allowed the teapot to fall out of my hands to the floor, splintering into hundreds of tiny pieces.

I never did go to a hotel that night. Instead Joel and I stayed up all night, sitting in the living room talking, and I remember clearly what Joel said about the teapot: "I just thought you ought to have it because, the way I was feeling, I might have done some damage to it."

Those words never really penetrated. Was Joel telling me he could be violent? If he was, I never heard it. I was just so glad that he'd not "kicked me out."

So Joel got 100% on his own test. He could manipulate me at will, and I wouldn't resist.

Not Criticizing

April 1976. We're taking a Sunday evening after-dinner stroll, and Joel hasn't taken my hand; when I try to take hold of his, he pulls away. This makes me feel horrible, unwanted. So I say to him, "Joel, why won't you hold my hand? I feel so rejected."

"I'm not rejecting *you*," he answers. "It's just that your hand is so tense. You've gotta relax. It's the same with the way you walk. You're not at ease even with walking. Your knees are stiff. You have to bend them when you walk. See how I do it?"

So I try. I try to relax my hand and bend my legs when I walk. But Joel's still not happy.

Later, at home, he repeats all the stuff about the hand and the legs.

"Relax," he says. "It's so easy. You've got to let yourself be you. It's that you that I care about, that I want to be with. Stop being in control of yourself all the time. Let it be."

So I keep trying to relax, to let go of the control of myself. It's funny that no one else has ever complained about it before. Well (sigh), if Joel thinks I need to relax more, I'll work at it.

Yet there's no way I can do it. It's a double-edged sword: If I don't try, I'm too stiff to please Joel. If I do try, I can't relax for trying so hard.

And I get the same criticism in bed.

"You've got to be more spontaneous," my lover demands. "Let go."

But the result is the same. I'm damned if I do and…

It's all very stressful because I'm so in love with this man; I've got to make him feel the same. I can't lose him. He's everything I've ever wanted. I don't know what to do.

If he would only stay happy with me, as he seems to be half the time. At those times things seem so good; it's like paradise to me. We laugh and have fun. Like when we do the *Times* crossword puzzle on Sunday. There's no criticism when we're working on the puzzle. It's pure play for us.

We have a system. We always do the puzzle together, and neither one of us is allowed to write in an answer until we both know it. Sometimes I don't know an answer when I first look at the puzzle, and then, later, when Joel says he knows it, suddenly I do too. I'm certain I'm getting it from his mind somehow. And even that's fun and proves how close we are.

If only he weren't so critical of me. Oh, he says he's not criticizing me; he's just trying to help me grow. Criticism is negative, Joel tells me, while what he's doing is positive: "It doesn't tear down, it builds up," he repeats. So why do I so often feel like I've been razed?

Isolation

After first moving in with Joel, I'd felt I should spend all my non-working time with him (I spent much time working both at my job and on my book), so I was hesitant to make appointments with my friends.

Joel would say, "No, I want you to see your friends. That's so important. Please don't stay home on account of me!"

He asserted this sentiment again and again. Soon I felt comfortable enough to see them as well as to try to include Joel in my time with them, even getting dates for them with Joel's friends and double dating. However, that only gave him more time to observe their less favorable traits, which he highlighted repeatedly.

I prefer not to mention names here when I note the negative characteristics that Joel attributed to each one. Each friend actually had those undesirable traits—to some extent, at least. Only, I'd overlooked those things, preferring to emphasize each one's positive qualities.

"X is really selfish. She never thinks about you, only herself." Well, except for the "never" part, this had a lot of truth in it. So eventually, though not right away, out went X.

"Y has no class. You deserve friends who can build your image. She brings you down." So, after many months of Joel's friendly persuasion, although Y was a kind and caring person, out she went too.

"Z is so shy. You need to hang around with friends who can bring more people and excitement to your life. I really don't know what you see in him, anyway." And yes, of course, Z went the way of X and Y.

Etcetera, etcetera, etcetera.

Critiques

February 21, 1977. It's been nearly two years now since I've known Joel, 21 months to grow to love him more and more. But day and night I get from him not "I love you," but, "You don't want to work to grow. You want someone's magic wand to do it for you. You want me to take care of you, work for you, teach you. You don't want to take care of me, or anyone else. You don't want to give. You just want to take."

That's not true. I do so want to give. I give to Joel every minute. I give him my love, my soul, my everything. And I try so hard to change, to be everything he wants me to be, everything I want me to be. But it doesn't happen. If only he could see that I'm his one thousand percent. But he doesn't.

Life is a constant struggle for me, not only in trying please Joel, but in trying to please myself. He's invited to so many parties and dinners, and of course, I go too. But they're uncomfortable for me. Always have been. I just have nothing to say to strangers unless someone interesting starts a conversation with me first. Then I can handle it.

To help me with this, Joel's been tutoring me in party behavior. No, actually, he's been tutoring me in sociability. Yeah, that's it, and although I've definitely become more sociable in my own office with people I see every day, it's so much harder when I'm at parties and dinners with Joel's friends and clients. So when we go, I try, real hard.

Like last night. We drove out to Long Island to the home of some old friends/clients of Joel's, whom I'll call Dennis and Stephanie. Well, they're friends for whom he's done some legal work.

So we're in their basement, and while Joel was going around charming all the women and shmoozing with all the men, I was standing around shyly, smiling—and feeling awkward. The women, to generalize a bit, wore lots of makeup, had on cleavage-revealing blouses, and overindulged in alcohol. Not exactly my type.

I was wearing a very simple, sophisticated outfit— a tailored skirt and silk blouse (no cleavage showing, of course) with a pair of black heels, small silver earrings, and the silver, brass, and copper bracelet I had made in jewelry class a few years ago. Joel said I looked "elegant." But I felt "different."

Oh, the women were nice to me, and they tried to make conversation. I did my best, but the evening was a struggle for me. Entirely.

At least I got a few compliments on the bracelet.

"Ooh, where did you get *that*?" a woman would coo.

"I made it," I'd reply shyly, feeling very proud.

But except for the bracelet praise and the pleasure I got watching the handsomest and most charming man in the house (Joel, of course), I had a really lousy evening.

So right away in the car (we had borrowed Daddy's car) as we were driving home, Joel started in telling me that I have to be more outgoing at these parties. Like I don't want to be. I put that very same burden on myself, but I don't do outgoing very well.

And then all the way home—it was a two-hour drive—Joel critiqued my behavior, step by step. When I came in I should have done such and such. And then when I was talking with Annie, I should have said such and such when she told me about whatever. And on and on it went. He went through the entire party. How the heck did he seem to be enjoying himself so much when he was watching me all the time?

And this is a pattern now. I mean, this isn't the first critique after a social event. When we go out to dinner with people, I get the same step-by-step analysis. I know he's trying to help me. He's great that way. But gosh, I feel so inadequate.

And that's what happens in our nightly critique sessions, too. Somehow, with all Joel's help, I end up feeling worse instead of better. The only time I do feel really good is when I see that Joel's tutoring is coming to fruition, and it's actually happening at work these days. I come into the office and just talk to people. I don't wait for them to talk to me first like I always used to. But that's just not good enough for Joel—I have to be that way all the time, he says. It's never-ending.

Here's what a session sounds like:

Joel, pacing beside the bed: You've got to let go, be yourself. Stop always being in control of yourself. Just be. You're afraid to be yourself. You know that? Afraid. You think that if you're you, maybe everyone won't like you. To hell with other people! So they don't like you? Who are they, anyway? You're better than they are. Right? So just be you. You're afraid they won't like you even if you don't like them! That makes no sense, does it? Does it?

ME: No. I guess not.

JOEL: You *guess*? Of course not.

And it goes on for an hour or two like that. And then maybe we watch Johnny Carson before we put out the lights and make love. So that's life with Joel—lectures and growth. But never enough of the latter for him. So then there are more lectures, and more therapy sessions, and more and more, every night. And I keep trying. Sigh. And he's never satisfied. Sigh again.

Overindulging

When I met Joel, and for several years thereafter, he refused to put any kind of drug into his body, even aspirin. In fact, I'd plead with him when he had a headache to take one, but he'd say, "I'm not going to put any foreign substance into my body."

I'd shrug and think he had to be nuts, yet admire him for his strength.

I'd found it really mind boggling when he'd come home from the dentist once after having a tooth pulled, and told me how very stalwart he'd been by refusing Novocain.

"I can't allow anything like that into my body," he had insisted.

On the other hand, he drank cups and cups of coffee every day at the office, and he had no aversion to alcohol. In fact, around 1977, he went through a period of drinking excessively every time he went out to dinner or a party, which was several times per week.

Joel assigned me the responsibility of watching him carefully and making certain that he kept his alcohol intake moderate. At dinner in a restaurant, I'd mind how many glasses of wine he drank, and nudge him when he'd had enough. Then after dinner, I'd watch and warn again as he drank espresso with sambuca or anisette.

"Joel, you'd better cool it with the alcohol. I think you've had enough…"

I'd generally have to remind him a few times, and sometimes he'd have an after-dinner brandy or two before he actually stopped.

But the lord help me if I were ever distracted by conversation with others, especially with another man, and Joel overindulged. Then it was all my fault.

"You were too busy talking with Dick to pay attention to me, weren't you? You were so busy talking with him about all those important things that you could just ignore your own man. Don't you have any sense of caring? Don't I help you out all the time? If the roles were reversed, I'd be there for you. You know that. But you don't want to take care of me. You want me to take care of you all the time. You just won't hold to your responsibility to me. A fine partner you are, letting me get drunk! Now I'll have to clear myself out so I won't be sick in the morning."

What Joel meant by that was this: He'd stick his finger down his throat, much like a bulimic would, and vomit up all the alcohol—as well as anything else that was in his stomach from dinner. I'd stand beside him to comfort and encourage him as he hung his head over the sink. It was a thoroughly gross experience, and yet fascinating in a bizarre way.

I especially remember one night when Joel became extremely drunk. We were in New Jersey at the wedding of a client of his.

"Joel," the client said. "Let me put you and Hedda up at a hotel tonight. I think it'll be better for you."

"Good idea," I said. "Let's stay, Joel."

"No, I don't need to shtay. I'm in full control; no matter how much I've had to drink, I can drive. No problem."

The client continued to prod him, and Joel kept on insisting he could drive and not to worry. Mr. Big Shot could make it home easily. So, finally, the client gave up, and that was well after I'd stopped nudging Joel to stay. After all, if Joel Steinberg said he could stay in control, as far as I was concerned, he could do it.

So Joel got behind the wheel of the car. Of course, I could have driven, but that wasn't even considered an option by either of us. And I remember feeling perfectly safe. I had complete and total faith in him, and I wasn't a bit drunk.

I don't know how he did it, but we reached home safely, and I recall that he did seem in full control, which of course encouraged my reliance upon him.

However, not long thereafter, Joel had to cut out all over-indulgences. One evening in 1977, Joel met with an old Air Force friend of his, Joe Penner, a dermatologist. And, as Joel told it to me, Joe had looked at him and said, "I don't like the way you look."

Dr. Penner then took Joel's pulse and listened to his heart. Joe, who liked to play the clown and act bizarrely sometimes, simply pulled out his stethoscope and listened—right in the restaurant where they were having dinner. Thinking he detected an arrhythmia in Joel's heart, he recommended a cardiologist.

So, one day, Joel went out to the town on Long Island where the cardiologist—I'll call him Alan Gross—whom Joe Penner had promised would treat Joel "right" (meaning cheaply) had his practice. Joel spent the entire day there having tests and then had dinner with Dr. Gross. A few days later, both Joel and I went to Columbia Presbyterian Hospital in Washington Heights (about 30 blocks from where my parents lived) to meet Dr. Gross for another test.

Both Bonnie Gross, the doctor's wife, and I were left in a classroom together for well over an hour while Al gave Joel the test. And, boy-o-boy, was I bored!. Bonnie, a sloppily overweight woman of about 30 with a droning voice, was clearly not someone I could relate to.

When we got home, Joel told me that Al had told him he wanted to spend more time with him—on a personal level.

"But I don't really enjoy Al. What do you think I should do?"

"Well," I said after thinking about it for a while, "why don't you give him a chance, spend a little time with him, and then see how you feel?"

"Good idea. I'll do that. And then if I still don't enjoy the guy, I'll just give him the polite heave-ho. Good thinking."

When the test results came back, Joel was told that he did indeed have a heart arrhythmia. So he'd have to stop smoking (he smoked about two packs a day—Marlboros), stop drinking caffeinated coffee (he drank it all day long in his office, totaling maybe 10 cups a day as well as consuming a pot of espresso every night after dinner), cut out alcohol, and get plenty of exercise—that is, if he wanted to escape having a heart attack.

Joel took this very seriously and, amazingly, stopped smoking cold turkey. He also switched immediately to decaf coffee and quit the espresso— for a while, at least. I was impressed with the strength of his will.

However, when it came to exercise and alcohol, he had a bit more trouble. He reduced the alcohol but never totally quit, and I had to keep pushing him to exercise. He loved to play paddleball, and used to play often, but he rarely did it anymore.

"What I need to do is get together a racquetball game. I hear that's the big thing now, racquetball."

"Well, then, do it."

Roles were reversed here for once. I kept coaxing him to get a group together for racquetball, and he kept promising to do it but failing to follow through.

But finally, Alan Gross said he'd come into the city one night a week to play, as did another new friend of Joel's, a man I'll call Sam Altman, a lawyer from the suburbs north of the city. When they found a fourth player, Joel began getting his exercise.

David's Bar Mitzvah

Judy's son, David, turned 13 in March of 1977, and as most Jewish families did, Judy and her husband were having a large reception after the religious Bar Mitzvah services, with everyone who could be considered a family member or friend invited.

By this time, I'd learned enough about quality from Joel to purchase for the occasion an elegant, gray, scooped-neck Diane Von Furstenburg dress at Bloomingdale's for half price. And what's more, somehow I'd shrunk from an average-looking size 11, which I'd been from age 18 on, to a much more favorable (to me) size 7 when I met Joel, and now, incredibly, to a diminutive size 5!

I'd always dreamed of being tiny like Judy, my older sister by two years, who was exceptionally small. And Mommy's efforts to ensure that Judy didn't end up with what everyone then called "an inferiority complex," had ironically served to increase mine.

"Good things come in small packages," she had reminded Judy over and over while I listened.

My package, however, had been decidedly larger, even though I was younger; and from age eight to fourteen I'd been chubby, a condition I hated. Oh, how I wanted to be tiny and slender like Judy. She, however, wished she were taller, like me—in spite of Mommy's declarations about good things and small packages. The proverbial grass is always greener.

And now, at age 34, I'd finally become a good thing in a small package! My recollection is that I'd had a change in metabolism that allowed me to eat all I wanted and never gain an ounce. A dream come true! Judy, however, recalls Joel keeping an eye on every bite I took at the Bar Mitzvah and seeing me sneak some cake behind Joel's back afterwards. His restrictions came, she says, at a time when I was already so thin that my cheeks were hollow and drawn.

But I glowed with pride at that family affair because Joel impressed my relatives with his charm and his obvious devotion to me. I especially remember my Aunt Gerdie fascinated with one of his monologues. At last I was able to show the family, who probably considered me an old maid at 34, that I had snagged a "fantastic" man. This made up for the fact that Joel was slow in getting ready and caused us to arrive late to the reception. It also made up for my missing the temple services earlier that day. Joel had persuaded me to miss those and go only to the celebration that followed.

"What do you need to go to the services for? You know how boring they are. What's the big deal about being there for that? You'll be there later for the party, and you'll dazzle them with your great looks. That's what counts."

So I was persuaded, and I missed David's official passage into manhood, something I knew he would want his only aunt to witness.

A Dream Come True

I don't recall the exact date it happened. It could have been in 1977 or '78. Joel had, several months earlier, graduated from Ed's group—the only member who'd apparently learned "the work" well enough to earn that honor. Apparently even insightful Ed had become convinced that Joel kept his focus, was centered, and spoke his feelings honestly.

Now Ed had left New York to work in Europe, and the rest of us in the group tried for a while to make a go of it with a replacement whom Ed had trained, and then with a self-appointed successor. However, as far as I was concerned, neither had Ed's capabilities, so I left. And although I'd stopped seeing Dr. Norton and no longer went to his group, I remained friendly for a while with several of its members.

A party given by one of them became the actualization of a dream for me. Joel's tutoring had come to fruition.

Could this be me with a crowd listening to my animated conversation? Yes, there I was with a group of people, male and female, standing around me—all evening—listening to me talk freely and comfortably. And these were people whom I'd never met before! And, amazingly, for the first time in our relationship, a couple asked *me*, not Joel, if we would join them on their sailboat the next weekend, and Joel stood back quietly in the background, *kvelling*. That's a Yiddish word that usually describes a parent's or grandparent's feeling of happiness and intense pride in the behavior of his or her dear, little child. And yes, that was our relationship: Father and child. Joel had successfully taught me how to behave in the world. And I was overjoyed that my man's superior talents had brought me so far.

At the office, I was now comfortably talking with people at every level from my boss to my secretary. In a conversation with the typographer on the *Charlie Brown* Super Books I was editing, I learned that she and two of her friends were going for a few days to a tennis camp, and I said, "Ooh, can I come too?"—a request I'd not have dared to make at an earlier time.

And indeed, I did go with them. The camp turned out to be fun, I got on well with the other women, and I even learned to play a bit of tennis.

On the drive home we sang camp songs all the way—a forte of mine, since I have the strange ability to remember every word to any song I learned before about 1964. At last I was making new friends. Joel could be proud of me now, and he seemed to be, or at least he seemed to enjoy, as much as I did, some of the advantages my new sociability brought.

For example, one night we were on our way out to a party at the home of an attorney and his wife, old acquaintances of Joel's.

"Let's play a game tonight," suggested Joel with a twinkle in his eye sharper than his usual one. "No one at the party knows you, and there'll be lots of people there. So let's pretend that we don't know each other. You just go out there and charm all the men—have a good time. Don't worry about me; I'll have plenty of people to talk to."

"Really?" I giggled. "You won't mind?"

"Would I suggest it if I minded? Have fun. I've trained you for this long enough. Flirt! Enjoy yourself!"

Although this would seem a strange approach for a man to take with his lover—that is, had it been any other man—it made perfect sense for Joel to exhibit such hubris. He knew of my unfailing devotion to him and him alone. In fact, he savored seeing men falling all over me at parties (and I had become, I must admit now, quite a *femme fatale*), sure all along that I'd be leaving with him with no temptation to go elsewhere.

Our little charade this night wouldn't really be so unusual. It had become our custom since I'd come out of the wallpaper for Joel and me to separate at a party and spend the evening on our own, each chatting with a variety of people. And I'd come to enjoy my separate conversations with men. I could show off my new-found confidence, my intelligence, and my charm, and feel great seeing men drooling over me. It sure beat feeling lonely and desperately uncomfortable in a crowd like I always had in the past.

This night was even more fun than usual. From time to time I'd see Joel, beaming with pleasure, sneaking a look at me toying with some guy's sexual appetite.

What other woman was so lucky? I thought happily. *Who had a man who not only wasn't jealous but encouraged her to flirt and have fun?*

We went home happy and made fiery love.

But the next day Joel spent two hours lecturing me on being more relaxed and spontaneous.

Sex, Marriage, Houses, and Babies

Not only was life becoming much more fun since I'd come out of my shell, but my hopes of permanently settling down with Joel Steinberg were heightened. Now that I was starting to be me—just what Joel wanted for me—we'd find a house, get married, and have those children we both wanted so badly.

So you can imagine my excitement when, in the spring of 1977, we finally found a house. It was on the New Rochelle/Larchmont border, had the requisite acre of land, and although it wasn't on the water, Joel decided he'd supply that himself by building a motor-run waterfall. Certainly the price was right: $67,000. How could Joel pass up a bargain like that? (As it turned out, he did. I now believe he was too frugal to put up the money for even a deal like this one. But then, he claimed that the house wasn't perfect, and Joel demanded perfection.)

Believing that, how did I ever think I'd live up? How could I ever feel secure in the belief that he'd love me enough to want to stay with me forever? Guess what? I didn't, even though Joel finally said those precious words to me on occasion: I love you.

And although, through programming me with a repetition of: "Why do you need a piece of paper to make it official? If two people are committed, that's enough," Joel had convinced me to outwardly go along with his beliefs about marriage, I most definitely still wanted to get married to Joel.

Once I turned 35 in August of 1977, I had trouble hearing any sound other than that of my biological clock: tick-tock, tick-tock, ticking away like mad.

And then one night we had dinner in a restaurant across from Lincoln Center with Joel's old friend Joe Penner (the doctor who'd first detected Joel's heart arrhythmia) and a woman he knew named Trudy. What I remember of this evening is an intense conversation with Trudy about having children. I don't recall what was said, but I know this: By the time Joel and I went home that night, I'd made a decision—marriage or no marriage, I was going to become pregnant with Joel's child ASAP!

And contrary to the way I'd consistently behaved with Joel all along, I didn't say a thing about it to him—not right away. Instead, I simply stopped taking the birth control pills I normally popped every morning. I suppose I must have strongly feared that Joel would turn tail in terror if he knew I was seriously committed to having his child.

But I was wrong. Because after a few days, I told Joel of my plan and my subsequent action. (That's me. How could I possibly keep a secret from my soul mate?) And to my great shock and pleasure, he was thrilled.

"I've wanted children so badly," he told me, holding me close to him in bed. "And since Dawn's death, I've felt a real emptiness that needs to be filled. So I'm elated that you feel as strongly about this as I do. We're gonna have a baby!"

But that didn't happen so easily. We had two issues to face first: fertility and fidelity.

Winning and Losing

December 1977. Life doesn't always turn out the way you want it. Since I met Joel, I've believed that once I came out of my shell and became more outgoing and freer with people, he would be satisfied. And then I'd be content. But that's not the reality. I've definitely come out socially, and yet Joel's still not happy with me.

Sex. That's what he says is the problem. I'm not spontaneous enough. And it's true, I guess. During lovemaking I tend to concentrate real hard on how I'm moving my pelvis—is it the *right* way? Is it the way Joel wants me to move? Will I please him? So how can I be spontaneous? I'm caught in a trap because if I don't think about it, I may not move exactly as I'm supposed to, and then Joel will get angry again. In fact, his dissatisfaction over this issue is why I started concentrating on my pelvis in the first place. Sigh.

And my failure to satisfy Joel has caused my worst fantasy to become a reality: he's dating other women!

But at least he's being honest and up-front about

what he's doing. Most men who cheat on their partners try to cover their tracks, but not Joel. And I admire that. So I don't feel I can complain, especially since it's all my fault. That's so ironic, isn't it?

I learned the other day, for the first time, what's been going on. Listen:

JOEL: You know where I was so late tonight?

ME: No. You're always ending up going somewhere with somebody, so I don't worry about it. I know I can trust you.

JOEL: Well, I want you to continue feeling you can, and that's why I want to tell you the truth. I had a date tonight.

ME: A date? With a woman?

JOEL: You know I've been talking myself blue in the face for years to get you to be more spontaneous, but you just haven't gotten there. You refuse to satisfy me sexually, and I need a woman who can fulfill me in bed.

So what could I say? How could I complain? He's being honest, and now it's up to me. But how will I survive this one?

Truth, Lies, and Joel Steinberg

Clearly, Joel was honest with me about his infidelity because that served his purposes, but when dishonesty brought him closer to his desired ends, that reigned. From the time I first met him, Joel would tell extravagant tall tales to friends and clients. I'd hear him on the phone saying something like, "That new client of mine is really a representative of my old employer, the DIA [Defense Intelligence Agency, which had, in fact, been his employer], and he's going to get me involved in some spy stuff again," (which was not true).

And I'd scold him when he got off the phone.

"Joel, that's not true. You shouldn't tell lies. You need to tell the truth."

And he'd counter, "Well, this kind of untruth does no harm. I need to do it for business, to impress people. They need to see me as someone special if I want them to call on me to represent them."

And when I'd admonish him for telling clients that we owned things we didn't, like boats or horses, he'd come back with, "People need the image of material success to appreciate my value to them. In fact, you need to do a little of that yourself. Let people see you as someone with a lot to offer them."

And I'd be the one ending up changing my way of thinking. "Yeah, I guess so," I'd finally say.

So as time passed, I came to accept his exaggerations and distortions of the truth—for that's what they usually were, as opposed to outright fabrications from whole cloth.

Convinced of Joel's business motivation, I not only accepted, but actually verbally corroborated (when pressed), his story about *our* horses. I realized that unless I chose to expose him and embarrass him horribly, which I'd never do, I didn't have much choice.

That "our horses" tale arose because Joel's friend Joe Ferranti, another lawyer, owned a beautiful steed named Pegasus, which he stabled at a ranch in Wayne, New Jersey. On a visit there with Joe, Joel turned on the charm with the stable owner, spouted a little professional advice, and was invited to return and use any horses he chose in exchange for giving the owner free legal counsel. So the stable horses acquired the title "our horses." When Joel brought friends or clients to Wayne, New Jersey, for a day of riding, they were suitably impressed, having no knowledge of the truth.

I never became comfortable, however, with Joel's exaggeration about my success or about that of one of my friends. Barbara, a friend since college, was someone Joel didn't separate me from for a long time. I think he believed he was charming her into being one of his faithful fans. For people either despised Joel or adored him, and he dealt only with the latter. As long as Barbara seemed to be in his corner, I was allowed to remain her friend.

Joel would introduce Barbara, who worked for New York City's Housing Authority, as "the head of rent control." She'd stand there looking very embarrassed because, in truth, she had nothing to do with rent control and didn't head up any department. But how could she say, "Oh, no, I don't have such a prestigious job. All I do is…"

I believe that Joel had a desperate need to feel that those who surrounded him would impress others as much as he made sure he did. And I think that's the reason he began pushing me for promotions: he wanted me to have an awe-inspiring title at Random House to feed his own ego needs.

"How long have you been at Random House?" Joel asked me one evening.

"Since September, 1974."

"And you're still an Associate Editor! It's more than time for you to ask for a promotion."

"But, Joel, I can't do that. I don't deserve to be promoted."

"What do you mean!? Of course you do. You're the best editor there. Jenny [a senior editor in my department] sees it. You know she does. In fact, she's jealous of you. Don't tell me you're afraid to ask for a promotion because you don't think you're as good as she is? You know you shine above her, and all the rest! And what about Bernette [an associate editor]? She can't hold a candle to you."

"Well, thank you, Joel," I said, omitting what I was really thinking: that I disagreed with him, and that both Jenny and Bernette were excellent editors. Instead, I just countered with, "But I still don't think I can ask for a promotion."

"You were afraid to ask for a raise last spring, too, weren't you?"

We'd argued for weeks about this issue back then. Finally I'd taken the plunge and asked.

"And you got that raise, even though you insisted that you get raises only on your anniversary, once a year? Right?" Joel persisted.

"True. But I only got it because you trained me so well to ask for it."

"Well, then I'll train you just as well to ask for the promotion."

And so he did, night after night.

"Did you ask for the promotion?"

"No, I can't do it."

"Don't you know that you're…"

A week later:

"Did you ask for the promotion yet?"

"No."

A month later:

"Well?"

"No, Joel, I don't deserve a promotion. The raise was a different issue. But this…"

Finally, of course, Joel convinced me to ask for the promotion, and—guess what?—I got it. On February 10, 1978, I was promoted to Editor.

"Joel," I exclaimed over the phone to him when I heard the news, "I got the promotion. How can I ever thank you enough?"

Yes, there I went, giving all the credit to Joel. I didn't realize that Random House wouldn't have given me a promotion unless I deserved it, that I got it because of me and not simply because of him.

Hopeless

March 2, 1978. I'm so miserable. When will he love me the way I love him? I guess never because I can't seem to do anything right. I don't grow enough so I can't seem to make him love me.

He tells me I won't let go. I need to be in control of everything around me. He says that being me scares me so I won't *be*. He says that I'm afraid to take the risk of really living.

Risks! I'm sick of hearing about risks. I try. I really try. Day after day, I try. I work. But to no avail. Joel just keeps hounding me that I'm not doing it. I'm not changing. Excuse me. I'm not supposed to "change." I'm just supposed to take the risk of being me. Well, I'm sick of it. I just want Joel to love me for what I am *now*. Not what I am potentially. I've done all I can. It's hopeless. I'm hopeless. I can't go on without Joel's love. So I sit down and I write:

1. I must have Joel's love and approval to survive.
2. I'm worthless and helpless. I'm a piece of shit.

3. I can never do anything right, and I'll always be rejected for it.

4. I can't change. I need someone's magic formula or magic want to do it for me.

5. I don't want to take care of anyone else. I want to be taken care of.

6. I want to be loved the way I am. I don't want to change to be loved.

7. I deserve to be loved because I exist. I don't have to do anything to earn it. I don't have to give.

8. I'm not going to do anything I'm told to do. I'll do what I want. So there!

9. I've got to BE.

10. I've got to control myself and everything around me. I can't go out of control.

11. Being me feels so good it scares me to death.

12. I'm afraid I might be happy. I don't deserve it, and I don't want the responsibility for keeping it up.

13. I need everyone's love and approval, even people I don't like. I must please everyone.

14. No one has a right to criticize me. I'm such a good girl. I try so hard to please.

15. I don't want to take the responsibility for really living. I want someone to do it for me. I don't want to take the responsibility for dying. Maybe if I'm lucky I'll get hit by a truck.

16. I'm hopeless.

There! That's all of it, all mixed up. That's me, and that's Joel, and that's what I think and what he thinks. I'm not sure I know the difference anymore.

The First Time

How it first happened, I can't recall. It was a major change in the relationship, but I hadn't a clue. In fact, I decided pretty quickly that it had brought us closer together. In case you haven't guessed, I'm talking about the first time Joel hit me.

We were in the bedroom—I recall that much. That's where most of our interactions took place: sex, "therapy" sessions, crossword puzzle sharing, and finally, assaults. I have no idea what led up to it, what sort of exchange we'd had. All I can recall is the impact, the blow with the heel of his right hand, karate style, to my left eye. Blammy!! That's all.

And then he embraced me, held me close. To me, that meant he was sorry, although he never uttered those words. It was just a fluke, I thought, something that'll never happen again. After all, no one who claimed to love me had ever hit me before, not even one of my parents when I was a child.

The next day I went to work, just like I did every weekday morning, but with one difference: I had a black eye and a cut under it.

After I'd exclaimed that I couldn't go to work looking like *that*—what would I tell everyone in the office?—Joel had insisted, with what I now consider incredible hubris, "You don't have to tell them anything. You don't owe anybody an explanation. It's your own business and none of theirs."

So I went. But I did feel a need to explain.

"Would you believe I was mugged *on East 57th Street*?" I told everyone.

In fact, I had been to that posh street the day before, and that's why it was so easy to come up with that particular story.

"Did you call the police?" I was asked.

I don't recall what I said in response to that question. However, whether I said yes or no, I'd already lied. And that was something I rarely, if ever, did. It just wasn't my way to tell an untruth to anyone. Oh, maybe at first I'd avoided telling my parents that I'd been living with Joel or, when I was 14, that the piano teacher had taken a quick feel, stuff like that, which I'd thought they couldn't handle. And although Joel considered those "lies," I never had before he kept telling me, "The sin of omission is just as great as the sin of commission." So I now considered those kinds of things "lies" too. But to deliberately make up a story, no, not Hedda.

Anyway, about three or four days later, I started to see lights flashing from that eye, which scared me but good. Was I about to lose my vision? When my co-workers suggested I ask the company nurse to have a look at the eye, I did. And she advised me to get on over to an emergency room. I did that too.

I chose an ER not far from Random House, in a hospital that specialized in eyes and ears. Being truthful by nature, as I just said, I told the female doctor that "my boyfriend hit me." But as I saw her writing that down, I immediately regretted my words. *They could get Joel in trouble, especially since he's a lawyer,* I thought.

So I quickly recanted, "No, no, cross that out!" And she did.

I'm sitting here now, as I write this, looking at a copy of that ER report. The doctor had written:

Thurs nite hit ~~by boyfriend~~ fist…

"black eye & lacerations."… sutured…

Actually, "by boyfriend" had scribbles through it, not just one line like that. But those words were still visible, and yet, no one ever followed up on the report. This, you must remember, was March, 1978, when the battered Women's Movement was just beginning. And as I now say in my talks about domestic abuse, oddly using an expression I picked up during my years with Joel, "In 1978 it was "domestic WHAT?"

So, neither the hospital staff nor me, the patient, was acting in my best interest. Since I valued Joel so highly, I thought of him first. But had you told me a few years earlier that I'd behave in this way, I'd never have believed you.

One summer evening while I was living with Risa a few years before I met Joel, I heard a terrible ruckus emanating from an apartment in my building. I knew that the man who lived there was an alcoholic, but I didn't know that he sometimes became violent toward his wife. That night, the wife ran into the street in her robe, and Risa and I, like many others in the building, peered out the window at the scene. The wife stayed in front of the building and didn't return inside until the police had arrived, even though her husband kept up a steady stream of abusive hollering at her. Two policemen escorted her back in, she packed a bag, and left him that night. You can imagine how completely shocked I was when I saw her return the next day. I absolutely couldn't understand her. I remember saying to myself, *If my husband ever hit me, even once, I'd be out in a minute, never again to return.*

When the reality of the situation faces us, we don't act in such idealistic ways. Love often interferes with reason, and because of my intense feelings for Joel, I dealt with the circumstances in a way that may seem mystifying. I now think about what I did like this: I put the incident in a drawer in the back of my mind and shut the drawer. And there the incident stayed for a long, long time.

Weekends at Jacques'

"Country roads, take me home…" Joel and I sang at the top of our lungs as we drove through the Westchester County roads, just north of the city. Since we were best buddies again, we were on our way to the modern, extravagant home of an attorney I'll call Jacques Finemann from whom Joel was now renting office space. Although Joel couldn't sing for beans, my voice was pretty good, and he followed along.

Singing like that had become a ritual with us whenever we borrowed a car—usually Joel's mother's—to drive to a weekend of freeloading at a friend's home. Having our own car in crowded New York City wasn't practical, and it certainly wasn't cheap! But, of course, Joel was, so he'd never have paid the extravagant bucks per month necessary for a parking garage in New York City. Fortunately, we had the city's extensive subway and bus system to rely on for daily travel. (A token in the 1970's cost 15¢.)

Weekends at Jacques' consisted of swimming in his pool; playing extensive backgammon; mingling with party guests often there for the day; listening to Barry Manilow tapes—favorites of Jacques', which we also grew to love; Joel's lecturing of his fellow attorney, a pastime both men seemed to relish; and eating large protein-rich dinners. For years Jacques had been on the Atkins weight loss diet and had gone from someone "who couldn't see his shoes when he looked down," as Joel liked to describe him, to an attractive slender-looking man when fully dressed, but one who was rather soft and

103

lumpy in a swimsuit.

In the next few years, Joel and I spent many free weekends at the homes of his various friends and acquaintances and a lot of time on the sailboat of another. What did Joel offer in return? Well, he was an excellent sailor, and for that he was always welcome on a boat. But in exchange for bed and board for two at someone's house, he'd offer a day riding "our" horses, or a sail on "our" boat, which belonged to us as much as did the horses.

The sailboat Joel loved to tell people was ours really belonged to an old friend of his named Richard Brignoli. We had bumped into him one day in our then-favorite restaurant, Portoroz, on Lexington Avenue and about 40th Street, and the two men had renewed their acquaintance. Of course, we soon joined Richard for a sail.

He owned a 42-foot Morgan with two cabins on which he was living full time ever since he and his wife had split. On weekends his two boys, nine and eleven, had been allotted visits with Richard, and so they all sailed.

It wasn't long before Joel and I began spending weekends on the boat with them. Richard appreciated Joel's skill, and I learned to sail. In fact, the Morgan eventually became our second home, meaning that we spent almost every weekend on it for a full year. (Fortunately, we had a mild winter.) Weekends on the Morgan, in Joel's mind, were enough for him to dub it *our* boat.

On this boat, Joel was in his element. Not only was the sea his natural home, but he knew everything there was to know about sailing. Being a seafarer made Joel happy, and seeing him joyous and spirited made me feel content. Wanting to participate in what Joel loved, I easily learned to steer the boat, and because I needed to stay on deck and busy when the weather was rough, I became the helmswoman during every storm. But Joel made certain that I never learned to handle the sails other than to re-furl the mainsail at the end of a trip. So I became useful on the boat but never could I have taken control of it, or as Joel called it, "taken the con."

Joel and the two boys had a great time on the boat together, roughhousing, laughing, and even playing backgammon. Joel loved kids, and although I did too, I always wished that I had the instant rapport with them that he did.

Because Richard seemed lonely to Joel, he was perpetually fixing up the boys' dad with one woman or another. One time Joel even convinced me to introduce my then-secretary, a young woman in her twenties, to Richard, who was somewhere in his forties. I didn't think it would work; it didn't.

One night Richard, Joel, and I sailed to the Glen Island Casino off New

Rochelle where there was a dance, and the men came up with a plot. I guess it must have been Joel's idea. Now that I easily socialized, I would strike up a conversation with whichever woman Richard found attractive and invite her back to the boat. It seemed like a challenge to me, as well as fun, and I did it. Amazingly, the maneuver worked, and the young woman selected returned with us to the boat and spent the evening astounding us with stories of her experiences as a former heroin addict. Never once did it cross my mind that I, too, would someday develop an intimacy with drugs.

The Gordon Lightfoot Concert

"I bumped into Gary Balken today," Joel told me. "He's the guy whose marijuana case I won a couple of years ago and made new law. Remember I told you about him? That was quite some case. I convinced the judge that Gary shouldn't be prosecuted, although he really was in possession of all that grass." And then Joel described in long detail how he did that.

"Anyway," he went on, "Gary said that he and his brother Ken want to take us out for my birthday next week. I told him about you, and so of course, you're invited."

So, on or about May 25th, 1978, the two brothers I'm calling Gary and Ken Balken showed up at our door with tickets to a Gordon Lightfoot concert being held at Lincoln Center.

"We picked Gordon Lightfoot especially for you, Joel," said Gary. "You know, we thought it's the kind of music you guys can relate to."

Gary was a tall, fair-haired man in his late twenties, dressed in a brown leather jacket and neatly pressed jeans. Ken was a younger, thinner version of Gary, with a friendly, innocent face. They were both drug dealers.

We took a cab to Lincoln Center and proceeded into the theater. Our seats were in the third row, so we had a long walk down the aisle. As we approached, a few heads turned, and then the entire third row stood to honor Joel. Friends of the Balken brothers, most of whom had met Joel before, had come for the celebration as a surprise tribute.

Wow! I thought, *These guys really appreciate my Joel.*

I felt happy and was set to have a really fine evening.

As it turned out, everybody in the row was a coke user, and during the concert, one or two of them laid a line of coke along the indentation of a house key, snorted the drug, and then passed the key to the next person. *What fun!* I thought, doing this in the third row at Lincoln Center.

What!? Is this really Hedda Nussbaum, the good girl? I think the marvelous reception Joel received that evening had inspired me to feel happy, even adventurous. And since I'd previously taken a few snorts of cocaine via the generosity of Jacques Finemann, I felt no compunction about joining in that night.

During the period that Joel was renting space from Jacques, our offices were just a few blocks from each other. So often, after I'd finished work, I'd walk over to pick him up. Then we'd take a leisurely stroll all the way to 10th Street and home.

On evenings unfit for walking, Jacques would sometimes give Joel and me a lift home. As soon as we'd be on our way, he would invariably snort some coke in the car—though I never saw him use any when we spent weekends at his home. Like a good host, whenever he would take out his stash of coke, he'd offer some to us. In those days, Joel would always refuse. He seemed horrified and disgusted by any drug.

He told me a story about once finding a client laying cocaine lines across the law office's conference table as he had walked into the room. Joel had angrily wiped the table clean, knocking the white powder to the floor.

"I told him never to do such a thing in my office again," he declared.

On the other hand, I was intrigued by the cocaine. Why not be naughty for once and try just a little snort? It might be fun. Besides, I was sure there wasn't any danger. Marijuana had had no effect on me the few times I'd tried it back in the '60s. I enjoyed having a drink occasionally but certainly didn't overindulge in that. So one day I took the plunge and accepted a snort of cocaine. And, as I'd expected, I felt nothing.

Still, from time to time, when Jacques offered me a snort, I'd take one. I relied on being unaffected, and I liked appearing worldly for a change. Joel never attempted to stop me.

But that night at Lincoln Center, Joel was incensed, and like a parent reprimanding naughty children, he collected all the keys being used for snorting. Already a bit high, I guess, I felt disappointed; Joel was spoiling all the fun. So I reached into my purse and pulled out my own key and passed that around. Amazingly, Joel didn't protest.

I remember that concert as something strictly visual—the lights, I just watched the lights all night. That's probably because someone had also started passing around a joint, and I gladly joined in that caper as well. So although neither marijuana nor cocaine had ever had any effect on me before, by the time we left the theater, I was quite stoned. The few drinks I had later at dinner in a nearby pub went right to my head, and I became maudlin and cried in the restaurant.

After dinner, we moved on to someone's house and sat on the floor all night, snorting more cocaine. Although Joel eventually used cocaine, too, I'm quite sure that he didn't that night—though my own condition certainly couldn't guarantee clear memory. Yet I do recall him sitting there talking and talking, which was possible even if he were the only sober person in the room. You see, with cocaine, as opposed to marijuana, the user doesn't become antisocial and go off on a personal trip. Cocaine is a more social drug, so Joel certainly could have had a good time even if he was the only one not high on coke.

But I certainly was high, uniquely so. Never before and never again did I indulge to the extent I did that night. And I must confess that I look back on the experience with a smile.

Turning the Tables

Not much had changed in my relationship with Joel in spite of the black eye he'd given me and the occasional announcement that he was going out on a date. I continued to focus on all the wonderful things he did to help me. So during this period, I was pretty happy most of the time, and I considered Joel's lecturing and preaching a marvelous benefit. For example, I considered it strictly my own shortcoming that I wouldn't dare ask for raises and promotions without Joel's prodding.

Although I'd been promoted to Editor in February of 1978, not much more than a year later, Joel began pushing me to ask for another promotion.

"But I just got one," I protested.

"It's not 'just;' it's been over a year, and you're entitled to another," was Joel's retort.

"But I just got a raise in September."

"This has nothing to do with a raise. This is a title. You should be up there as an executive. Then they'll be sure to put your name first in the *Charlie Brown* books."

"That's history, Joel. You convinced me to insist my name be listed ahead of the art staff, and they did it in the last book. And yes, I understand the point. I have to be the one to insist so that I don't get taken advantage of."

"Well, so my words aren't lost on you, after all… [smile]. Then go in there and ask for a promotion to Senior Editor."

"But Senior Editor is such an advanced position, I don't see how I…"

"You deserve it, and you can ask for it."

This conversation continued on and off for months, but at last I asked for the promotion, and just as Joel had insisted, I got it. I was promoted to Senior Editor, almost as a birthday present, on August 10, 1979 (my birthday is August 8th). I saw it in the same way I'd seen the first promotion: as an accomplishment gained because of, and only because of, Joel Steinberg.

I also didn't see my success at socializing as anything but more evidence of Joel's marvelous abilities. We continued to go to plenty of parties and dinners with Joel's friends and clients. I'd never had such an active social life before, and I was thrilled with it, and with Joel for "giving" it to me.

At one party, I spent a great deal of time talking with a lawyer named Larry Phillips. Discovering that we had some interests in common, we exchanged business telephone numbers. And, in fact, Larry did call me to have lunch with him one day; I said I would. When I told Joel, he beamed eagerly, enjoying his fantasy of Larry, a married man, being interested in me.

Joel also had another motive in this. He was unhappy with his office arrangement, which seemed to be the status quo. He'd already left Jacques Finemann's office, and his business was now headquartered elsewhere, but not too happily. A proposed partnership with yet another attorney had fallen through, and so Joel had been searching for the "perfect" situation, without success.

Larry had already informed me that he rented a suite and that two offices in it were vacant. Lunch would be a perfect opportunity for me to ask him if he might like Joel to come into the suite with him. And if so, since there were two vacant offices, it seemed like there'd also be room for Joel's associates, Mel Sirkin and Marty Rappaport, who continued to travel with him from office to office.

Joel did rent an office in Larry Phillips' suite as did Mel and Marty, and I was exhilarated by my part in it. Joel had been looking for an appropriate opportunity for months and had been unable to find it; but I had. How, I thought, could Joel help but hold me in high esteem for this achievement?

Because I was advancing in so many areas, I started turning the tables on Joel and playing *his* therapist for a while. I got him to talk about the feeling that his father was never really fully present. Morris Steinberg would sit and read his newspaper, and Joel's mother would run the show. I got him to talk about competitive feelings with other boys when he was in high school.

I would also keep an eye out to see when Joel was feeling stressed. I had a foolproof way to tell: under stress, Joel's eyes bulged, giving him a wild-eyed look. When I'd see those popping eyes, which was particularly easy in those days before he wore eyeglasses, I'd try and soothe him and encourage him to relax. And Joel praised me to the skies for caring about and helping him. But even these accomplishments of mine weren't sufficient to satisfy Joel Steinberg.

More Assaults

When Joel hit me that first time, I was sure it would never happen again. But I was wrong. It did.

The incidents were momentary. The extent would be, as the first time, one hit with the heel of his hand (he'd been trained in karate). Again, I have no recollection of what would occur or why. I know that I developed another black eye or two that year—1978—and the next as well. But as amazing as it now seems to me, I thought little of it all then and had no plans to leave Mr. Steinberg. My former psychiatrist, Samuel C. Klagsbrun, has put it this way: I split the "good Joel" from the "bad Joel." I held onto and protected the idealized image I'd fallen in love with, the one I'd waited nearly 33 years to find, and I put the significance of my black eyes out of my consciousness.

After that first black eye, I stayed home from work whenever any bruises were apparent—two weeks each time. But then Joel insisted that I go in anyway. "Why did I have to worry about what people thought?" he said. I owed them no explanation. The words were familiar, and as a result of them, just as I did that first time Joel hit me, I went in to work with black eyes. And as I did that first time, I also gave explanations. I couldn't use the "being mugged" excuse again, but one time I said I'd been horseback riding (I had been) and that the horse had run off through the trees resulting in my face getting all messed up. Another time I gave the old "I walked into a door" routine, a cabinet door that had been left open.

I thought everyone in the office accepted my alibis. Why shouldn't I? No one questioned me. No one interfered. It was only nine years later, after our tragedy hit the newspapers, that everyone in the Random House Juvenile Department said they'd known all about Joel's abuse.

Getting Pregnant

Not only wasn't I planning on leaving Joel, I was trying desperately to bear his child, and that persistent biological clock of mine was continuing to tick. *Why am I not conceiving?* I worried. Joel and I had been trying to make it happen since the summer of 1977, and it was already 1979 with no signs of progress. I decided I'd better see a doctor.

Naturally, the first one I went to was my own gynecologist, Mike Bergman, also Joel's closest friend since their Air Force days together. I'd been using Mike as my OB/GYN for the past few years, free of charge in exchange for Joel's work on Mike's divorce and custody battle, which Joel had won.

This was something Joel liked to brag about: "In these days when custody always goes to the mother, I got Mike custody of the only one of three children that he wanted—the *girl*."

Joel emphasized *girl* because he felt that getting just the female child for a father was a feat requiring extraordinary skill, which, the point was that of course, Joel had.

Since the easiest test is of the man's sperm, that's done first in any fertility workup. Mike, said Joel, told him that his sperm were fine and so the problem must be mine. Before we saw a specialist, however, Mike suggested the following: Quit having sex every night so as not to deplete the sperm and also put a pillow beneath my buttocks so the sperm would travel in the correct path. We tried these, but to no avail.

So I asked around for the name of a fertility specialist and made an appointment to see a man highly recommended—Dr. Charles Debrovner. He, in turn, sent me to a long line of subspecialists. The whole process took more than a year during which, I might add, Joel, the father-hopeful, continued to date other women.

I still didn't satisfy him, he'd proclaim, the words tearing out my heart and guts. The thought of him making love to another woman was painful enough, but, I agonized, it was all my own fault. It wasn't Joel who was to blame; it was *me*.

Happily, Joel's infidelity ceased at about the same time as my fertility tests. I now wonder if there was any connection. Perhaps the thought of having a family scared Joel so much that he needed to sow his oats. Of course, he'd never admit his actions were due to *his* problems; *Blame it All on Hedda* was his theme song.

Putting Joel's infidelity aside, I concentrated on becoming pregnant. I had a series of six tests, the last two of which were a laparoscopy and a D & C for which I had to enter the hospital and stay overnight. Joel inexplicably refused to go along with me to the hospital. I had to take a cab and sign in all by myself though the object of the visit was to help the two of us conceive a child.

Why wouldn't he go? He didn't tell me until years later, but this is what he said: It was because two summers before that, while swimming, I'd cut my foot on a rock and then allowed a male friend of ours to drive me to the ER.

"You wanted Chad to take you and not me," Joel declared, though the truth was that Chad had offered, so I told Joel he could stay at the lake (he was having fun) and didn't have to drive me.

The results of that laparoscopy and that D & C were the same as all the other tests: negative. Not a clue as to the problem.

But perhaps I should have come to a different conclusion from the following incident:

During the workup, I was supposed to visit a doctor on Central Park South who specialized in giving antibody tests. Joel was to come with me and give a sperm sample, which, in turn, would be used to see if my body produced antibodies that rejected it.

Well, picture this: Joel and I entered the examining room, and the doctor told us that we both needed to participate. He would take a tissue sample from me while Joel was to leave a sperm sample in a test tube. Then, in typical doctor fashion, the specialist left the room for a while. I encouraged Joel to go into the bathroom and leave his donation. He said no, he wanted *me* to stimulate him to produce the sperm—right then and there in the examining room.

"No," I said, flabbergasted by the suggestion. "I can't do that here! The doctor could walk back in at any time."

"Then come with me into the bathroom."

"No, Joel, I can't. Do it yourself."

"I thought you really wanted this baby!"

"You know I do. I just can't do that here."

Getting even angrier, Joel continued, "And here I thought you really wanted a baby. But you won't do what's necessary to conceive one, so I guess you don't!"

And he turned around and strode determinately out of the office.

Startled, I followed close behind Joel, embarrassed as we passed through the waiting room, exiting onto Central Park South. He was moving at a rapid, irate pace, and I was trying to keep up, continuing to walk ten paces behind him. Tears were falling as I hurried along near the park, feeling that I'd blown it. Now I'd lose both a baby and Joel.

The point is this: Joel had wormed his way out of having a sperm test. Could it be that he knew that he had a low sperm count but had kept it a secret from me? I say this because years later a test indicated that his sperm count was, indeed, below normal.

PS: Eventually I had the courage to return to that doctor's office and was tested for allergy to sperm, though not specifically Joel's. The results were negative.

Is There Such a Thing as Free Lunch?

I wasn't expecting any company that day at my office on the sixth floor of the Random House building on East 50th Street. That little room was as full of plants as it had been when a comment about them some five years earlier had inspired me to write *Plants Do Amazing Things*. Their presence gave the office a homey feeling, as did the empty paper wasps' nest hanging from the ceiling. I'd found it at a ranch on Lake George—Joel's latest freeload. The paper wasp chapter had never made it into *Animals Build Amazing Homes*, but I still found its construction quite wonderful and enjoyed the fact that my office probably looked more like an elementary school classroom than a place of business. The bulletin board above my desk certainly added to that feeling. It held a display of cover proofs of books I'd recently edited—the latest in the *Charlie Brown Super Books of Questions and Answers* series, four "Snoopy" books based on the Charles Schulz beagle, and *Wonder Women of Sports*, a Step-Up Book like the two I'd written for the series.

The phone rang, and the receptionist announced that Charles Schulz was there to see me.

Charles Schulz! Could this be? I'd never met the man personally, although I edited books that used his Peanuts characters. But those books were created by Random House, not Schulz, so why would he be here to see *me*?

I told the receptionist I'd be right out to show him in.

Smoothing my hair, I proceeded to the reception room, there to find not Charles Schulz, but Joel Steinberg.

"Just as I thought," he grinned. "You came right out for Schulz, though you usually make me sit here forever."

Joel didn't like to be ignored, and the few minutes I'd usually take before escorting him in when he visited seemed to offend him. He liked to be number one all the time.

I guess he sensed the truth. In my work environment, I saw Joel as less than perfect. His aggressiveness seemed out of place in the peaceful juvenile publishing office, and I felt that the other editors didn't appreciate his friendly but overbearing chats with them. I was uncomfortable having him there. So I quickly suggested we go out to lunch.

We left for lunch, strolling through a warm spring day with the sun beating down directly on our faces. We found a cute little Italian restaurant a block or so from Random House where we enjoyed a delicious three-course meal— with wine, which is certainly more than my usual workday lunch, but it also cost quite a bit more than I would normally spend.

So right then and there while eating our salads, Joel started in on me with, "You really ought to put this on your Random House expense account."

"But I can't do that!"

"Sure you can. Just write in that you had lunch with an author or an agent. You sometimes do, so how will they ever know?"

"But that's not ethical!"

"Ya know, you're still a child. You're dealing with a big corporation here. Do you believe a few extra dollars means anything to them? Of course not! You'd think they paid you what you're worth, the way you act. Why, they give you *bupkas*! You know that. And they must make millions just on your *Charlie Brown* books alone. Come on, grow up, Hedda. Don't start giving me 'ethical' as an excuse for your being unable to stand up for yourself."

"Joel, you know it's not that; it's just that I don't like to do anything dishonest. Haven't you gotten used to the way I am by now?"

"Bull! The real you isn't afraid to get what she deserves. And that's what's the issue here, not ethics. Anyway, do you think Random House is ethical when they make a fortune off your work—work, I might add, that is superior to that of any of the other editors in your department—and then they pay you 20-something a year? That's what big corporations do to employees they consider little schmucks: they take advantage…"

I just sat there taking it all in, saying nothing.

"So then it's agreed. You'll pay for this lunch and put it on your expense account."

"Yeah, I'll pay for it, but I'm not so sure about putting it…"

"But I AM sure: You'll charge it to Random House. By the end of this month, when it's time to put in your expense account, I'll have you charging not only this meal, but lots of meals. Like it's a big deal, a little $20 lunch!"

The sad part is, Joel was pretty much on target. He kept after me about that lunch so much that I finally gave in and put it on my expense account.

And that wasn't the last time he had me adding extras to my expense account, either. Once in a while, I'd have a nice lunch out with someone, and of course I'd tell Joel about it. No need to go into details about the rest, is there? He'd win me over to his way of thinking every time. And naturally, because I kept getting away with it, he was encouraged to continue pushing me into this kind of deception, which was entirely against my own sense of morality. Well, maybe not entirely—because I did it, didn't I?

And speaking of deception, Joel Steinberg loved to play tricks on everyone's minds, to fool folks, to make them believe the most improbable things. On the other hand, I hated lies. Although I'd gotten used to Joel's exaggerating and aggrandizing, I put a high value on honesty. So, Joel came up with what he called "Honest Dishonesty."

Here's how to play the game: 1) Be clear and deliberate inside yourself while you do something dishonest, 2) share the deception with someone else; 3) make certain it hurts no one, and 4) have fun doing it.

One example, which he and I practiced frequently, was putting cut-rate store-brand liquor into an expensive brand-name bottle and serving it to guests. Then we'd have fun listening to them coo about the wonderful liquor we'd served them. I say "we'd" have fun because I enjoyed it as much as Joel did. Although he was doing it out of stinginess, I took pleasure in observing the tremendous power that suggestion has on the human mind.

And I realized that my own mother had practiced a bit of honest dishonesty herself. Because brewing coffee for a large number of guests had been impractical for her, she'd mixed some instant into a carafe, letting it pose as fresh-brewed. Even one friend of my parents', Murray, who wouldn't touch a cup of instant coffee, would praise my mother's delicious brew. If Mommy could do it, I reasoned, there was no harm in us doing the same.

The Haircut

"I need a haircut," Joel announced one day. "And since I haven't found a barber I really like ever since Tony stopped working across the street, why don't you cut it?"

"Me?" I responded, astonished. "I've never cut a strand of hair in my life! That's always been my father's province." Daddy owned a small neighborhood beauty shop in the Washington Heights section of Manhattan where I'd grown up.

"Good," Joel responded. "That means you'll be overcoming another block. It'll be good for you."

"Why don't you just find another barber, Joel," I continued, feeling trepidation at the thought of putting scissors to Joel's head. "I don't want to even attempt to cut your hair."

But, of course, Joel convinced me to try. So I began, very hesitantly, feeling a lot of tension.

"Hold the scissors loosely," he stated calmly at first.

But when I still exhibited tension, he barked, "Relax!" Then, "You're not doing it the way I told you!" And finally, "I'm getting a knot in my stomach from the way you're doing this!"

But still, he insisted I continue until he had the haircut that satisfied him.

And, probably as a means of saving money—a constant concern of Joel's—several weeks later, he asked me to give him another trim. And so whenever Joel's brown, wavy locks had grown too long, a haircut by Hedda became the ritual, a ritual of agony for me, and who knows of what for him.

And although I began to gain a little skill, because of Joel's critical attitude, each time I approached the task, I was a little more nervous than the time before. And my anxiety would drive Joel crazy.

In fact, Joel never seemed satisfied with me, and I don't mean just when I gave him haircuts. As a consequence, I tried a whole series of ways to relax and improve myself: dance therapy, biofeedback, a deep massage called Rolfing, and around 1980, a few visits to the well-known psychiatrist Albert Ellis.

Ellis and I met perhaps three or four times, and, at his suggestion, I recorded one of the sessions. An excerpt follows about Joel's anger and my response during a haircut:

> HN: It's not just anger, it's like the wrath of God.
> ELLIS: He recently bawled you out for what?
> HN: I was trimming his hair. We've had a history with that, of where I feel a lot of anxiety about doing it…We've had arguments about it before…And then…he just started saying, "You're not holding the scissors the way I showed you,"…and he's saying, "Do it! Do it!" Com*man*ding! And that just in*fur*iates me. I got so mad…that I behaved very childishly. Rather than saying, "Don't talk to me that way!" because that's how I feel,… I just put down the comb and the scissors and said, "No!"…And he said, "Pick it up, and you'd better do it!"… And I said, "No!" And he punched me in the arm, hard. And that infuriated me even more. Because I don't want to be treated that way.
> ELLIS: And then what happened?
> HN: …I said, "NO!" And I got punched again.

It's evident that at that point, I still had some sense of who I was, and I could get angry. But, as the following excerpt from later in the session shows, I wasn't able to conceive of walking away from the situation.

> ELLIS: What could your sane conclusion be?
> SILENCE
> ELLIS: An obvious one you're avoiding.

SILENCE

ELLIS:…Here you are, he's yelling and screaming, and you're saying, "Oh, shit, there he goes again. He's really got a problem in dealing with ME…" What would be your next conclusion after concluding that?…What would any sane person, a woman like you, conclude?

SILENCE

ELLIS: Well, you're ignoring the very obvious conclusion which is stopping you from solving your problem, and that is if he continues like this enough, who the fuck needs him?

I never did really "hear" Dr. Ellis' final conclusion. I never said to myself, "Who the fuck needs him?" because I felt that I did, desperately.

A Fiasco

During the summer of 1980, a friend of Richard's, a Wall Street man named Jon, whom we'd gotten to know, invited Joel and me to sail with him and several others from Block Island to Newport where the America's Cup Races were being held. Jon's 51-foot sailboat was even larger than Richard's Morgan 42, and was sleek and modern in design. To board the boat, we flew to Block Island on Jon's private airplane for which he had his own personal pilot: a handsome, Swedish blond named Stein.

Such adventures were an element of living with Joel Steinberg that went beyond my most extravagant expectations. Life had never been like this in the working class neighborhood of Washington Heights where I grew up, nor when I'd dated other men who lived relatively quiet lives.

A woman Joel and I had met socially, whom I'll call René, had rented a house in Newport for the summer, and Joel invited her to join us in sailing while we were there. As the week ended, Jon and most of the other guests were planning to sail back to New York and Joel to be flown in another private airplane, that of a relatively new client, a man I'm calling Milo Handler, to his vacation house on Martha's Vineyard. René had invited me to stay on at her house to work on some writing ideas I'd been toying with. Although I scarcely knew René and didn't feel very comfortable with her— she seemed awfully sophisticated to me—I decided to accept. I'd be independent for a change and get some writing done at the same time.

Besides, I felt honored that someone like René wanted me around. Apparently she valued me for myself, and not just because I came with the Joel package.

That weekend at René's was a sweeping fiasco. My first mistake was to ask if I could join her and a friend at a party rather than just stay at her house and work. My second mistake was to socialize freely at the party and even flirt with a man. I didn't realize that with Joel away, my now-habitual routine of flirting was out of place and easily misinterpreted. After all, I'd been playfully coming on to Stein all week, and nobody had seemed to mind— especially not Joel, the man who'd trained me to act that way in the first place. But boy, was the flirting at *this* party ever misinterpreted—or so I eventually understood.

When at last, after an hour of chatting with a gentleman of whom I've no memory at all, I looked for René among the party guests, I couldn't find her anywhere. And when I called her house, she answered the phone and then hung up on me. I panicked. What had I done wrong? My old insecurities about myself returned, especially when the next day René was cold and abrupt. Without Joel around to guide me, I felt lost, scared, and inadequate. I must have done something terrible; I must be a horrid person. I was sorry that I'd ever ventured out without my mentor by my side. Not a very good omen for the future.

Belize

In spite of an occasional fiasco, the excitement of life with Joel continued. After Newport, our next trip via private airplane was to Belize, the small Central American country that used to be called British Honduras. Milo Handler was going there with his girlfriend, whom I'll call Noreen, and he took us along as his guests.

In the 1960's Joel had worked for the Defense Intelligence Agency (DIA), and whenever Joel told anyone about this Belize trip, he made it sound as though it were connected to secret intelligence work. He'd frequently told me stories that allegedly described his work with the DIA—how he'd traveled with an attaché case hand-cuffed to his wrist, entrusted with carrying *the* Vietnam war plans, how he'd learned to brainwash people, and how he'd collected the feces of Premier Khrushchev from a hotel's basement plumbing so the government could analyze the Russian's health. Trusting Joel, I believed every word of this outlandish drivel.

But the Belize trip was simply play and adventure with no government work involved. We drove through a rainforest where our personal guide, Godwin, after shinnying all the way up to the top of an incredibly tall coconut palm to get coconuts, tossed a tree snake down at us. EEK! But no damage done. I got to see leaf-cutting ants marching along, each holding its piece of leaf. (I'd read about those when I'd done research for my nature books, but now I was actually seeing them!) We tasted a palatable creature called a gibnut, something in the rodent family that is a popular food animal in Belize. And Joel later told people that we also tasted armadillo. We didn't.

Though I was aware that Milo's legal case involved his allegedly selling cocaine, I certainly never saw him with any on this trip. Still, we nearly got into drug-related trouble. On the way back from Belize, a marijuana-growing country, carrying another American couple, Art and Jane, we landed in Florida to refuel; and the airplane was thoroughly searched by uniformed policemen while we waited in the tiny airport. Two marijuana seeds had been found on the floor of the cockpit, we were told, and as a consequence, these men would have to body-search each of us.

At that point, Joel spoke up "Oh, no!" he bellowed, "Show some respect for these women. You get a female examiner in here NOW if you want to search them."

Joel's brashness paid off, and a woman was brought in for the job. My hero, Joel. But in fact, the search was quite superficial. Even so, Joel later told everyone all about "our harrowing body-search."

While examining Jane's bag, one of the women police officers found a small vial of white powder. "Aha!" her eyes announced, and the container was quickly seized to be tested. While we waited in the airport lounge, the six of us howled with laughter because the white powder was Jane's supply of baking soda, which she used as a feminine deodorant. When the policewoman abashedly returned the vial to her, Jane impishly opened it, stuck in her finger and put the powder to her nose. I quickly snapped a photo, preserving on film forever the image of Jane with a ring of baking soda around her nostril.

Leaving Art and Jane in Florida, the rest of us flew back to Westchester Airport. During our flight home, Joel, who'd flown in the Air Force twenty years earlier but not since, took over as pilot while Milo and Noreen napped and screwed around in the back of the plane. Sitting beside Joel in the cockpit, I quietly and calmly read the flight manual to him—after all, planes had changed quite a bit in twenty years, and Joel needed a little guidance. In spite of his rustiness and apparent unfamiliarity with flying a modern airplane, I wasn't a bit anxious (nor, for that matter, were Milo and Noreen, who did their thing in the back). I had full confidence in Joel, just as I'd had when he'd driven home drunk from the wedding a few years earlier. Again, we made it without a problem.

Freebasing 101

Joel had often socialized with his clients—most notably Gary and Ken Balken—but there had been others. However, beginning in 1980, hanging out with drug dealers became a common practice. That may or may not be related to the fact that Joel first tried coke sometime that year. Although he refused to snort it, he tried rubbing the white powder on his gums and liked it. But certainly he didn't seek it out, not just yet.

Such rubbing noses with drug dealers (pun intended) probably escalated when in that same year Joel began representing Milo Handler. And although Milo claimed that his arrest for selling cocaine had been a setup, entrapment, and that he wasn't a dealer, he certainly was a user. Both he and Noreen smoked the drug, though I wasn't given the privilege of observing them doing so until after the Belize trip. Since they knew both Joel and me better by then, I think they felt more comfortable indulging in our presence.

What enticed Joel to want closeness with Milo, however, had nothing to do with drugs. I believe the lure was his client's perfect setup for freeloading. Milo lived in a beautiful old house in one of the elite towns of Westchester County with his common-law wife and their young son. He also owned a restaurant near his home and managed it with Noreen. (She and Milo's common law wife were not one and the same—in case that's not clear.) So when Joel and I spent a weekend at Milo's, we also got extraordinarily good meals at the restaurant, not to mention personal service.

One night when we were at the restaurant, Milo convinced Joel to go across the street with him and Noreen to his office and try some freebase; naturally, I went too. In case you don't know it, freebase is homemade crack cocaine. And in those days, people made it in the same way that the comedian Richard Pryor was soon to make famous—by using ether and a blowtorch. In Pryor's case, there was an explosion and he was badly burned. However, Milo was, besides a restaurateur, also a trained chemist, so there was little of that kind of danger when he made the drug.

When I studied chemistry in high school, I learned the difference between an acid and a base, which are opposites. Apparently, cocaine is a base, and the substances dealers utilized to cut the coke were acids. Anyway, I think that's correct. During the 80's I knew this information inside, outside, and upside down. I studied it—probably to distance myself from the drug in which I was indulging. And eventually I did indulge fairly often, although not then in 1980.

Today I'm at least sure of one thing: that the purpose of using the ether and the blowtorch was to separate the cocaine—a base—from the cut; and what you'd get was free base—namely pure cocaine. It would be in crystallized or rock form that would be smoked in a water pipe.

I remember the evening well. The four of us sat around the desk in Milo's tiny office while he played freebase chef. Then he passed around the water pipe with a small lump of cocaine in it (known as a rock in cocaine lingo). Each of us would take a deep pull on the pipe, hold it in our lungs for a few seconds, and then pass the pipe to the next person.

You had to wait until the pipe came around to you again for your next "hit." And that was difficult to do—difficult for me because the freebase made me want more, and more, and more, which was strange since I didn't like the high it gave me. I just felt unbelievably greedy.

"I hate that stuff," I told Joel later.

But apparently, Joel, the man who wouldn't put any foreign substance into his body, liked freebase. Hence, the next time Milo offered him some, he was quick to say yes.

However, in spite of the myth of crack's power, neither he nor I became instantly addicted. Only when we spent time at Milo's home or when he came to our apartment, which was rare, did we indulge. And that wasn't just because Milo was our exclusive chef. I, for one, had no appetite for any form of coke between sessions, and Joel gave off no signals of desire for it either.

In fact, when Milo gave us a sizable rock of freebase, we took it home, pondered where the safest place to hide it would be, and finally stashed it behind one of Joel's law books, leaving it there for weeks. When Milo informed us that cocaine loses its potency after a while, we said, "Oh," and shared some of the hidden coke with Gary and Ken. The rest of the rock remained behind the book for months and months.

Adoption?

And then I thought I was pregnant. Could it be at last? I hoped and prayed and had a pregnancy test. While I excitedly waited for the results, Joel and I were invited to the house of some friends who were occasional freebase users, kind of like us. Everyone there was indulging, but not me—not if I were pregnant. I watched the goings on, feeling above it all, steadfastly sticking to a simple, "no thanks" when prodded with, "Come on, Hedda. Have a hit."

As it turned out, I wasn't pregnant. This was sad news for both me and Joel. Even though I'd undergone all the tests possible, no cause for my infertility had been found. That's when Joel suggested adoption. Getting a baby, he indicated, would be much simpler for us than for most couples.

As part of his law practice, Joel regularly handled private, legal adoptions, and his good friend and my OB/GYN, Mike Bergman, occasionally had unmarried patients who wanted to give up their babies. "And," Joel grinned, "Mike just happens to have such a patient right now! She's Italian, and so she has the same brunette coloring as we do. Mike thinks her baby would be perfect for us."

"Well," I hesitated, "I don't know...I really want our own."

"So do I," he responded, "but this is a great opportunity. And you know how often it happens that as soon as people adopt, the woman finds herself pregnant!"

"True, Joel, but..."

"Well, think about it."

So I did, but I couldn't get away from one conclusion: no. I wasn't ready to adopt. I still wanted to go on trying to have Joel's baby. And so we passed on that one.

A Real Beating

February 1981. I'm sitting here in the big, green velvet chair in the living room. Joel's in bed, asleep. I tried sleep, but failed. I can't lay down! The pain was too excruciating whenever I made any attempt. But sitting's not so bad.

I'm trying to make sense of it now, but I can't. How did it come about? The beating, I mean. This wasn't just one smack like the others. This was a real beating. Why? I don't know. He didn't seem any angrier this afternoon than usual, and I certainly didn't do anything special to provoke it. But the pounding, that's what's clear in my mind. Joel's pounding on my lower back over and over again in that same spot near my waist. I'm down on the floor, but he keeps pounding.

Fortunately the doorbell rang, or who knows what my condition would be now! Joel stopped and went to the door. It was Gary Balken with a friend; Joel hadn't been expecting them. But Steinberg, totally calm and collected, sits down in the living room with them to discuss a possible new case with Gary's friend.

I was still in the bedroom getting myself together. After a trip to the bathroom to wash my face and catch my breath, I joined the two visitors on the couch. Joel has always allowed me in on private discussions with his clients, and none of them mind. They know I respect client confidentiality. That's one of the nice things about my relationship with Joel; I'm included in all aspects of his life and business.

There are so many good things about us, so why does he have to do this? I can't understand it; I can't think about it. I'll think about other stuff. Like work. Yes, that new Step-Up Book we're planning … OUCH! I shouldn't really move, I guess. This pain seems to be getting worse.

Ya know, this didn't even hurt me for hours. After Gary left, Joel and I went on as if there'd been no beating. Ignoring it is so much easier for me, I guess. Being loving and close again is a total relief. As to Joel, I guess he was feeling too good to even think anything but positive thoughts. That's because Gary was clearly showing his adoration for Joel. He's one of Joel's true fans. And such veneration gives Joel a high. So the subject of the beating never came up all evening. Quite frankly, I'd rather put it out of my mind.

5:50 a.m. The pain has gotten so much worse. I guess I should go to the hospital. I can walk to St. Vincent's; it's only a few blocks away. If I'm quiet, I won't wake Joel. Can I stand up? Slowly. OOH! That hurts, but I did it. I'll just grab my pocketbook and my jacket and be out of here.

So, I'm in the street, but I can't do this. I can't walk; it's just too painful. I hope a cab'll come by at this hour. Well, maybe on Sixth Avenue—if I can make it that far. Oh, great! There's a cab now. TAXI!

Midnight. They have to remove my spleen! I told the doctor I wanted a second opinion, and you know what he said? "You don't have time for a second opinion!"

Well, if they hadn't waited so long—all day, in fact—
to decide that I was bleeding internally, there'd be
plenty of time!

I called Joel immediately—for the fourth time
today, in fact. Thank goodness for him! When I called
him from the ER this morning, he was sweet and eager
to know what was going on, and I told him I'd keep him
informed after the tests (and no, we didn't mention
the beating or my leaving the house without waking
him). I just called him again after I heard the news,
and he said not to worry. He'd call Mike Bergman, whom
he was sure would know a good surgeon who works out
of St. Vincent's. And he does! Mike woke up a Dr.
Martin Rosenzweig who's on his way to operate. Again,
I'll say it: thank heavens for Joel!

<> <> <> <> <>

So that's how I continued to see Joel—as my hero and not my abuser.
Now, Joel, being someone of considerable intellect, apparently knew that for
this astounding mindset to continue in his lover's brain, he'd have to be as
attentive and supportive as any mate could be, which he was all during my
recovery. And, as you might expect, I consistently protected him from being
linked to my injury.

While still in the recovery room, a doctor asked me, "Did the man who did
this terrible thing to you at least come to visit you?"

"No," I answered, because Joel had visited, and I didn't want anyone to
think that he was the culprit. He, in fact, was there to see me every day, and
together he and I crafted a story to tell friends and family about my infected
spleen.

Did they believe it? I certainly thought so.

Once I was home again, we had what's known in the domestic violence
field as a "Honeymoon period." Not only was there no violence, but Joel
treated me like a princess.

He cooked and brought me meals in bed. It was great, and of course, I
expected the loving behavior to last forever.

He told me how fortunate I was that Mike Bergman was his friend and that
he'd been able to get the best surgeon for me, and at midnight, too, which only

134

served to reinforce my own feelings. But those resident doctors, Joel declared, had done a messy job cutting to test for internal bleeding and should probably be sued. Now *they* were the villains; Joel was the hero. And in this way, Joel the Honeymoon Man fooled me into agreeing that the scar below my navel was entirely the fault of the hospital.

A Fateful Decision

As you might guess, Joel's talent for charming and fast talking extended well beyond the gullible mind of Hedda Nussbaum, and that means he could convince just about anyone of anything—that is, as long as that person trusted Joel enough to allow it. And apparently, Mike Bergman allowed himself to be bamboozled by his old Air Force buddy's tale of how my spleen had ruptured. Oh, it must have been a doozy of a yarn to fool an MD.

Ergo, about a month or so after I came home from the hospital, Joel brought up the idea of adoption again. Mike Bergman, Joel told me, had another patient whom he thought would be a good candidate for us. And this time I felt more inclined toward saying yes.

Since the incident of my ruptured spleen was now sitting comfortably in that drawer in the back of my mind, I reasoned this way: Why not? I wanted a baby desperately, and I was fortunate that Joel had easy access to perfectly legal private adoptions. Most people had to remain years on waiting lists before getting a comparable opportunity. And if we adopted, I thought, it didn't mean that I'd never have my own child. Returning to Joel's earlier theory, I rationalized that maybe I'd become pregnant right away after the adoption; then I'd have two kids and catch up a bit. After all, I was almost 39, and time was getting short.

"Go ahead," I told Joel. "Check this one out."

He did, and in the spring of 1981, he met with 17-year-old Michele

Launders, Lisa's natural mother.

And that's the way it happened. I was definitely "Cleopatra, Queen of De-Nile," as the song goes. I believed that Joel would be a fantastically wonderful father. After all, I believed he was a definite caretaker, earned enough to support a child comfortably, and was so bright that a child would be very fortunate to have him as a father. Of course, he also along got great with kids as well as with dogs. Dogs and children know, or so goes the myth.

I doubt that I thought about these things consciously. I was simply positive that Joel would be the best Daddy in the whole world.

When Joel returned home after meeting Michele Launders and her mother, he said that the situation looked good. "Michele's an attractive young woman, even while pregnant, so we have a pretty good chance that the baby probably will be nice looking too. And two such good-lookers like us gotta have an attractive kid, right? And she told me that the father was an athlete, a football player in school. This is, as you know, very important to me. I want a well-coordinated child so we can play football and basketball together, and...Don't look at me like that! You know I'm a feminist. Whether it's a boy or a girl, the kid needs to be athletic. Maybe you'll learn a thing or two from an athletic girl." (Smile)

"What about religion?" I asked. "You said she's Catholic."

"Oh, no problem there," Joel replied. "Michele told me she didn't mind what religion the adopting couple was. Then I deliberately added, 'What if they're Jewish?' and she said 'I have no problem with that either. As long as they love the baby. That's all that counts.' 'Even if it's a single parent?' I asked, just to cover all bases, and she's fine with that too. I'm really pleased here. Everything seems just right."

Since Joel was pleased, so was I. And, of course I believed every word he told me. But Ms. Launders' version of that meeting differs quite a bit on a couple of important points, notably religion and marriage. She says she insisted on two things: 1) the couple be married, and 2) they be Catholic. Well, it would certainly have been like Joel to tailor his version to foster my wholehearted desire to proceed. Had I known that she'd not have approved of us as the potential parents of her child, I probably would have fought Joel on the subject. Chances are I wouldn't have won the battle, as usual, but I'd certainly have tried—that is, until Joel had convinced me to go along with his way of thinking.

The reason Joel had brought up "single" parent, even though we were two people, stemmed from our legal situation. Since our union hadn't been sanctioned as a marriage, we knew we wouldn't be able to adopt as a couple. One of us would have to be the legal parent, the other making an application to adopt at a later time.

"I want you to be the initial adopting parent," Joel told me. "I know how much that would mean to you." He certainly was right about that, and I felt overwhelmed by his generosity and love. Such a man would be a wonderful father!

Planning for Baby

Constrained by the wisdom of "don't buy anything for an expected baby until it actually arrives just in case anything goes wrong," I didn't go crazy buying baby stuff. Not yet, anyway. But I couldn't wait to make the announcement to my family. So the next time we visited my parents, now living in Teaneck, New Jersey, I told them the good news.

"*Mamale*," my mother burst out, "*Mazel Tov!*" And she kissed the two of us.

"So, you're finally making me a grandfather again?" my father remarked wryly with a twinkle in his eye and the Jewish intonation I always hear in my mind's ear when I think of him. As usual, Daddy's attitude was easygoing and playful, which was why just about everybody loved him.

Daddy had always been an entertaining father. I recall him bouncing tiny me on his bent knees as he lay in bed, and then at a surprise moment, his legs would open wide and I'd fall between them onto the bed. What fun that game of "Horsey" was!

Daddy had a great sense of humor and loved to tease. For example, when Judy and I were young teens, we once played a game of scrabble with Daddy, whose English spelling was often phonetic rather than correct since he'd been born in Poland. During the game, time and again, he misspelled a simple word, by, for example, putting down "menny" instead of "many." Each time he did this, Judy and I exclaimed in unison, "Daddy, that's not a word!"

139

He'd say innocently, "Oh, yeah?" and then proceed to put out the correct letters, which he apparently had known all along. In fact, Daddy won the game.

Whenever I complained that he, who always did all the haircuts in his beauty shop, cut my hair too short (which was the usual state of affairs), he'd say with a good humored smile, "Don't worry about it; *tsee voxen*," which is Yiddish for, "it'll grow."

And that was Willie's attitude about life. He'd take in stride most situations that didn't go his way and encourage me to do the same. He wasn't a worrier like Mommy was, making true that age-old saying, opposites attract.

Nervous, that's how I think of Mommy. She'd get nervous when the teenage me went out with friends, insisting that I call before I left wherever I might be to come home. Then she'd sit at the bedroom window, which faced a subway entrance and a bus stop, watching for my arrival. I hated it, especially the necessity to call; it was embarrassing. And if I expected to be even a minute late, I'd have to call again so she wouldn't worry. When I WAS slightly late, her face would turn gray with anxiety, and I knew her blood pressure would be rising. The specter of causing a potential stroke always hung over me.

In spite of their different approaches to the news, I recognized that both Mommy and Daddy were as thrilled as I was. After all, they really admired Joel and considered him my husband. I knew they dreamed of the grandchildren we'd produce.

The only problem connected with the adoption came up when Mike informed us that Michele Launders had tested positive for toxoplasmosis, a blood disease that could cause birth defects in the baby.

What should we do now? I did some research and found that toxoplasmosis causes serious birth defects in a very small percentage of cases. The area most often affected is the eyes, and blindness may result eventually. This was a critical issue, and we discussed it exhaustively. Eventually, however, Joel and I decided that since the likelihood of a grave problem was small, we would take a chance on the Launders' baby.

So I asked my boss at Random House for a maternity leave beginning some time in May, and she agreed to give me the three months I'd be entitled to if I gave birth. Then I announced joyfully to everyone else that Joel and I were adopting a baby.

Jenny, another senior editor in my department, who'd obviously figured out what I'd been trying desperately to hide, said to me, "Who's going to protect this child from Joel's abusive behavior?"

I was outraged. Joel would never be abusive to a child! The remark offended me so much that I didn't even bother to respond.

Mother's Day: An Idyll

On May 14, 1981, I arrived in my office at 10:00 a.m., my usual time since Joel had convinced me several years ago that I didn't have to appear compulsively at 9:00 every morning. After all, I was an executive, wasn't I? And there on my desk was a bouquet of flowers and a note from several of the office secretaries: "Congratulations! It's a girl!"

Oh, my goodness! I thought. *I'm a mother! The baby's really here!*

While I'd been on the subway en route to work, Joel, who now practiced law out of our apartment because he hadn't been able to find the "perfect" office situation, had received word that a girl had been born to Michele Launders.

My leave of absence started immediately. With a quick farewell to all office mates, I happily dashed off to shop. With caution about layette buying now banished, I hurriedly bought infant kimonos, baby bottles, diapers, etc. and returned home to celebrate with Joel. But first we started a marathon of phone calls to deliver the good news to everyone.

At dinner that night at Gene's, our favorite Italian restaurant, a business client of Joel's—Lisa was her name—brought us the antique wooden cradle she'd promised to lend Joel for the baby who'd be delivered to us the next day.

May 15. The wait seemed interminable. I sat on our beige corduroy couch cuddling the tan crewel pillow I'd painstakingly embroidered in shades of

142

beige and brown a few years earlier (these days, Joel was my only hobby). I walked to the kitchen to get a Pepsi with a wedge of lime for Joel (a treat he often required, but this time I offered it voluntarily). I sat down on the couch again. I got up and stopped to straighten the crisp, new, yellow-and-white plaid bumper I'd carefully tied to the tiny wooden cradle; then I was back on the couch. Anxious? Not me!

At last came the sound of the downstairs doorbell. I practically flew to the buzzer.

"Who is it?" I asked excitedly.

"It's us," came the male voice cheerily in reply.

Buzzzzzzz! I let our callers into the building. Simultaneously I opened the apartment door and looked over my shoulder at Joel. To him I must have resembled a little girl about to open her gifts on Christmas morning. My eyes, I'm sure, were wet and shining, my smile was beaming hugely and nervously, my heart was pounding in my ears. Joel was happily smiling but looked cool and calm to me.

And then the elevator door opened. And there she was, wrapped tightly in a navy blue plaid wool blanket, though it was May, and held securely in the competent RN arms of Mike Bergman's new wife Jackie, while Mike, who'd delivered the baby the day before, walked behind, grinning. As they entered the apartment, Jackie smiled too and handed the baby to me—absolutely the happiest moment of my entire life. *My* baby. At last, at last!

Joel rushed over to look at her in my arms: tiny, only a day old, and already beautiful. Our baby. Her skin was a soft, smooth pink, not red and wrinkly like some infants. Her blue eyes were wide open. She looked right at me, making eye contact—or so it seemed.

"Oh, Joel, " I breathed, "isn't she beautiful?"

He looked at her carefully, removing the tiny pink hat from her little head.

"That she is," he said smiling. "You'd better sit down with her now," he added, the concerned father. And I did, in the rocking chair, Jackie showing me the correct way to hold the baby's head to support her neck.

"Perfect in every way," said Dr. Mike. "Ten fingers, ten toes, and a pretty face, too."

"Oh, and here," added Jackie, "we brought her a present. Open it, Joel."

"A teddy bear!" he exclaimed after impatiently tearing off the white paper with tiny pink and blue bunnies on it. "Every baby has to have a teddy bear," he added with a grin. "Thanks, Mike, Jackie." That was all he said, somehow hushed of his usual bluster, apparently awed by this wondrous child.

"The blanket, sweater, and hat are also our gifts," Mike added.

"Would you like something to drink?" I asked from my seat in the rocking chair, not forgetting my role as hostess. But both Mike and Jackie politely refused.

"Speaking of liquid," I added, "I think the baby has…"

"Let me show you how to change her," Jackie quickly offered. And she did. Then she showed me how to wrap the tiny newborn in receiving blankets so she'd feel as comfortable as in the womb. Next was a lesson in feeding her a bottle. The previous day I'd purchased all the supplies I needed for these tasks and beyond.

My new daughter seemed like such a "good" baby. She didn't cry. She sucked at the bottle eagerly and then fell asleep. I'd been holding her for quite some time and finally, reluctantly, put her into the cradle.

"Boy," I thought, "taking care of a baby is really easy!"

Holding my new baby.
(I keep this photo in a frame with my most
precious possession—a lock of Lisa's hair.)

A Name for Baby

Now that we had our baby, we had to find a name for her, and it took Joel and me nearly two weeks to agree on one. We'd had the traditional Jewish names selected longbefore her birth—Moishe (after Joel's father) if it were a boy and Ruchel Molya Toba (after my two grandmothers) if it were a girl. But we could not decide on an English name.

Girl's names that begin with R for Ruchel: Rachel, Rochelle, Rose, Robyn, Roberta. No.

Girl's names that begin with M for Molya: Molly, Mildred, Marcia, Maria, Merry. No.

Girl's names that begin with T for Toba: Toby, Theresa, Peter, Tonya, Tillie. No.

Problem: Joel wanted his daughter to have an elegant name like Jennifer or Elizabeth, neither of which began with the appropriate letters of the alphabet. Since I found the name "Lisa" quite appealing, we finally came up with a compromise that did not begin with R, M, or T. We'd name the baby "E*lisa*beth," and call her Lisa.

And then Joel had a brilliant idea for a middle name: Erin.

"Since her heritage is Irish," he said, "it'll be appropriate."

So that was our baby's name: Elisabeth Erin Steinberg.

The Honeymoon of All Honeymoons

Now that I had Lisa, life was beautiful except for the obvious: I had to get up during the night to feed the wailing infant, so I got very little sleep those first few weeks. There were diapers to change, there was formula to mix, bottles to sterilize and then to warm at feeding time. But believe it or not, I loved every moment. When I'd not become pregnant and no reason for my infertility had been found, I'd begun to fear that I'd never be a mother, that my lifelong dream would remain a fantasy. But here was current reality: the tiny person in my arms was mine! Neither sleepless nights nor dirty diapers could ruin my bliss.

"Well," you must be thinking, "and of course she had help: Joel." Ha! Think again. Although Joel bragged to everyone that he and I took turns getting up nights to feed the baby, that never happened. I was the only one doing the job. I didn't complain, however, because I had no objections. Holding the baby was pure joy at any hour, so why should I demand that Joel, who had to save his energies for legal work, spoil his sleep? As to diapers, well, Joel may have changed a grand total of two during Lisa's diaper days.

Except for these small deficits, Joel's behavior seemed impeccable during those first few months of our parenthood. He was loving, never even

146

approached being assaultive, and was very supportive. It was another "honeymoon period," and it lasted a full six months.

Most importantly, it seemed to me, Joel began encouraging me to communicate better with my own family, insisting that I get them to "go on the line" more often and to be more direct about feelings. You see, my parents had been raised to be indirect, to be polite, never to confront; and certainly they'd be evasive if they thought something would upset me. Joel called them "liars." But they weren't lying, just not coming out and saying directly what they felt. And it was my assignment to get them to do that very thing, which Joel declared would bring us closer together. So he'd counsel me to say to my parents things like, "What do you *really* mean by that?"—something we'd never have dared say in my home growing up. But now I'd say it and would actually succeed in getting Mommy and Daddy to verbalize their feelings.

In fact, sometimes during phone conversations with my parents or with Judy, Joel would mouth words for me to say to them. And when I repeated the words exactly, they seemed to have the desired effect. I was *so* pleased.

The Baby Shower

Judy decided to give her little sister and new niece a superb gift—a baby shower. I supplied the guest list, which consisted of the few old friends I was still in touch with, the wives of the couples with whom Joel and I often socialized including Bonnie Gross, five or six women from my office, Joel's mother, his Aunt Florence, my mother and Judy. The shower itself, held in our favorite restaurant, Gene's, seemed perfect to me, and the photographs taken that day show me all aglow.

I was, in fact, feeling so blissful that the absence of most of my Random House colleagues didn't faze me. That only two of the editors invited showed up, one of whom was, ironically, Jenny, the only person ever to have commented on possible danger to Lisa, held a meaning that totally escaped me: *they were all aware of the abuse in my home*. This I learned years later.

It Seems like Old Times

In the months that followed Lisa's birth, Mommy and Daddy visited us often and even bought a small portable crib for their granddaughter's visits to their New Jersey home. For Mommy's 72nd birthday when Lisa was only six weeks old, we barbecued in Judy's backyard.

"I never thought that at my age I'd be a grandmother again," exclaimed Mommy ecstatically, while everyone, even Mommy's first grandchild, the awkward teenage David, took turns posing for photos with the sweet and loveable baby in their arms or on their laps.

My parents with Lisa.

That summer of 1981, the Nussbaums and the Steinbergs all got together much more often than usual—a real family—even spending days at Joel's mother's pool club. Once again we took pictures of the proud grandparents, all three of them, posing with the new baby, as well as pictures of me with Lisa, and Joel with Lisa. In later years, when we weren't taking many photos, I was disappointed to note that Joel and I had not posed together with our baby. That may be simply because he and I took turns as the photographer.

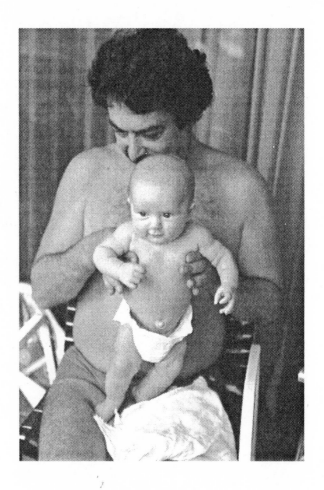

Joel and Lisa.

Now that my parents were regular visitors to 10th Street, Daddy began cutting my hair again. He'd always acted as my personal hairdresser (that is, until Joel had insisted I go to a more modern beautician). But there was a difference this time around: The haircuts were done in our apartment, as opposed to Daddy's store, and both Joel and I supervised every snip.)

"Now hold the scissors loosely."

"Cut just a little over there."

"Make sure you make both sides even."

And Daddy put up with it, good-naturedly, although he'd been cutting hair for more than 40 years. And he even trimmed Joel's hair once or twice.

We began entertaining Judy more frequently, too. Because she was seeing a therapist weekly not far from where we lived, Joel encouraged me to invite her to have dinner at our place on those nights. Later, when Lisa was a few months old, I would meet Judy in a local restaurant, and we two sisters would sit and chatter all evening while baby Lisa slept in her stroller. This felt almost like old times.

Judy and I had been each other's best friend growing up. Because I'd been diagnosed with a heart murmur at age two, and although the doctor had put no restrictions on my activities, Mommy and Daddy, who were over-protective anyway, had felt these instincts zooming to a new high. I had had to stay quiet, and for the most part, inside the house, missing out on learning to roller skate, to ride a bike, and to make friends.

Trying to show no favoritism, Mommy and Daddy had placed the same restrictions on Judy. So we became each other's playmate and closest friend, not to mention a pair of terrible athletes!

When Judy started school, I missed her terribly. During the hours she was gone, I sat near the door at the end of our apartment's long hallway, playing with my dolls, waiting until my big sister and best friend came home. In fact, I'd become so reliant on her company that I hadn't learned to make friends, so all during my childhood, I shared Judy's playmates until I became determined to change that situation and make my own friends in high school.

After Judy got married at age 19, our relationship changed, of course; but still we continued to be extremely close. However, recently, we'd seen less and less of each other. So I was thrilled that we were close again. And, of course, in my mind Joel was the key to it all.

The House in Connecticut

Now that we were a family, finding a house seemed essential. Since Joel's latest freeload was in Westport, Connecticut, at the home of the client who'd lent us the antique cradle Lisa slept in, Mr. Steinberg decided that this upscale community had all the right elements: water, class, and houses with lots of land. So we began a house search there. Joel talked of spending just weekends living in Westport—at first—until he could establish a Connecticut clientele. Eventually, we'd move in full time, and I would become a railroad commuter to midtown Manhattan and Random House. If we couldn't find a house, Joel assured me, he'd find land and build the beautiful dream house he'd designed many years before—a hexagonal fieldstone dwelling with all rooms emanating out of the central fireplace. Of course, he spent hours describing the house to me and drawing diagrams. *Oh, Joel was so talented*, I thought.

Amazingly, it took only a short search to find the house we wanted, so no need to build one, just add on to it. With an acre of land (plus public land all around so that no one would build on it), water on the property shallow enough to be safe for Lisa (the Aspetuck River flowed through the backyard as a stream), and a low asking price, we were both thrilled. And to top it all off, our next door neighbors would be Paul Newman and Joanne Woodward! Joel started talking to his bank about a mortgage. Never before had we gone this far in the pursuit of any house.

But as anyone who is familiar with my story knows, we were still living in Joel's one-bedroom apartment on 10th Street in New York City six years later. The problem, as Joel told it, was that this house, like all the others we'd seen, wasn't perfect; he claimed that this one was too close to the road so you could hear the cars going by. I remember sitting beside Joel in back of the house near the stream, the two of us listening intently. Yes, you could, indeed, hear cars whizzing by if you tried hard enough. The real problem, of course, wasn't the noise, it was Joel's miserly nature. So although he actually put in a bid for this house, he knew it was too low, and so did I, but I'd been convinced, as usual, that unless the house was just right in every way, it wasn't for us.

Baby Days

Although our baby seemed perfectly healthy, the specter of toxoplasmosis was never far away. When Lisa was a month old, I took her to a specialist at one of the large New York City hospitals where a blood sample was taken from her tiny foot. I think the needle prick hurt me more than Lisa because I don't even recall her crying. Naturally I felt anxious until we got the results: Lisa was fine, no sign of toxoplasmosis in her blood. Phew!

But then when she was about three months old, the late afternoon crying began—colic. It was quite distressful because in spite of my marching up and down with the baby in my arms and other futile attempts at quieting her (made by me, never by Joel), Lisa's crying would continue steadily for an hour or two every day. Fortunately, the colic lasted only a few weeks, and once again we had a thriving baby. No earaches like some kids get. No fevers. No problems.

The pleasantest time of day for me as a new mother was evening, when I'd put the baby to sleep in her cradle. I started a habit that lasted for years: I sang Lisa lullabies. For at least the first year, I held her in my arms in the rocking chair as I'd rock and sing.

My favorite song was "Summertime," you know, the one that ends, "There is nothing can harm you, With Daddy and Mommy standing by." I surely believed this was true, that my baby would be safe in our loving care. Today when I try to sing the lullaby, I weep instead.

But back then in 1981, seeing that Lisa was healthy and letting me get a good night's sleep, it seemed like time to return to work; my three-month leave of absence was just about over, anyway. But, with Joel's encouragement of "You're entitled", "Don't worry; they need you", and "You should be able to make your own schedule. After all, you're an executive," I extended that leave by working at home. This time, I didn't need a lot of prodding. I really wanted to be home with my baby. So why not take the editing to my apartment and just go into the office from time to time? Random House seemed to have no objections.

But on days when I went in, Joel was left at home with the baby and that wasn't to his liking. "You really should be able to take the baby into the office with you," he proclaimed often. "This is the ideal for a feminist mother like you." And he would paint a verbal picture of the paragon of jobs for a professional mother: there I'd be, the hard-working editor with baby fast asleep in the office beside me. The image appealed to me, and so I tried it. On days when I went into Random House, I brought Lisa along, keeping my office door closed so as not to disturb anyone, although she rarely cried. However, the office secretaries were forever finding reasons to come in and play with the adorable infant. Who could blame them?

The management of Random House's Books for Young Readers certainly didn't. They blamed me and told me they'd prefer it if I didn't bring the baby into the office again because she was too distracting to the secretarial staff. So much for feminist dreams.

New Mom's Group

I don't recall where I'd learned of it, but I began going to a support group for older new mothers, older being over 30. But by no means was I the most senior, although I'd turned 39 that August. We had one member past 40, and she'd actually given birth to this first baby. I was impressed.

We moms would sit around and discuss baby issues while the little ones slept. How can I convey the mixture of emotions at being there? Joy at motherhood, desire to make friends, and my old, inherent shyness all played a part.

Did Joel have any objections to my newfound companions? Seemingly none at all. However, even though we mothers would meet in each other's homes on a rotating basis, my apartment was taboo since Joel ran his business from there. I, of course, didn't find any fault with that, but I quietly wished I could have brought the group to my house.

It was from one of those new mothers that I learned of a daycare play group for Lisa, ages six-months to five years, that I could use when I returned to work full time.

That happened in the fall, after Joel had gone to Vermont to try a case. As soon as Joel was gone, I started setting up a system for going back to work. I felt that I'd stretched Random House far enough on the leave-of-absence front, and if I wanted to keep my job, I'd better appear in my office daily again.

And at about that point, the best period of my entire life ended. Never again while I was with Joel would I be free from abuse, happily employed, very close to my family, and with my beautiful daughter all at the same time.

The Novak Trial

Representing John Novak, the chief defendant accused of flying marijuana into Vermont, was a big case for Joel, one from which he expected to get a fat fee. In fact, Novak had agreed to pay Joel at least 100 grand, as I recall it, for trying his case. For that purpose, Joel flew to Vermont in the fall of 1981.

The trial lasted about two months, and during that time, I started going back to work on a daily basis. After an unsuccessful few days using my mother as baby sitter (it was too much for her post-70 energy level), I put Lisa into daycare. However, on weekends when Joel was home, much to my dismay, I was getting criticized again with the same old stuff: "You're not giving; you're taking," (where, in reality, I gave and gave), "I need to be with women who can satisfy my needs," etc.

Apparently the "postpartum" honeymoon period was over, and I became increasingly anxious every time Joel was scheduled to return to New York. I remember pulling from the medicine chest one Friday night some years-old Valium, which I swallowed before he arrived home so that I'd be relaxed. I imagined him complaining, "Why did I have to come home to this tension? I should have stayed in Vermont." You can be sure I didn't want to hear that. *Was his conduct due to the stress of the trial?* I wondered.

But when Joel called to say he'd be going to Boston with one of the other attorneys one weekend rather than coming home, I couldn't handle it and told him that Lisa and I would be joining him. "Oh," was Joel's reply, "and Jeff was going to fix me up with a terrific woman," whom he proceeded to describe. To my horror, he didn't sound like he was joking.

Once I arrived with the baby, Joel's attitude changed, and he kept telling me I *must* come with him to Vermont to watch him in the courtroom. It was true that I'd never seen Attorney Steinberg in action, except during his frequent dramatizations of court proceedings put on for my benefit. And although I protested, "But I've just returned to work; I can't take off a week *now!*" Joel, of course, convinced me to do things his way. I will never know what the Random House administration thought of that inappropriate vacation, but I can guess.

During one of Joel's weekends at home, he told me that Novak had promised as payment his silver convertible Mercedes Benz sports car in addition to the pledged cash.

Joel's eyes sparkled when he described how dashing he'd feel driving around in such a vehicle. I was excited for him.

But the trial ended badly for Joel: out of all the defendants, only Joel's client and wife (for whom Joel had referred the lawyer she hired) were convicted. Because losing a case was a rarity for him, Joel was shaken. And not only that, he told me, Novak hadn't given him much of the promised fee and had been wavering about giving him the Mercedes.

That is why, Joel informed me, he'd enlisted the aid of an old client, one from the days he had represented Mafiosi. Jimmy was known for his techniques of persuasion. And one day, after the trial, Joel and I traveled to Long Island to pick up the car now parked in front of Jimmy's house. I never asked for details. If Joel said the car was rightfully his, I believed it. Period.

But, for reasons I couldn't have fathomed at that point, Joel informed me he would let the Grosses keep the car, "because it won't survive a night on the streets of New York City, and," he added, "it'll be good politics to register the car in their name." However, since Joel didn't have the title, getting it registered in any name would be difficult to say the least.

Now, don't ask how we did it, because I truly can't remember; but after an incredible series of maneuvers, during which I made all the telephone contacts, we managed to get the car registered, title or no title. That feat was another one of Joel's "talents" of which I was then proud. After all, I reasoned, he had a right to get what was promised for his excellent work, whether or not the client won or lost.

Return of the Dragon

In spite of getting the car, Joel wasn't happy. Perhaps it was a combination of losing both the trial and a valuable client, Milo Handler. Milo, who'd always proclaimed that Joel was the best of all possible lawyers, apparently felt abandoned while his attorney was in Vermont. No hand holding for a couple of months, no socializing; no freebase sharing. Milo transferred his case to another lawyer, one who apparently had agreed to something Joel had consistently refused to do: pay off the judge, or something shady like that, as I recall. But it didn't work, and Milo ended up in prison; of course, he blamed it all on Joel.

Joel's discontent became apparent to me, not only from his increased faultfinding, but because the assaults returned. Wham! Another black eye.

One night while Joel and I were having one of our long bedroom talks, one where we genuinely felt extremely close, I told him, "Joel, I hate it when you hit me. It's painful, it's embarrassing, and it makes me feel you don't love me, and I know you do."

"Of course I do," he responded. "I hate myself when I hit you. Hitting's not *me*; I'm not really like that."

This was the first and last time we ever discussed the subject. And, in spite of hating himself for the abuse, it continued intermittently, and very slowly, it began to escalate.

Goodnight, Lisa

When Joel was what I later came to think of as "The Good Joel," he was very, very good. And yes, when he was bad, he was horrid. The Good Joel used his superior intelligence to solve problems that had me stumped.

When Lisa was about six or seven months, whenever I would leave her in her crib for the night, she'd start to wail just as I was walking out of the room. I'd go back in, stroke her, talk to her a little til she got quiet, and then I'd walk out again. WAAAH! was the response I got every time. What to do?

Of course I asked Joel, and he had a solution that worked.

"She feels abandoned when you leave her alone," he said. "So here's what to do. Sing to her as you slowly leave the room, and she'll still be able to hear your voice even after your body is down the hall.

"Here, let me show you."

And he demonstrated with a song he composed on the spot. In his off-strain singing voice (the one and only skill I felt he lacked), he sang to the tune of *Good Night Ladies*.

> Good night, Lisa,
> Good night, Lisa,
> Good night, Lisa,
> It's time to go to sleep.

And it worked! I marveled at how bright, sensitive, and perceptive my man was.

For the next few months, Joel and I together sang Lisa's song each night as we tiptoed out of the room. Subsequently, I continued the singing tradition by myself, and did so forever after.

To me, Lisa was the best baby ever—the best and the smartest. We always took her with us to restaurants, where we had dinner a few times a week. At first I carried Lisa in the baby seat, which I'd place on the table while Joel and I ate and she drank her bottle. Later, when she was no longer a tiny infant, she sat in her stroller. One evening, when Lisa couldn't have been more than six months old, she initiated a game of peek-a-boo with a woman at the next table. Could any child be smarter?

Even though Lisa was growing bigger every day, because I loved carrying her close to my breast, I was reluctant to give up the Snuggly®with which we two traveled the streets. However, when a stranger in the supermarket commented, "Who's carrying who?" I realized she'd outgrown that contraption, and it was time to use the stroller Joel had actually spent his own money to purchase—and without complaint!

It was about that time, too, that Lisa became too big for the tiny cradle she'd been sleeping in, so I transferred her to the Portacrib® my parents had bought. Although they'd bought it for Lisa's visits to their own apartment, leave it to Joel to ask them if we could "borrow" it until we got a place big enough for a full-size crib. Of course they said yes, and the portable crib was now in Apartment 3W at 14 West 10th Street, and (surprise!) never again in my parents' possession.

To make the crib ready for use, I covered a layer of foam rubber with heavy plastic. Voila! A crib mattress. I did the same to create a second mattress to put on the window seat in our bedroom. Joel thought that this would be a great place for Lisa to sleep (when she got a little older) on hot summer nights or when we had company in the living room where we kept the crib.

As spring came around, on weekends I'd take my little girl to the park and put her on the baby swings. Joel most often stayed home. Other park mothers would remark, "Oh, she's going to be a redhead!" And that certainly did seem to be the case. As Lisa's hair was finally coming in (she was nearly a year old before we could see much of it), it appeared to be reddish.

Once a woman queried, "Who's a redhead in your family?"

I replied, "My mother," with a secret inward smile. That was actually true, although she'd been born a brunette. But here was a possible way to explain how Joel (a wavy-haired brunette) and I (a curly-headed one) came to have a strawberry blond offspring with straight hair.

Joel and I often discussed Lisa's status. We'd inform her from an early age that she wasn't ours from birth. It would be better for her that way. Meanwhile, I continued to press Joel to get the consent agreement signed so she could become officially ours. I never once thought about what apparently kept Joel from proceeding: the inevitable investigation was bound to expose his abusive behavior.

But life went on—whether or not our daughter was officially adopted. Whenever I'd pass a store that sold children's clothes, I'd stop in and buy something unusual for my little Lisa: tiny blue jeans, a romper or two, a pretty dress, although she certainly didn't need any of this. As a newborn, she'd received more gifts of clothes in all sizes up to 3 than she'd ever have use for. And the gifts continued to pour in from relatives, friends, and Joel's clients who didn't need any excuse to buy a gift for their favorite little beauty. Lisa had acquired so many stuffed animals (which Joel lumped into the category of dolls), that we didn't have room to store them all, so he'd tell everyone who said they wanted to buy Lisa something, "NO DOLLS!"

The Penthouse

It was at this point that Joel began his new fantasy: a penthouse.

"Can you see it, Hedda? Grand parties on our wraparound terrace, with guests oohing and aahing at the magnificent view. We'll invite Al and Bonnie, Stephanie and Dennis, Gary and Ken—with different groups, of course—and they'll all be *so* impressed. And my new clients will be willing to put a lot more up front when they see how well we live. Our butler, paid for with all that new income, will serve them drinks as we sit, sunning ourselves. The women'll be so jealous of your bikini-clad figure, their eyes'll pop, as will the men's, of course. But I'll know you're all mine."

And on and on he'd go for an hour or more at a time.

So, it was then that I began looking regularly in the Sunday *Times* for New York City penthouses. With Lisa in tow, I'd visit majestic apartments, high over the city, each one enhanced by a large terrace that wrapped around at least two sides of the building. The agents had no idea that my spouse wasn't about to put out the bucks for such a place, and amazingly, neither did I— after all, Joel had instructed me to look at only the one-bedroom penthouse apartments. These would be less expensive, of course, and then he would use part of the terrace to create a second bedroom—another intricately described Steinberg fantasy.

I guess I was still as gullible as I'd been at age three. That's when my sister had played a trick on me that was famous in the Nussbaum family. Knowing

164

that little sister Hedda would believe anything five-year-old Judy told her, Judy had informed me one day, "If you sprinkle pebbles here," in the gutter of a street near the curb, "tomorrow you'll find money." So I had eagerly sprinkled pebbles in that spot. The next day when we returned, there was a bright and shiny penny. *Wow!* I'd thought. *It's true!* And so I'd sprinkled pebbles there every day for a week but was greatly disappointed when no other money ever appeared.

The point is, I'd always been a very trusting person. Even at age eleven or twelve, I'd fallen for a goofy story Judy told me. She had sworn that the word "aspirins" was a dirty word and really meant "ass of prins." And, although I wasn't a baby anymore, still I'd believed her. So, although I soon got too old to fall for that kind of story, here I was at age 40, fully sucked into believing a tale as fantastic as pennies from pebbles or ass of prins: Joel was going to buy a penthouse apartment with a wrap terrace.

So, just as there had always been something wrong with every house we'd inspected, none of the glamorous penthouses were perfect enough for Joel either. However, when I found one on 14th Street and 7th Avenue, very close to where we lived, he was really quite taken with it—possibly because the price was relatively reasonable and the space a bit larger than the others we'd considered. As usual, for hours at a time, Joel enumerated the improvements he'd orchestrate and the additional bedroom he'd construct. But, he told me firmly, the final decision of whether to buy or not to buy was up to me. And this time, I think it actually was—but maybe that's only because I decided not to. I felt that the neighborhood wasn't up to par. With numerous derelicts hanging around 14th Street, it wasn't a safe place to raise a child.

Alas, probably because the price of real estate was rising so fast, this was the last penthouse apartment, as well as the last dwelling of any sort, that we viewed as a possible home. However, the housing search nearly led to another outcome: my beautiful strawberry blond baby becoming a professional model.

One of the real estate brokers, after meeting Lisa when she and I had visited a lovely one-bedroom penthouse on West 57th Street, told me that her friend represented child models. Lisa, she said, was so gorgeous, I should call her friend immediately and get my little Venus a modeling position. I couldn't wait to tell Joel all about it.

Since he certainly had no objections to the baby earning her keep, I dialed the number on the modeling agent's card and made an appointment—just like that, without the agent ever laying eyes on Lisa. I guess hearing her described was sufficient.

I was pretty excited when we got there. But it soon wore off after we sat and we sat in a tiny, crowded, noisy waiting room full of mothers and babies. At least Lisa didn't seem to mind it. But I surely did! Wailing infants, nervous moms, and a two-hour wait. It was almost too much to bear—not to mention the subway train that stood between stations for 15 minutes on our way there.

But at last we were called for a photo. Phew! I couldn't have taken much more sitting around and waiting, although the watching was interesting. The babies were all adorable, of course, but unquestionably none as precious as mine. And I'm certain I wasn't simply a biased mother. I held my breath, hoping she'd come out looking as great in the photo as in real life.

Two Polaroid shots later, I got my chance to look at the results. Oy! Lisa looked terrible. *How could she have a double chin,* I wondered, *when she doesn't really have a double chin!? It must be the way she was sitting.* I sighed. *I guess that's the end of her modeling career.*

And it was—fortunately for both Lisa and me.

Joel's ESP

By the time Lisa had her first birthday, she was walking and had even said her first word, "Mama," although I still wasn't her mother officially. That would come in time, Joel promised, and I believed him. Now that I'd come to know and adore my little girl, I wanted to be her lawful mother more than ever.

She had become a sprightly little person, comfortable and happy no matter where she was, including her play group, from which she'd return each day cheerful and smiling. Patty, who ran the group, told me that Lisa was also perfectly behaved there, as she always was at home.

But Joel soon began trying to tear down my confidence in Lisa's caretaker. First he told me he knew Patty was a lesbian.

"So?" I responded. "What does that have to do with how she cares for our child?" Shortly thereafter, he told me he knew through his ESP that Patty was a child molester and explicitly described scenes in which she'd do more than just wash the kids in the bathtub. I found this allegation hard to take seriously since Patty seemed like such a caring and able woman with whom Lisa appeared to be quite contented, even though I'd come to trust Joel's competence with ESP.

During our first few years together, Joel had never mentioned having Extra Sensory Perception. However, because I often spoke of my long-term interest in the paranormal, I think he was spurred on to claim he had such powers.

Ever since I was 14 and had read *The Search For Bridey Murphy*, I'd taken an extraordinary interest in reincarnation, hypnosis, and ESP, all of which are subjects of that book. Its appendix was possibly even more fascinating to me than the actual text. In it were descriptions of actual experiments done at Duke University, and the one I recall best tested people for ESP. One person would look at the top card in a deck and another who couldn't see the card tried to call it. Some people had scores too high to be possible through mere chance. Those scores were claimed to be due to ESP.

Judy and I had decided to have some fun and try the experiment between us. She held the deck, shuffled the cards, and looked at one at a time. I then told her what card she was looking at. Amazingly, my guesses were correct a huge percentage of the time. What a lark! We two teenage sisters repeated this little game over and over, day after day, week after week, with the same fantastic results. Wow! I had ESP! After several months of unfailing success, my scores suddenly dropped. I could no longer read Judy's mind. But I'd become a believer.

Of course, I'd told this story to Joel. And guess what? Little by little, he began to demonstrate "paranormal" powers.

The first time was a treasure hunt of sorts. One night Joel told me that if I walked to the corner of University Place and 9th Street (where, I was certain, Joel had not been all that day), I'd find something I'd like. So, hand-in-hand down the street with Joel I went with the object of finding the prize. And sure enough, sitting in the trash can on that very corner was a rattan window shade just the size to fit one of our bedroom windows! *Wow!* I thought to myself. *Without having seen it, he knew it was there!* And I certainly didn't question Joel's perception of trash as a treasure. He often picked up discarded household items and even clothes. I'd come to accept this eccentricity of his as just another of his ways to "avoid paying the exorbitant prices that stores charged."

So I was impressed, believing Joel really had ESP. After all, hadn't we been reading each other's minds all these years while doing the *Times* crossword puzzle? But then a disturbing thought crept in: the correct answers come to me after Joel says he knows them, but when did I ever see evidence that they come to *him*, too? However, I summarily dismissed the notion. Joel was just plain amazing.

Next Joel confessed to me that, although he didn't like to boast about it, he was a healer too. In fact, he'd been the cause of the disappearance of the chronic pains in my neck and shoulders. I didn't really believe that one session at Ed's had done that, did I? He'd also caused the disappearance of the spastic colon I'd had for years before meeting him. I felt dazzled. My wonderful Joel was even more extraordinary than I'd imagined.

Joel Loses a Friend

Mike Bergman, who'd been Joel's friend for nearly 20 years, had delivered Lisa from her birth mother's womb, and was also my gynecologist, discovered during a routine checkup a lump in my breast. Gulp! So off I went, at age 40, for my first-ever mammogram.

While I nervously awaited the results, Joel and I had dinner with Mike one evening as a gesture of support. You see, Mike, although only about 45, had learned he had a bad heart. The following day he was scheduled to leave town for a hospital famous for bypass surgery successes. Back then in 1982, such surgery was considered risky rather than routine like it is today.

Sitting in Gene's Restaurant, Mike and I kidded each other about our mutually threatening situations.

"Well, Hedda, which of us do you think will die first?"

"Hey, not me," I laughed. "I'm too young."

The joking continued back and forth all evening.

That was the last time I ever heard Mike laugh or even speak, the last time I saw him stand, walk, or feed himself. While my "lump" turned out to be nothing, Mike didn't fare as well. Instead of bypass surgery, he had a stroke on the operating table. It left him almost totally paralyzed.

Joel was, quite naturally, very upset by the news, but not upset enough, it appeared, to continue his friendship. One hospital visit after Mike's return to New York and one visit to his home was all Joel gave his longtime friend.

I often wanted to ask him why he didn't at least call Mike's wife, Jackie, to find out his friend's condition. But something held me back. I now regret not giving Joel at least a nudge or two.

When Mike and Jackie left Greenwich Village some months later to live in Mahopac, New York, the same community where Joel had spent his childhood summers, the same locale he and I had visited every summer for years, Joel neither called nor visited. When Mike died several years later, having never had his heart surgery, it was, of course, too late, and Joel knew it because he got into a deep funk and took his despair out on guess who?

Right after Mike's move, his medical practice had been turned over to another gynecologist, Peter Sarosi. Joel befriended Peter and became his attorney, financial advisor, confidant, and racquetball buddy. Peter, after all, could provide Joel with free GYN services for me, potential babies for the adoption aspect of his legal practice, and, as it turned out, a sailboat and a son.

Passing the Pipe

Although by 1982 Milo Handler was gone, one or another client of Joel's occasionally provided us with cocaine. Joel acquired such a client, whom I'll call Pete, through his brother, "Tony," who worked at the courthouse. Joel liked to shmooze with court workers; it helped him get quicker access to the files he needed. The charm with which he could affect this when required had endeared him to Tony.

One day, on a visit to our apartment to discuss his brother's case, Tony, who also smoked freebase, got in an instructive mode. He showed us how to make the drug the simple way. No ether was involved, he informed us, just plain old baking soda. Did I have any in the house? Since I did, Joel and I got our first cooking lesson, which was also the last, since the recipe was so simple: Put some cocaine in a test tube, add water and baking soda, and heat. That's all there was to it. The method was simple and safe, and you didn't need to be a chemist.

Disaster! That's how I see it now because we began cooking it on our own. At first we did so very occasionally, and only at night when our work was done and Lisa was asleep. But since Joel felt that we communicated well when we smoked, the idea was always somewhere in the back of his mind: Let's get some coke, cook it up, and smoke tonight.

Since our freebase sessions were awash with slow inhaling and lots of sensitivity, Joel claimed it was a tool in my "therapy," he could use it to help

172

me grow. Therefore, he needed to have some available fairly often.

Joel had become a cocaine user and not just the dealers' lawyer, although he felt he wasn't addicted to it. Unlike most, Joel and the intimate group of those with whom he often smoked did so with the intention of improving communication, getting in touch with their inner selves, getting to truth. Yes, folks, *truth* was the ultimate goal for Mr. Steinberg, and he used freebase "exclusively" as a means to achieve this end for himself and his beloved crew. Made up of his cherished partner, Hedda; the physician who had saved his arrhythmic heart, Al Gross; and a buddy of his, Sam Altman, who'd hide out for a while from his suburban wife, Star, they would meet secretly within the bowels of Joel's Greenwich Village apartment and pass the pipe.

Occasionally, Al and his wife Bonnie would visit as a couple. But more and more, Al began to come on his own to spend entire weekends on 10th Street. You see, Bonnie was of the sort who would never use drugs, so Al indulged secretly. All his spouse was aware of was that Al was visiting his dear friend, Joel Steinberg.

Sam also hid his drug use from his wife. He, however, didn't dare spend whole weekends with us as Al did. Instead, he indulged exclusively in stolen moments. He'd come by our apartment for a few hours after work in midtown Manhattan and then nervously depart to catch a train to his waiting wife. Star would never have a clue.

Of course, along with smoking cocaine went Joel's brand of psychotherapy.

"Inhale only a small amount," he'd direct. "That's the way. Now hold it in as long as you can and then let it out slowly...And feel. Feel the smoke, feel you, feel deeply. Be aware of all your senses—what you see, what you hear, what you are."

Ah, Joel was loving every minute of his guru status.

He'd direct his attention to one initiate at a time, asking tough personal questions and insisting that the disciple give direct, honest answers.

"Al, do you really like being with Bonnie?" he'd ask, for example. "Tell it straight. Put yourself on the line."

And eventually, truth would ostensibly pour from the mouths of his students. At first it was a struggle, pulling out bits at a time. But soon the words would flow, aided by the freebase, of course.

I would often join Joel with questions for the one in the hot seat. Or sometimes the men would get on my case. But Joel was almost never on the receiving end of the "therapy," but he was regularly on the receiving end of the pipe.

If ever Joel or I told other freebase users, like the Balken brothers, for example, how we smoked it, they'd laugh and say it was impossible. To them you had to inhale as much as the lungs could hold, get a quick high, and then strive to maintain it. Since, by the nature of the drug, matching that first high is impossible, they'd keep on chasing the unattainable. No matter how much they took in, no matter how long they tried, they could never equal that first high.

Although I've written most of this section tongue-in-cheek, it's fair to say that our little group did truly try to use the drug to get in touch with ourselves and each other. That is, Joel's satellites did, but I think that our mentor's first aim was to get high. As an added bonus, he attained a good deal of control over his crew of freebase users.

Of course what Sam, Al, and I did wasn't exactly noble. But because our use, and that meant Joel's too, seemed a lot more level headed than other peoples', I felt no shame about it and only a little guilt because the substance was illegal. And because I frequently checked that Lisa was either in her crib fast asleep or in her playpen happily surrounded by toys and stuffed animals, I was satisfied that she was neither being affected by the drug nor ignored because of it.

So where did the cocaine for four come from? Most often our source was one of Joel's clients who either gave it to us as payment for legal services, or we'd buy it from the guy. I say the client gave it to "us" as opposed to "him" because no one ever actually handed the coke to Joel; rather, I was the one who took all the risks of the transaction, insisting that Joel never involve himself directly in the process. After all, I contended, he had his professional standing to think of. I would protect my guru, my messiah.

So I made the coded phone calls. "We'd like two bottles of the best white wine you can get," I'd say, for example. Or else I'd ask for so many books. And I met with the dealers, usually in the street, and always after dark when my baby was fast asleep. A few times over the years, I took the subway to Brooklyn or Queens to complete a deal. But often the purveyor came to our apartment, and even in that private setting, I insisted that Joel never be seen touching the illegal substance.

Since most dealers cut the drug, not only to make a profit but also to replace the pure cocaine they've removed for their own use (don't forget, these guys are usually users as well as sellers), I quickly learned how to test for cut. The simplest test was to convert the powder to crystals and interpret them visually under a microscope, which Joel conveniently had around the house. Pure coke crystals looked different from those cut with amphetamines (which weren't going to cook out of the coke), which looked different from those cut with lidocaine, etcetera, etcetera, etcetera.

So imagine Johnny X, a client, has just rung our doorbell and delivered an ounce of coke into my hands. While Joel sits and talks with him in the living room, I cook up a very small amount in the kitchen, remove it to the bedroom, and check it under the microscope. Yeah, it looks good. So I go back to the living room and pay Johnny the stated price, the cash for which purpose Joel has previously left with me. If, on the other hand, the coke had been heavily cut, I'd have refused to purchase it.

A few years later, I sent away for a very comprehensive book for making and testing all kinds of drugs. From it I learned to do a full string of chemical tests, which I thoroughly enjoyed performing. I assume that approaching cocaine use scientifically helped me distance myself from the uneasy fact that it was illegal.

But, hey, at last we had an area that Joel quietly left entirely in my hands!

The Problem with Hedda

Freebase smoking wasn't exclusively left to sessions with Sam and Al. Very occasionally Joel and I would smoke some coke by ourselves—exclusively at night, long after Lisa's bedtime. Although the sensitivity Joel promised from it was rare indeed for me, I indulged because he insisted it was good for our relationship; it would bring us closer. As you might suspect, Joel used those occasions as opportunities to give me "therapy," which was the rule most nights anyway, cocaine or no cocaine.

The following are some of the "problems" Joel worked hard trying to correct during these sessions:

1. My stubborn rebelliousness. Who, me? Rebellious? Because of my experience with Baba at age two, I'd always tried to please and do whatever authority figures (parents, teachers, Joel) demanded of me. So, "Hedda the Rebel" existed only within Joel's need for complete control.

"You should rebel," he instructed, "when someone tells you to do something harmful to yourself, which, as you know, does not include me. When someone like me tells you to do something beneficial, obviously you should inhale it as deeply as possible and use it to your own benefit. So you MUST stop this juvenile rebelliousness."

Joel was apparently referring to my persistence in debating Joel's suggestions, even though he *always* won me over to his point of view—even when my ideas made better sense.

2. My inability to let go. This was a constant theme. I had to get looser, relax more, be me, etc., etc., etc. What did it matter that the harder I tried, the tenser I got? It was my duty to let go of everything I was holding onto and just be—not change, just *be*.

3. My inability to live "in truth." Joel talked of truth and being in truth for years. At one point he and I were even going to write a book about it. He'd supply the brilliant ideas and I the writing ability. But today, all I recall of the meaning of truth according to Joel Steinberg is that it had nothing to do with facts. You were "in truth" if you had the "right" state of mind, even while you lied.

My Sister, My Enemy

The phone rang. It was Judy, sounding unusually agitated.

"I just got a call from a woman who works with you at Random House," she told me, "Anne Something-or-other, and she said some strange things."

"Well, there's only one Anne there, so I know who it must be. But you sound upset," I noted.

"Well, I am. She told me that Joel is controlling your life, that you're in danger, and that I'd better get both you and Lisa out of his house as soon as possible."

"What?!" I was incredulous. "That's absurd. You know it is. She doesn't know what she's talking about!"

"That's what I thought, but why would she make up something like that?"

"Well...I don't know..."

I was horrified. I couldn't imagine where this idea had come from; she had not even been at the office long enough to have seen me with bruises.

But then I remembered—although her appearance had surprised me then, she was one of the people from my office who had visited me at the hospital after my splenectomy. So I assumed she'd made some assumptions, which, I believed, were completely wrong. *What a terrible thing to be saying about Joel!* I was thinking. *She has no idea how incredibly wonderful he is, how he inspires me, helps me grow—and is the perfect parent to Lisa.*

I could not wait to tell Joel what had transpired. As soon as he walked into the house from court, even before he got past the doorway, I immediately poured out the alarming tale.

"Anne?" he replied angrily as he removed his well-worn beige leather coat. "She's the one who used to be a missionary, isn't she?"

I nodded in reply.

"Still trying to be a do-gooder, I take it…but here it's entirely misplaced! Don't you see, she's the type who has to try and help people, even if they don't need any help? So she's not worth getting upset over…In fact, I'll bet she's just getting even with you for not inviting her to the baby shower."

"Gee, I never thought of that," I replied.

"But your sister!" Joel went on. "What did she do while Anne was saying all these things?"

"Well, she listened, kind of amazed, I guess."

"Oh, yeah? Your own sister, and she didn't even stand behind you, defend you from those awful accusations. And you think you can rely on her? Some sister she is! How could she allow a woman like Anne to say such things about you?"

The next time I talked to Judy, I surprised her with some anger of my own—a rarity for me. Repeating many of Joel's words, I ranted on about her disloyalty.

"How could you let something like this go unchallenged? You've betrayed me by listening to that crazy woman! Joel is a wonderful, caring partner; you know that! And you know how much I love him."

And Judy, who had grown up in the same environment as her little sister, with the same consistently loving parents, apparently felt no reason to doubt the conviction of my words. Today she admits she thought Joel was controlling, but if I was happy with that, then she had no reason to interfere.

But Joel couldn't be happy once Judy's image of him had been tainted. So began the tales about my sister and drugs. Because I'd told him that Judy had been experimenting a little with grass, he encouraged me to give her some marijuana—a gift from a client of his, which had been sitting around in a drawer unused. Judy's acceptance became fodder for Joel's tales. Judy, he now said, was a major drug user. She'd do anything for drugs. She'd betray me if I wasn't careful—seeds of distrust planted and ready to be sprouted when needed. One more step closer to my total isolation.

Good-bye Patty

One day I complained to Patty, the woman who ran Lisa's play group, about something pretty insignificant; in fact, I can't even recall what it was about. But her reaction was swift because the next day when I came to pick up Lisa, I found my baby standing alone in a crib in an isolated spot in the room. Patty said she was punishing my one-year-old for spilling her juice. Such punishment seemed quite inappropriate. It looked like my criticism of Patty was being taken out on my child. Then, when I met another mother in the street a few days later who had a similar tale of mistreatment of her child, I decided to remove Lisa immediately. Joel concurred.

"Remember I told you Patty was hurting those kids?" he proclaimed.

So what was I to do now? Without a babysitter or daycare group, I couldn't go to work. After all, Joel couldn't very well care for a toddler while running his business from our house. So I was home a few days. Luckily, I saw a notice on my pediatrician's bulletin board announcing a woman available to take care of a child in her home. I called her at once. That's how I found Annie.

Annie was compelled to stay home days because her two-year-old didn't take naps, and no nursery school would accept the little girl. Taking care of Lisa became Annie's way of earning a few bucks while doing her mother thing.

So, mornings I'd drop off Lisa at Annie's and then hop on the subway to

50th Street where Random House and the job I loved were located. But if you think for one minute that my life would now run smoothly, you…well, you'd better read on.

Judgment Day

The job at Random House was my all-time favorite. I'm not exaggerating when I say I *loved* being a juvenile book editor there—guiding authors, line editing their work, checking illustrations, writing text for *Charlie Brown* books based on TV Specials, coming up with the questions for *Charlie Brown* Question and Answer books, and lots of other awesome things. It was not just work; it was fun.

Although I was kind of compulsive about getting to work on time (even though "on time" now meant 10:00 a.m. since my spouse had pushed me into making that my norm), Joel still pressed the issue. He'd want me to stay home a little longer to do some task fabricated for the occasion: a letter *had* to be typed immediately, he *must* wear to court that day the suit that needed the pants hemmed, etcetera, etcetera, etcetera.

And when I'd object, he'd say incredulously, "Are you still worried about being at work at 'on time!?' I thought you'd gotten past that. My god! You're an executive, Hedda. Executives are free to come and go as they please. When will you grow up?"

And I'd feel sheepish. Why did I still worry about being late for work? What was wrong with me?

But as I suspected, my superiors at Random House were unhappy about my irregular hours and frequently missed work days. A black eye usually caused me to stay home for at least a week at a time until the bruise was light enough to cover with makeup. Gone were the days of going in blatantly with a shiner. I knew there was a limit to the number of times I could say I'd been mugged or had walked into a door. And then I got a warning.

"You can take a leave of absence," one of the vice presidents told me after I'd been called into his office, "or you can stay, but if you choose to stay, you'll have to be here on time and not take any more days off."

I promised I'd be a good girl from then on (how I saw resuming regular hours) and went back to my compulsively on-time schedule, telling Joel that I had no choice in the matter. I absolutely didn't want to lose my job at Random House and stay at home with Joel instead. As much as I loved being with him, I needed to be the Heditor (as someone dubbed me years later), a woman who was respected for excelling in a field that was *her* specialty, not Joel's.

But in late July of 1982, Joel gave me another black eye, and I was forced to stay home from work again.

"Don't worry," Joel crooned, comforting me. "Your boss is on vacation. You won't have any problem."

But I did worry, and I did have a problem after taking off a full two weeks, not returning to Random House until the day my boss was expected back. When she learned I'd been out the entire time she had been away, she appeared in my office.

"Hedda, as much as I hate to do this, I have to let you go," she said quietly.

It was hardly a real surprise, and yet I was stunned. How could I not work for Random House? I began cleaning out my office. Taking down the book cover proofs from my bulletin board, I wondered how I'd carry home the dozen or more potted plants that had inspired my first book. Should I take the paper wasp's nest? I felt a bit paralyzed. So I called Joel and told him the news.

"Come home," he said. "Don't stay there where you'll feel uncomfortable. Just leave."

So I did and was very thankful that Joel was so supportive about my failure.

Once home, Joel greeted me lovingly, gathering me in his big arms as soon as I walked in the door.

"Even before you left the apartment this morning," he declared, "I knew this was your Judgment Day. That's why I told you, 'Be strong today.' Remember?"

I didn't, but I was certain that if my wonderful, prophetic love told me that's what he had said, then that's exactly what he'd said. Joel's special powers, I concluded, had given him the insight.

The good part of this tale is that Random House seemed reluctant to let me go completely because they offered me some freelance editing. I was extremely grateful for this, even when it turned out that Anne was the editor I'd be working with. You remember Anne, the one who told Judy to get me and Lisa out of Joel's house immediately, the editor whom Joel had convinced me was trying to hurt me out of jealousy. Although I now harbored resentment toward her, I felt I could deal with it. Being needed for some editing and thereby maintaining my professional self-esteem ranked higher in importance. But the Random House work alone wasn't going to fulfill the need, so I began to apply for jobs advertised in the Sunday *Times*.

Apparently Joel also felt that I should be working full time—though his ideas didn't exactly match my own. Since freelancing occupied me for only a few hours a day, he considered me at leisure. Without my having to care for Lisa between 9:00 and 5:00 (she still spent days at Annie's so Joel could have a quiet house to work in) it seemed to Joel the time I spent cooking, cleaning, doing laundry, and tending his every need did not count as employment. After all, he offered, I'd done as much when I had worked full time. So, as long as I had so much un-regimented time, I may as well answer his phones, do his filing, etc. I'd already been doing his typing at night.

As should be evident, once he'd begun working from our apartment, Joel had not hired a secretary. Why would he spend a few extra dollars when he could get the same free from me? He had, however, tried hiring a young lawyer or two to help him out, but since Joel wanted his staff to do things his way, none of those associations ever worked out.

I had no objection to helping Joel until I found another editorial position. I was sure I would, and in fact, I assumed I'd probably get an even higher-level one. Why not? I'd been an editor for about eleven years, and Janet, my boss at Random House, had graciously promised to conceal from prospective employers the fact that I'd been fired. After all, I wasn't dismissed because of the quality of my work, which was highly valued in my department.

In fact, I probably could have prevented Random House from giving me the ax by confiding the truth to Janet, or to Jerry, the vice president who offered me the leave. Maybe then they would have understood why I was taking off all that time and pushed me to get help rather than firing me. On the other hand, I simply cannot imagine that I would have either told anyone the truth or gotten help had I been urged to.

Freelancing

With all I had to do at home, I made certain I set aside time for the freelance editorial work Random House had given me, and I got it done on time, as always. But suddenly Joel came up with a new way of "helping" me.

At night, our sessions now focused on me ending my "compulsive" work habits so I could be freer, less "obsessive." I'd never noticed that my work habits were anything worse than efficient, nor had anyone else. But Joel was now teaching me to let go of my intense concentration. And it worked! So well, in fact, that I found focusing on my assignments quite difficult. Still, I persisted in applying myself to them. Since being editor was a large part of my identity, I was not going to throw away this final opportunity.

And then on the evening before an assignment was due, I was unable to find the pages I'd completed. I was hunting for them frantically when, with a sly grin, Joel admitted that he'd hidden them. It was just a joke, he insisted, but he wasn't going to tell me where they were. I'd find them, he was quite sure. Ignoring my repeated appeals to reveal their location, he eventually went to sleep chuckling.

But to me this wasn't funny. So I continued to search the house, finally finding the missing pages hours later inside one of the rarely-opened compartments in the captain's bed.

End of story? Not a chance. One fine day, to teach me a lesson, Joel claimed, he tore up a few of the pages I was editing and threw them out the window. Horrified, I watched them fly down into a neighbor's backyard.

Seeing my panic, Joel calmed me down, saying, "Don't worry. Just call up the Bonanos [our neighbors downstairs] and tell them Lisa ripped some of your work and threw it out the window. They'll give it back to you."

They did, and I taped it (my only copy) together for submission to Random House, laying the blame on my innocent little daughter.

And then there were the arguments with Ole Risom, a vice president in our department. Ole and I had always gotten along magnificently. In fact, he was the one who had once told me I was the best editor they had. But now, for some reason, things were changing. Ole phoned me one day with accusations that baffled me. I'd stolen a book, he said, and that just wasn't true. I can't recall the details of the incident, but something was screwy, totally. Joel, of course, blamed it on Anne turning Ole against me. But today I know it had to have been Joel's doing. I don't know how this could be so, but I'm as sure of it as I am of my own name.

It may, therefore, come as no surprise that Random House gave me no more freelance jobs for the next six years, not, that is, until 1988 when the public saw me as the epitome of the battered woman.

Joel, the Anorexic

Random House or no Random House, I had work to do for Joel. Besides the legal stuff, I had an unofficial job: to see that Joel ate well, drank appropriately, and kept physically fit. Since encouraging my "employer" to get together a racquetball game, he'd established a weekly foursome. But the man had a tendency to eat large portions, and the exercise wasn't enough to keep him in shape.

"You've got to help me out, Hedda," he said, urging me to put him on a diet. "After all, you're the one who prepares and serves most of my meals."

I agreed, and cut down the amount of pasta, bread, and ice cream I served him, while increasing the salad and veggies. And it worked. Before long, he'd lost the protruding belly and double chin he'd developed. He was looking so good, I continued serving Joel the low-cal meals, and he certainly didn't object.

One night he came home from a racquetball game incensed.

"You did this to me!" he ranted.

"What? What are you talking about?"

"I'll tell you what," he fumed. "When I took off my shirt in the dressing room, Chasin [the matrimonial client who was part of his racquetball foursome] said, 'Joel, you look anorexic!' Anorexic! Do you hear that, Hedda? Anorexic! You've deliberately done that to me. You've starved me so that I'd get skinny, and people would assume it's from cocaine."

"What? Are you crazy, Joel?"

"Don't you call me crazy. You know exactly what you did and why."

"That's ridiculous, and you know it. You asked me to help you lose some weight, and I did."

On and on went the argument as it always did whenever Joel was off base about something. At times like that, I'd always try to set him straight, but he wouldn't listen, and especially not this time. He just kept up his absurd accusation: I wanted people to believe he was a drug addict, and that's why I had deliberately made him look emaciated.

"But you never told me you wanted to stop dieting," I protested.

This only met with another comeback argument. There was no way to win, so I agreed to comply with his next demand: fatten him up again. Okay, that would be easy. So here came nightly pasta and ice cream again.

Lisa's Back

With Lisa spending her days at Annie's, I would often pass an hour or so there, drinking coffee and gabbing. The talk was light—a great recipe, getting our daughters to sleep on time, which supermarkets were the best for bargains, stuff like that. And while Joel was away on a business trip, I spent even more time there. Annie had become a friend—my only friend now—except for Joel, of course.

Such a relationship must have been quite a threat to Joel. And when Annie and I had a disagreement about payment, Joel encouraged me to get rid of her.

"Since you're not working," he insisted, "you can handle taking care of a marvelously-behaved child like Lisa. What kid could be better? Annie should pay us for having the pleasure of taking care of her. Just tell Annie she's fired, and that'll be that."

So in short order, Lisa was back home during the day.

Not that I minded at all. I was glad to have her with me every day. Yes, in addition to all my other duties, I had to keep an eye on a toddler, too. But Joel was absolutely right about her; she was no trouble at all. Unlike many her age, a year and a half, Lisa wasn't the sort who would do what I'd blamed on her: tear up pages of my work. No, she never ripped books; she never broke toys. In fact, she was a pleasure to have around the house. I got much joy from her little laugh, her baby hugs, and her increasing vocabulary. Lisa loved going on the swings in Washington Square Park, and I always found the time to take her there—well, almost always. The only thing that ever kept me from it was the appearance of an occasional black-and-blue mark on my face, which would have spelled ABUSE to the world. No way was I going to let anyone see a bruise, so I'd stay home til it had faded enough to cover with makeup.

As this statement implies, from time to time, Joel would smack me in the eye, and I'd get another black eye. One such incident, however, doesn't stand out from another.

Each one is a part of a jumbled miasma in my mind consisting of hundreds of minor assaults between 1978 and 1987. It's the few major attacks that stand out very clearly.

Who did the shopping while I was quarantined with a black eye? Joel, of course. Who took Lisa to the park while I was locked in the house? No one. Occasionally, on bruise-free weekends, we'd all go to the playground. I felt so contented to be there with my family, feeling the sun on my face, listening to Joel's palaver about anything and everything, pushing my beautiful baby on the swings. Ah, life could be sweet.

Sexual Magic: The First Miracle

Because Joel continued to complain that I wasn't free enough sexually, I desperately wanted to please him and, in fact, become the greatest lover he could ever have. Then one night he lovingly told me that he could use his supernatural powers to make me all I wanted to be sexually. This deed, he said, would be totally selfless; this was for *me*. I begged him to try.

When we made love later that night, he whispered that his magic was taking place. And it did! Or so it seemed. Today I believe it was the sorcery of the suggestion that did the trick. After all, I believed in Joel totally.

Whatever the cause, my body now began moving freely; our nightly lovemaking became idyllic. Never before had Joel seemed so pleased with me, and I'd never felt so joyful. Not only had I become the woman of *my* dreams, as Joel had promised, but I'd become the woman of *Joel's*—even better. And, I believed, it was all due to his special powers. What an incredible man!

The extraordinary change in me showed itself in more places than bed. For the first time ever, Joel would proclaim, "I love watching you move," and he'd smile and stop whatever he was doing to observe me walking across the room. Ah, heaven on earth for me.

How could I not venerate this magician? How could I fail to kneel down before his extrasensory abilities? If I'd been a believer before, I was now a worshiper.

We began making love as often as we could, even during the working day while Lisa was napping. On would go the answering machine so we'd not be disturbed. But Joel thought it would be fun to have me answer the phone and chat while we were in the midst, so I did—a few times. He felt like we were fooling the world, and he relished doing that. But me? I just loved making Joel happy.

The Caring Closet

There we were in the bedroom where we had spent most of our time lately, and I said to Joel, "Joel, you know how much I love Lisa, and I know that you do too. Yet she still isn't ours legally, and it's been nearly a year and a half. We really need to get that consent agreement finalized. I want her to be ours."

"You don't know how to express your caring feelings," Joel responded, totally ignoring the content of my statement. "You've got to say such things like you really mean them, with passion; you have to stay clear and focused at the same time.

"Come here," he said, and I followed him to my closet, which he opened.

It was a small closet, tightly packed with all my blouses, dresses, slacks, and skirts, as well as some of Lisa's since her one big drawer was crammed full.

Joel reached in and yanked out my best black dress. It was elegant: a straight short shift with billowing, see-through sleeves, quilted across the bodice and cuffs with narrow gold thread. I'd bought it at Bloomingdale's off one of its drastically-reduced-price racks. I loved that dress, and I'd had a chance to wear it only once, to a New Year's Eve party at Dennis and Stephanie's where I'd felt I looked as splendid as any of the Long Island princesses in attendance.

"You like this dress, don't you?" Joel asked rhetorically, looking at me solemnly and straight in the eye.

"Well," he continued as I nodded yes, "I'm going to rip it, right down the middle, unless you ask me not to in a way that shows you really mean it."

I stared at Joel and the dress, wide-eyed, disbelieving.

"Don't rip it!" I gasped. "Please! I want that dress!"

"Now, let me hear how you mean it," Joel said calmly with a smile. "Show me you care for it."

So I tried, hard. I strove with all my might to stay centered as I said it again: "Please don't tear it. I really love that dress and want to keep it."

"Sorry," was Joel's reply. "That's not good enough."

Rrrriiiiipppp! Right down the middle.

I was horrified. My dress! Tears sprung to my eyes.

"Let's try again," he said calmly with a hint of a smile around his lips, taking out the jacket to my plush corduroy olive-green suit, which Joel knew I loved and wore often to work. "Tell me why you don't want me to tear this."

Before I could do more than open my mouth to speak, Joel added, "Now, be sure you stay focused and say it in a clear but passionate way, or else it's next…"

I took a deep breath, squeezed up my cheeks like I'd learned in Ed's group, and said, "Joel, please don't rip that jacket."

But there was a catch in my voice, so…*Rrrrriiiiippppp*!

Now Joel was reaching into my closet again. Oh, no! I felt panic looming up. What would go next? The olive-green corduroy skirt that matched the jacket? The beloved brown tweed blazer I wore so proudly because Joel had had it made to order for me? One of my silk blouses? I waited in horror.

The exact inventory of what Joel ripped that day has flown from memory, except for the black dress, which I've saved (almost in two separate halves), and the corduroy jacket. What I can recall is that slowly a pile of destroyed clothing—my finest—lay on the floor in front of the closet, and I was feeling more and more distraught, even though I believed Joel was simply trying to help me. I certainly wished that he'd not "had to" use the method he'd chosen, but I didn't hold against him the results over which I was grieving.

Apparently, I'd forgotten that he seemed to have a penchant for ripping up things I cared about. A few years before, he'd torn dozens of my personal snapshots, most of them with old boyfriends. He'd also ripped the two old books I'd sentimentally saved—my two favorites as a preschooler—*Mumpsy Goes to Kindergarten* and *The Bouncing Bear*, which first my family and then I had preserved for so many years.

But what Joel demolished next destroyed a piece of me with it. That was the extraordinary-looking marriage-of-metals cuff bracelet I'd made in the one course free to employees—in my case a silver jewelry course—I'd taken when I'd worked at Teacher's College, Columbia University, right before my job at Random House. Joel knew how much I treasured that bracelet and always seemed pleased by the frequent oohs and aahs I got on its uniqueness. Soldering together a variety of metals is supposed to be too difficult for a beginner because each metal needs a different temperature to succeed. But I didn't know that, and so I'd tackled the job and succeeded admirably.

"Okay," he said, pulling the silver, copper, and brass bracelet out of the drawer where I kept it, "this gets squashed unless you can tell me how much you care for it—in the proper way, of course." And he posed with his large hand gripped around the bracelet, ready to squeeze.

Destroying this would be too much for me. Clothes could always be replaced, but this bracelet… I couldn't control the tears. I pleaded tearfully with him, "Please don't smash that bracelet. Please," I slobbered—obviously the "wrong" approach.

And he crushed that beloved bracelet in his hand. I can still see his fist closing tightly over it, leaving it as flat as the proverbial pancake.

Next came the 14 karat gold Mathey Tissot watch I'd treated myself to after my first year teaching grade school (right after college). God knows, I'd earned that watch, and I'd felt somehow specially connected to it for perhaps 17 years by then. Joel squeezed the two edges next to its dainty face between a pair of pliers he had pulled from the tool closet, which stood at right angles to my clothing closet in the hallway. The glass popped off, the edges received permanent dents, and the delicate mechanism broke.

By the time Joel had finished with my clothes and the bracelet and gotten to the watch, I'd felt so drained there was no way I could have expressed anything in a focused voice. However, I rather think that even if I had, Joel's behavior would have been the same. He was demonstrating his power. My alleged inability to express caring in a specified way was just another excuse. Unfortunately, it would be many years before I realized that, and by then it would be too late for all of us.

Who Called BCW?

After the clothes-destroying episode, did I decide to leave the beast forever? No. Rather, I reasoned that Joel had only been trying to help me. So the incident became just one more to stick into that tightly shut drawer in the back of my mind.

But someone, probably a neighbor who was obviously aware that I was being abused, called the Bureau of Child Welfare (now called Child Protective Services) for fear that Lisa was being abused too. I was stunned that the secret I'd thought so well kept apparently wasn't.

The big topic of conversation between Joel and me became, "Who called BCW?" Joel, in fact, made quite a large issue of it, once again taking the focus off himself. But neither of us was very worried because we knew that Lisa was healthy, happy, and well cared for.

Still, I felt anxious on the day of the social worker's visit, imagining him entering our apartment and inspecting everything. Knowing I'd cleaned the living room, kitchen, and bathroom thoroughly, putting into the bedroom and out of sight all the excess junk we normally had around the living room (like the broken lamp Joel had been "fixing" for the past four months) helped me feel more secure. I was proud that the sinks, bathtub and refrigerator sparkled, as did the newly polished furniture. And Lisa looked especially pretty wearing, for the first time, a birthday gift she'd just grown into: lilac corduroy pants with a lilac and white matching shirt.

I met the BCW man at the door hesitantly, but he wasn't a bit intimidating. Rather, he seemed friendly and too young to be very experienced. He smiled as I led him in. Lisa was used to meeting new people since we took her with us everywhere we went. She greeted him with a happy face and a picture book in hand and immediately started to babble, pointing to a page she'd been "reading."

Joel and I, with Lisa sitting on Joel's lap for most of the visit, talked with the young man for a half hour, and then he left. The interview was obviously a success because BCW closed the case. The report said that Lisa appeared to have an excellent relationship with her father.

And that was true. Joel adored Lisa and treated her wonderfully, giving her plenty of love and attention while never being the least bit abusive to her either physically or verbally. As far as I was concerned, he was as wonderful a father as I'd always imagined he would be.

A Night at the Opera (Without the Marx Brothers)

Joel had always loved opera and often played Jussi Bjoerling records, howling along in his off-key voice. Because I didn't have much of an understanding of the art form, appreciating little more than Joan Southerland singing the mad scene in Lucia di Lammermore, for the first few years with Joel, I'd felt rather intimidated by his grasp of opera. But after listening to his albums often enough, I'd grown to enjoy them.

So when someone gave Joel two tickets to the Metropolitan Opera, of course we wanted to go. This would be our first trip since tickets cost more than Joel was willing to put up, even for something he adored. However, we had no babysitter to call on since we'd continued to take Lisa with us everywhere we went.

For our operatic evening out, we asked my mother to babysit. She'd travel in from New Jersey and spend the night at our house. She was, of course, thrilled. What an opportunity to spend time alone with her granddaughter! I was happy to give my mother this chance, and Joel was glad to have a free babysitter.

But one thing worried him: she would see the freebasing paraphernalia we now owned.

"But we keep it in a drawer in our room," I protested. "My mother won't even come into the bedroom since she'll be sleeping in the living room where Lisa is. And even if she should for some reason or another, she'd never look into our drawers!"

Joel, however, had a different opinion.

"Your mother can't be trusted," he declared. "After all, she wanted to turn you into a whore, a painted woman, when you were 13!"

"Joel, that's not true, and you know it," I retorted, outraged at his take on a story I'd once told him. At 13, I didn't want to wear lipstick, which to this day I don't like and refuse to wear. But Mommy wanted me to look pretty and coaxed me to wear it. I finally gave in and wore the red stuff until it went out of style in the 1960's.

"Look, I know my mother," I argued when Joel kept insisting she couldn't be trusted. "I kept a diary for years, and I never had to worry that she'd go to my drawer to look at it."

Although Joel was not convinced, Mommy did arrive, all excited about staying the night. Joel and I left for the Met. But the shadow of his fear about her snooping remained much of the evening.

After the opera, Joel and I ate a late dinner out, during which time Joel was unusually quiet. *Uh-oh*, I worried. *What's next?*

Then we began to walk more than fifty blocks home. Long walks had always been a treat for us, a special time to converse, laugh, and observe the city, too. Happily this occasion turned out to be no different. We joked, sang, and had fun all the way. Phew!

But the next day Joel accused me of deliberately delaying our arrival home to give my mother time to study our drug paraphernalia and take pictures of it.

"Joel," I declared, "you're being absurd."

Today, however, I realize he was being paranoid from the cocaine he used, of course.

And from then on, Joel began to implant in my head negative ideas about my mother. Although neither my father nor Judy was exempt from his criticism, Mommy got the brunt at this time. She was a liar, she couldn't be trusted, she wasn't supportive enough, she wasn't a good example for me, and she tried to interfere with my having a relationship with my father. Although I loved and believed in her, constant disdainful remarks about her coming from a man I also loved and trusted caused me doubts about my own mother.

He also began calling Judy a whore, suddenly "recalling" so-called indiscreet behavior at her son's bar mitzvah years earlier with a man whom Joel claimed had to have been her lover. According to Mr. Steinberg, she, too, couldn't be trusted.

Disaster Draws Closer

Picture a Saturday all-night freebasing session. Joel and I hit the sack at about 6:00 a.m. and made love before falling asleep. When Lisa awoke at about 7:00, I got up, changed her diaper, dressed her, fed her breakfast, did a few chores, and spent time playing with her before she was ready for a nap at about 10:00. Once she was tucked into her crib, I went back to bed fully clothed, knowing I'd have to get up soon because my parents were expected in two hours. Exhausted, I fell fast asleep beside a dead-to-the-world Joel.

Suddenly I was awakened by Lisa crying. And then I heard the doorbell ringing like mad, *Briiiinmmmg! Briiiinmmmng!*

Oh, my gosh! The doorbell! Mommy and Daddy are here!

I saw that Joel was still lying there, quite unconscious. I ran into the living room while smoothing my hair, picked up Lisa, and let in my anxious-looking parents almost at the same instant. Mommy's face had that look I know so well; it said, *I'm close to having a stroke.*

"What's wrong?" I asked as I seated my parents on the living room couch. "Were you ringing the bell a long time?"

"We were so worried!" Mommy began, taking comfort from holding Lisa whom she'd snatched from my arms. "Oy, Mammale, we didn't know what happened. Thank God you and Lisale are okay."

"Let me tell her the story, Em," said Daddy. "You'll just get all excited again."

Then he went on, "We got here at about twelve o'clock like we said, and we rang the downstairs bell. But no one answered, so we rang and rang, again and again. Right away you're mother starts to get all excited.'What if something's happened?' she says."

I could just picture how Mommy must have looked—even worse than she had when she'd walked in: tight face, gray complexion, blood pressure rising.

"'Relax, Em,' I tell her," my father continued. "But I was getting worried too."

"Well, you know what happened," I felt it necessary to put in, "we all took naps. Joel and I were out late last night, and I guess we were just too fast asleep to hear the bell. I'm so sorry."

"It's okay, Mammale," Mommy said. "As long as everything's okay." She was looking more composed now.

"Anyway," she continued, "we decided to ring the bell of the apartment above yours. Your upstairs neighbor, Blum is the name, buzzed us into the building after we said we're Hedda's parents—Hedda in Apartment 3W."

"Ya know," I said, concerned what my neighbor must have been thinking, "it might be a good idea to go upstairs and tell Mr. Blum that everything is fine down here."

Both Emma and Willie agreed with that. So while they were upstairs, I went into the bedroom and awakened Joel.

"Not getting up," he grumbled, scarcely opening his eyes. "I need my sleep." And he steadfastly refused to budge.

So once Mommy and Daddy returned to our apartment, Lisa and I spent a few hours alone with them. Then finally, at about 4:30 p.m., long after my parents had gone, Joel reached full consciousness. At that late hour, I brought him his "morning" coffee, as always, and told him all about Emma, Willie, and the doorbell.

Finally awake, his day beginning, Joel came into the living room where my parents had been, and right away, he noticed a book entitled "Cocaine," which I'd been reading as part of my constant research on the subject. I'd apparently left it sitting on the desk since the day before. The sight of the book set Joel off into a tirade.

"You've deliberately left that book there for your parents to see! Now they know we use the stuff. What are you trying to do? Ruin my reputation?"

"Joel, I didn't even notice the book there," I protested, "and I doubt that my parents did either. Besides, reading about cocaine doesn't mean we're using it. It could be something you're reading because of your drug clients."

"Don't give me excuses!" he roared. "You did it on purpose, and there's nothing you can say that will fool me!"

And then, "And sending your parents up to that guy upstairs. Did you have to do that? Did you have to deliberately embarrass me? You know how class-conscious he is…" and Joel proceeded to call my parents classless, common, crude, and too-obviously Jewish. "You'd better keep them at bay from now on," he declared.

So I saw less and less of my family, had no friends left, socialized almost exclusively with Joel's associates, worked at home with him all day, and spent my nights in his bed. And I started to come apart.

Joel had always relied upon me to remember our social schedule; now I began to forget dates and times. He'd always counted on me to know exactly where any item we owned was stored, but I was no longer sure where to find things. He'd put me in charge of handling the trivia related to his finances; now I was neglecting to mail checks. Even worse for me was the shock of finding a lost item in a place where it didn't belong: a sock in the refrigerator, one of Joel's files in a kitchen cabinet. And I had no memory of putting them there.

But something even worse started to happen: falling asleep at inappropriate times, like while talking on the telephone, which was embarrassing, to say the least. And horror of horrors, I found myself suddenly awakening while walking in the street wheeling Lisa's stroller. I was terribly frightened.

The first time wasn't too bad. I was walking down the street pushing the stroller, apparently fell asleep momentarily and then awoke. Nothing had changed except my realization that this was unnatural and possibly dangerous.

The second time I suddenly found myself in the lobby of a building I didn't know I'd entered. The doorman was questioning me: whom did I wish to see? I quickly excused myself and ran out, wondering what he thought about a sleepwalking woman with a toddler in a stroller.

But the most frightening incident happened in a supermarket. I'd apparently fallen asleep while pushing a shopping cart and suddenly awoke. My first instinct was to check on Lisa who was quietly munching on a cookie in the child seat. Phew! But then I noticed that my pocketbook was open and my wallet had been stolen. *Thank god it wasn't my child!*

Why was this happening to me? Was it due to lack of sleep? I didn't think so. Even though I'd lost some sleep staying up with Joel on our sporadic freebasing nights, the total wasn't nearly enough to cause such a severe reaction. I couldn't understand the phenomenon at all. I knew only that I was terrified, both for me and for Lisa.

Today I agree with the conclusion of Dr. Samuel Klagsbrun, the man who became my psychiatrist in 1988: it was an unconscious cry for help.

Of course, I told Joel about each incident immediately after it occurred. He was my Mr. Fix-it and would tell me how to make everything right. It didn't cross my mind then that he probably would—probably should—forbid me to take Lisa with me when I went out. Not until I got help, that is. But he didn't. Maybe that's because he didn't want to be burdened with having to watch her and run a business at the same time. So I continued to take her with me, praying that I'd stay awake—and, praise be to the heavens, after the third incident mentioned above, I did.

What Joel did say, repeatedly, was, "You're having a breakdown."

I probably was having a breakdown. But instead of being genuinely supportive about it, to my utter humiliation, Joel began to back up his analysis by telling me that others had come to the same conclusion.

"Bonnie told me you'd be better off in an institution," he asserted, putting the idea into someone else's mouth.

And since Bonnie was one of the people who'd been on the other end of a phone conversation when I had fallen asleep, I believed Joel. But quite frankly, I don't think she ever realized what had happened during that conversation. That, however, is the Hedda of today speaking. Then, I just felt more and more frightened. Although I probably could have benefitted from a stay in a peaceful, supportive, therapeutic hospital where, most especially, I could have been away from Joel and begun to regain myself, the image his threat conjured was right out of *The Snake Pit*. And he'd repeat it every time I'd forget something or fall asleep on the phone. So, to avoid this phantom, surreal asylum, I tried even harder to be a "good girl" and to do everything that would please my guru.

Escaping I

In spite of my attempts to make Joel happy in every way I could, he was never satisfied. In fact, he began threatening to throw me out of the house if my behavior didn't improve—and that terrified me. I did not want to be apart from Joel, the man I'd come to depend on for just about everything, and certainly I wanted to be with my little girl. But I obeyed when Joel ordered me to keep a bag packed at all times.

Amidst all this nuttiness was a moment of sanity on my part. *He doesn't have to throw me out,* I decided. *I'll go on my own.* But where could I go? To Mommy and Daddy, of course. In my hour of need, the horrid things Joel had been saying about them went out the window.

So, one day while Joel was out with Lisa, I took the packed bag out of the closet; I was going—alone—sure that Lisa would be in good hands with her Daddy. I called *my* Daddy on the phone, saying, "Come and get me," but I didn't say why.

However, before my father arrived, Joel returned, just as I was taking a jacket from the hall closet. My small suitcase stood on the floor beside me.

"What's going on?" he boomed.

Trained to be truthful with him, I answered, "I'm leaving you. My father's on his way here now to pick me up."

"You're going nowhere!" was Joel's response, and before another word passed between us, he'd struck me with the heel of his hand. The next thing

I knew, I was down on the floor, pain coursing from the leg I'd fallen on and sprained.

Grasping the situation immediately, Joel ordered me to soak in a cold tub to take down the swelling. Brrrr, the bath chilled me through and through, and my depraved "physician" saw my discomfort and took note.

When my father arrived, Joel greeted him while I was hidden behind the closed bathroom door.

"Willie!" Joel exclaimed, "Hedda's busy in the bathroom right now, so why don't you take Lisa out for some ice cream." And he did.

By the time he returned, the cold water had done its job, the swelling had disappeared, and I was just emerging from the bathroom, wrapped in my robe.

"Oh, Daddy," I smiled, "I'm really sorry for making you come so far, but I've changed my mind."

"Everything's okay?" he asked.

"Of course it is, Daddy." And then I changed the subject. Things seemed fine, and I didn't think his suspicions had been aroused.

But then the reverse of that scenario happened, and it shocked me totally. I'd just come home from a dead-end job interview—one last attempt to regain my identity. It was a Friday evening, and Al Gross was visiting. Although Sam Altman no longer risked his wife's becoming wise to his drug use and so declined to visit, Al continued to show up more and more regularly. Now, over a freebase pipe, Joel was unbosoming himself to his friend.

"Hedda hasn't been relating up to expectations. She's not even trying to stay in focus. She's never in truth."

And after giving several grossly distorted examples, he continued with, "What should I do with her, Al?"

Taking this newly bestowed power very seriously, Al told Joel, "Throw her out of the house. Let her go to her parents."

To my utter amazement, Joel agreed. He began gathering up all my shoes and boots, put them into a carton, and placed it outside our apartment door—a symbol to take with me.

In shock, I think, I obeyed and once again called my father to come and fetch me, telling him merrily that I'd decided to visit for a few days. When he arrived, I kept a smile on my face and explained the shoes with, "We have no room to store them here, so could you and Mommy please keep them for me?" The rest of what I needed to take along was already packed and waiting.

I stayed in New Jersey for about 24 hours, putting on a continual charade.

When Judy visited the next day, she and I went shopping; and I talked about Joel constantly while hunting for the brass lamp he wanted for his desk. I was determined to give my family no clue to my shame: Joel had thrown me out.

After arriving back at my parents' apartment, I received a phone call. It was Al, phoning from his home on Long Island. He and Bonnie were coming into the city that night to see a Broadway show, he told me. Joel was coming too. Would I like to join them?

"Of course!" I exclaimed, paradoxically, assuming that Joel had asked Al to invite me, that all was forgiven and that I could now go back home to the man I loved.

But when my father drove me to 10th Street in Saturday night traffic, we arrived slightly late, and Joel was angry.

"We're not going to the theater!" he proclaimed. "I don't want to get there late. It's just like you to pick this night to make a belated appearance."

"But there was traffic," I protested.

"Don't give me excuses," Joel snarled. "We're not going, and that's final."

When Al and Bonnie called, he told them to stop by after the show and take me back to their house. He didn't want me anymore.

I cringe now when I think about what happened after the Grosses arrived. I pleaded with Joel, literally on bended knees right in front of Al and Bonnie, to let me stay. And so I did. Joel had obviously gotten all he wanted out of the exercise—my total debasement—and had no reason to insist on my departing.

Escaping II

More and more, Joel kept telling me that I was the cause of all the problems in our home. Because of my breakdown, he needed to discipline me all the time, set me on the right track. Oh, he and Lisa would be so much better off without me. After all, then there would be no yelling, no fighting, no stress, just love. And so I became convinced; since I seemed to be denying peace and joy to Joel and Lisa, the two people I loved most, then I should go. And so I did in the spring of 1983 when Lisa wasn't quite two years old.

Joel had left early for court that morning. I dressed Lisa and myself, stopped to write a note to Joel, and was out the door. I was leaving because I loved him, I'd written. Lisa would be at Patty's; he could pick her up before closing time at 6:00 p.m. That was all.

I tried to stay brave while I dropped off Lisa at her old play group one more time. Kissing her good-bye, I hid my tears. I knew I'd see her again, but not when.

Then I walked a few blocks to the office of the brother of an old childhood friend. I'd bumped into Michael on the street a few months earlier and had learned that his business was headquartered not far away. I'd even taken him up to our apartment to meet Joel. As always, my man had charmed the visitor.

I'd chosen Michael this day because he was *my* friend, not Joel's. Well, he was the closest thing I had to a friend at that point. At least I knew him through a source other than Joel Steinberg. I felt that was an essential ingredient, and there weren't many left who qualified.

I told Michael that I'd left Joel. Could I stay with him and his wife for a few days until I could figure out what to do next?

He was polite but advised me, "You owe Joel more than that. You can't just walk out on him."

Had Joel impressed him that much? Or was Michael projecting—how would *he* feel if *his* wife simply walked out the door one day?

If I'd told him about Joel's abuse, I'm quite certain Michael would have talked a different talk. But I wasn't willing to do that. No one could know. I'd learned my lesson after the ER visit back in 1978 when Joel had given me that first black eye.

"You have to call him," he told me as he dialed our number. Taken aback, I accepted the phone he handed to me as it started to ring.

Joel had just come home, and he instructed me to do the same. Feeling defeated, I walked the 20 or so blocks back to 10th Street trying to convince myself that this was for the best. And when I walked in the door, Joel merely sighed and shook his head, thereafter treating me exceptionally sweetly. After all, losing me was not part of his plan.

And so we had another few days in the Honeymoon Phase of the abuse cycle, which Joel began by holding my hand as we walked to Patty's to pick up Lisa.

The Cycle of Abuse

I've learned that there are definite phases in the cycle of abuse, and they've been observed and studied. Although it's a mystery to me how any man "follows" the pattern, Joel surely did. He had a Tension Building Phase followed by a Serious Battering Incident, and then came a Honeymoon Phase where he treated me just like he might on a honeymoon—it was all sweetness and love. But soon the tension began again, and the cycle continued indefinitely.

Early in our relationship, it often took Joel months or even years to complete a cycle. But as time went on, the cycles got shorter and shorter.

The so-called Honeymoon Phase, when he was attentive and loving, could sometimes last for months, and sometimes only weeks or days. But it always roused in me the abiding hope that our early, idyllic era would return. Need I add that it never did?

And I really couldn't see the approach of a battering incident. Some women can see a man's aggression escalating, know that an assault is coming, and get away—anywhere—before they get hurt. But not me. The periods when Joel's offensive behavior was intensifying were short and so very subtle that I never realized that an attack was close at hand.

One day, for example, Joel had been doing some mild complaining—nothing to write home about. Hours later, while I was in the living room with Lisa in her playpen and Joel and Al Gross were in the bedroom installing a new telephone system that Joel had acquired from a doctor friend of his (the OB/GYN who eventually got us our little boy), the phone rang. I answered it in the living room and called Joel in to talk to a client. I was standing directly behind him when he picked up the phone. With no warning or provocation at all, and without even looking, he lifted his leg karate style and kicked behind him. It was a perfect hit. He got me right in the eye, that same left eye his right hand always smashed .

The force of the blow knocked me to the floor, and blood spurted from under my eye. I just sat there completely stunned, but Joel cut his conversation short and called to Al for aid.

I'd tripped on the shell of an old phone on the floor and fallen on one of the cradle prongs, Joel told him. As always, I backed the story. The old, large black phone minus its insides, now a toy for Lisa, lay right where I'd fallen.

With Joel directing his friend, the physician, they treated my wound and washed the eye all night long—literally. Al kept urging Joel to take me to an emergency room, but Joel always had an excuse. Time has erased from my mind his justifications for keeping my injury away from educated eyes, but you can be sure they were excellent. The cut below my left eye eventually healed, leaving no apparent scar; I credited this miracle to Joel's magical healing powers.

Only recently, some 18 years later, a small scar has appeared in that very spot. Mornings when I'm putting on my makeup and looking closely at my face in the mirror, I recall the incident and feel the fury I didn't experience back when it happened. It's a fury that's meant not for just this one tiny scar, but for all the scars—on my body and within my heart—that I wear because of Joel Steinberg.

Family Matters

Regardless of all that was going on in our home, Lisa seemed unscathed. She'd become a cheery, active, talkative, and bright little girl—my little "Pumpkin," as I often called her because of the color of her hair, or "Monkey," a pet name both Joel and I used.

On May 14, 1983, Lisa's second birthday, Mommy and Daddy— Grandma Emma and Grandpa to Lisa—insisted on taking her to Central Park for the day. With pleading, I was able to get Joel to agree.

When my parents arrived to pick up their granddaughter, I met them downstairs in the street. With his old-fashioned camera from the 1940's, Daddy took a snapshot of me holding Lisa wearing deep pink bibbed pants, size nine months, which now fitted her quite skimpily because Joel insisted she wear out her clothes before donning the new ones in her drawer that would have fit properly. I look quite normal in that photo; you can't tell that I'd hidden under makeup the yellow remnants of a black eye—nothing unusual about that anymore. Joel was giving me black eyes now nearly as frequently as the kisses he'd bestow upon me during our sexual exchanges, which still occurred nightly. Yet I continued to believe he loved me.

Daddy's snapshot of me holding Lisa—May 14, 1983.

When my parents returned hours later with Lisa carrying a Mickey Mouse balloon, a client I'll call Jerry and his Colombian buddy, Jorge, were sitting with us around our dining table. The two, who were accused of dealing cocaine, had become our suppliers, and we'd spent the day with them working out the contents of a motion for Jerry's defense. The two had become "friends" who often hung out at our house, had spent the previous New Year's Eve with us at a party given by Al and Bonnie, ate the dinners I cooked for them, and sometimes even smoked freebase with us.

That day has particular significance for me because it was the last time my mother ever saw Lisa. The two continued to speak weekly on the telephone, and Lisa kept her treasured Mickey Mouse balloon in her toy chest long after the helium had escaped from it, but grandmother and granddaughter were never again face to face—until maybe now, since they've been reunited in a better world.

Liar, Whore, Pig

In time, Joel would repeatedly call me three names— liar, whore, and pig—but the sobriquets were first applied to my mother. And it was because of Joel's claim that Mommy was a liar that he prevented her from ever seeing Lisa again. You see, ironically, to Joel, being a liar was the worst sin possible. And because *he* was one through and through, he probably delighted in his job of convincing me that my honest mother was the prevaricator. I should also mention that by keeping my mother away from our home, I too was prevented from seeing her for nearly five-and-a-half years after one last, brief visit when she was in the hospital for a stroke. The next time our eyes met, I was handcuffed to a hospital bed, bruised and scarred, and the life of my child hung by a thread.

I remember perfectly the events that cut the visual link between Mommy and me. For days, Joel had been constantly repeating, "You're mother's a liar," or "She's indirect, which makes her a liar," and, "She doesn't go on the line; she's a liar," and also, "She doesn't say what she means, so she's a liar," spoken each time with one of his famous sermons of distorted truth. At first I disputed his statements, as usual; eventually, I had no arguments left standing.

This red-letter day, he insisted I call her on the phone so he could talk to her. I pretty well knew what he was going to say, but he'd convinced me that we'd be better off without her around. So I obeyed and dialed her number

215

from the phone on Joel's big partner's desk in our living room. He repeated the same words: that she was a liar, indirect, not truthful, liar, liar, liar, and then he forbade her from ever returning. Next he motioned to me to back him up. I reluctantly took the receiver he held out to me and repeated the litany of her offenses but without much conviction in my voice. Then I said flatly, yes, it was true, we didn't want her to come to our house anymore. I wasn't happy about this, but Joel's indoctrination had convinced me that such action was necessary. Anyway, it was done, and there was no point in arguing now.

But Joel didn't stop with this. He continued to insist Mommy was a whore—the absolute last word anyone would think of using to describe my mother. Mommy was not very sexual; in fact, she was quite the wholesome mother figure, someone who had been brought up to value family, children, and love. Sex wasn't something very important to her. Still, Joel had always insisted that she was coming on to him. In fact, the first time my parents came to see Lisa when she was only two days old, Joel had appeared with nothing on but a towel wrapped around his waist—to tantalize my mother, he had said, because of her attraction to him. And my protestations to the contrary had no effect whatsoever.

He also began calling my mother a pig. I'm not sure exactly what that meant to Joel, but he eventually used the term to utterly debase both Mommy and me.

One day Joel and I saw a drawing in a magazine we were reading together—possibly *The New York Times* Sunday magazine, from which I often selected articles he'd like—about the US Supreme Court, spies, etc.— and I'd read them aloud to him. Anyway, this drawing was of a fat and grotesquely unattractive woman—a caricature; Joel insisted that this looked like my mother. So he told me to put a backing of cardboard on the drawing and hang it in our bedroom, and I did. Thereafter, when instructing Lisa about one of a variety of subjects, like manners, for example, he'd point to the picture and say, "You don't want to be like THE PIG, do you?" Fortunately, Lisa didn't connect this picture of the pig with the grandmother she enjoyed talking to on the telephone.

With Joel behaving so abominably about my mother, it's not surprising that he reacted as he did when one day I got a phone call from Daddy. Mommy had finally succumbed to the stroke we'd always feared her high blood pressure would bring about. And although Joel had banned visits with her, she was still my mother, and I wanted to see her.

"Please, Joel," I begged. "I really want to see her."

"You'll be putting yourself in danger; you know that, don't you?"

"But she's in the hospital and in bad shape."

"I don't know if I can allow you to do that."

"Please, Joel."

"We'll see. But what I can do is have Al call the hospital. As a physician, he'll be able to get more information about your mother's condition than we could."

And so Joel made a big deal to me and my father about how he was doing this great deed for my family while several days passed without my getting permission to visit Mommy. Al's information was one thing, but I still wanted to see my mother.

Finally, Joel relented, and Daddy came and picked up me, Lisa, and her stroller. At the hospital, my mother's cousin Temi and my father took turns watching Lisa in the waiting room while I visited with my mother. It was the first time I'd been with relatives in a very long while.

Thankfully, Mommy healed well; the stroke left no lasting aftereffects. But we did not meet again until our roles were reversed five and a half years later when she visited me in the hospital.

Fortunately, even though Mommy had been banned from visiting us, Daddy and Joel had always gotten along well, so the visitation prohibition did not apply to him.

On a day when Willie was scheduled to visit, Joel struck me in the eye. Knowing from an expanding accumulation of experience that I bruised easily, I panicked.

"Joel, my father is on his way here! What are we gonna do? My eye'll turn black and blue, and he'll see it!"

As you can see, at this point I was more upset about being found out than about being abused.

"Don't worry," Joel replied with a smile, "I'll get rid of that black eye. Here, I'll just do this," and he proceeded to rub the spot round and round quietly but quickly for a maybe a minute and a half.

"See," he then proclaimed, "the bruise is gone."

When I looked in the mirror, sure enough, I saw no bruise. Of course, I'd never seen one in the first place, but I'd become convinced that Joel had used his powers to rid me of it. I was *very* impressed.

When, years later, I mentioned to Joel that, come to think of it, I'd never seen any black eye that day, he insisted that of course I had. That was during his, "Don't you remember...?" period, when he was trying to convince me of many absurdities. For example, he insisted that my parents had told us I'd been adopted from somewhere in Europe, that my cousins had described their frequent use of hypnosis (a familiar theme at that point) on unsuspecting people, etcetera.

"Don't you remember?" he'd say, implying that something was amiss with my mind. Of course I didn't remember any of it—because those things had never happened. But by that time, Joel had messed up my mind so much that I was unable to distinguish between the truth and lies of his statements.

Joel Saves the Day—Or Does He?

Now realizing that I wasn't functioning well, I stopped answering employment ads. I knew I could no longer handle a job and felt doomed to staying home doing work for only Joel.

"There's one other solution," Joel offered. "I can get you back to being yourself. I just need a lot of intense time with you."

To effect that, he decided to ship Lisa off to spend a few weeks with Al and Bonnie. That way, he informed me, whenever he had some free time, he and I could concentrate on getting me back in shape.

I thought the idea made sense. Joel had successfully guided me in the past, so he would be the ideal one to help me now.

I also reasoned that a visit to the Gross's house might be good for two-and-a-half-year-old Lisa because she'd be away from my present unsteady influence. Since I loved her dearly, I didn't want her being affected by poor parenting, which I feared might now be what I was offering her. Also, at the Grosses', Lisa would have the company of Al and Bonnie's three-and-a-half-year-old son, "Noah."

"She's all yours," Joel told Al and Bonnie when he handed her over to them, demonstrating complete trust in his friends. "Treat her as if she were your own." But he then added an exception, one he and I had discussed in a moment of normalcy: "But make sure you don't cut her hair. We want it to grow long."

So now Joel and I were alone for some intense therapy. But, to tell you the truth, I can't recall any of it specifically. I assume it involved freebasing. And I know that at the end of week one, I was limping on a bandaged foot injured when Joel repeatedly pounded the denuded broomstick he called "magical" onto my instep. Both insteps, as a matter of fact, still have scars from this manner of rehabilitation.

The stick had a history with us. Joel had claimed for some time that it had special powers, imputed to it through him, of course, which he'd demonstrated to me and Al one cocaine-filled weekend. We two disciples had put our hands on the stick at Joel's direction and "felt" it pulse. It was alive! Such is the power of suggestion while using drugs.

The second weekend of my so-called "intensive therapy" was spent alone at home while Joel went to the Grosses' to be with Lisa. Since I was still limping, I was not only prohibited from joining him, but I was forbidden to leave the apartment at all during his absence. I remember it as a very lonely week of incarceration, but I believed the isolation was the price I was paying for my guru's help. I believed that very soon I'd have all my sensibilities back intact—thanks to Joel Steinberg.

At this point, events began to get weirder and weirder, more freakish and frightful. Lamentably, I was unable to comprehend the horror of what was happening. If, today, I spoke to an abused woman (as I do in my job) with a tale of such horrors as Lisa and I were living through then, I'd advise her to take the child and run as fast as possible to a battered woman's shelter and to be sure to call the police. But there was no one to advise me and no one I'd have listened to—except, of course, my abuser himself. Therefore, be prepared to read about some extraordinarily bizarre occurrences.

During the third week that Lisa was staying with the Grosses and I was having my mind reconstructed by Joel, he began telling me stories about our daughter's caretakers.

They were into hypnosis, he said. Bonnie had learned it in college and had taught it to Al. Okay. There was nothing too weird about that, I thought.

Then he dropped the bombshell: "Bonnie's been sexually abusing Noah," he said, just as calm as if he were telling me that he'd had a turkey sandwich for lunch. "Didn't you notice the last time we were there the way the kid walks?" And he went on to elucidate while I sat there with my mouth hanging open.

"But Lisa!" I cried, a little hysterical. "Why did you send her there?"

"Relax," Joel said. "You know that I wouldn't put Lisa in any danger. I told Bonnie and Al that because you were having such severe problems, I was arranging to have them adopt Lisa; you know how crazy they are about her. They wouldn't dare take a chance on doing anything to hurt her now. She's okay."

Two such shocking revelations in a row were too much for me. "You're not really going to give them Lisa, are you?" I gasped. Since she wasn't ours legally, anything might be possible.

"Of course not," Joel replied. "I just told them that to make sure they'd take excellent care of her."

I sighed with relief, feeling reassured by Joel's words. Lisa was still ours, and she'd be okay. They wouldn't harm her in any way. Such was my thinking. *Hello?* I say now to that Hedda of 1983, *Noah was the Grosses' child, and if they did indeed abuse him sexually, then how could Lisa have been safe?*

The next Saturday when Al brought Lisa home, I saw instantly that she was different; it wasn't just the new haircut and new dress. It was the flat look on her usually vibrant face, and she wasn't chattering as usual. She was quiet, withdrawn. I hugged her; she was unresponsive. What was wrong? She wouldn't say.

I felt panicky about this aberration. Normally, Lisa wore a smile and prattled about everything going on around her. But Joel didn't seem concerned. Only one thing was on his mind: the Grosses had defied his instructions and cut Lisa's hair!

As Joel went on and on about their disregard for his direction, Al blamed the haircut on Bonnie.

"When she took Noah for a haircut, Lisa went along and came back with one too. I had nothing to do with it."

"Well," Joel said to him, "then let's discuss this over some freebase. Perhaps you can learn how to be more assertive with your wife."

And off they went into the bedroom to smoke the base I'd already cooked in anticipation of Al's arrival.

Meanwhile, I tried to talk with a silent, grave-looking Lisa. She'd brought home some drawings that Al said she'd made in nursery school, and I made a fuss over these and proudly hung some on the refrigerator. At that, she did say something.

"I didn't do that."

"Who did?" I asked, thinking that they certainly looked like the drawings of a two-year-old.

When Lisa didn't reply, I left the artwork on the refrigerator.

Since she was wet, I took my baby into the bathroom to change her diaper. With that removed, I got the shock of my life: her vagina was black and blue. Now I knew the reason for her odd behavior.

When I revealed this event to my attorney years later just before Joel's murder trial, he insisted that I must have seen diaper rash. But he was wrong! Although my reasoning wasn't very clear in 1983, my vision was 20/20; that was no diaper rash. I saw black and blue, not red, except maybe figuratively.

"Joel!" I called. "Come here."

He took a look at Lisa's bruises and told me that he'd take care of it with Al.

"Don't worry," he promised, looking determined as he left the room.

I relaxed a bit, knowing Joel would take charge of the situation; he always did. He was so together, not like me.

In the meantime, Lisa needed my love and care, and I attended to her until dinnertime when the two men sat chatting comfortably together. *Had Joel confronted Al about Lisa?* I wondered. *Why were the two so chummy?* I felt confused, but who was I to question Joel's strategy? He knew what he was doing.

Later that night, after the two men had spent several more hours over a freebase pipe, I got the report from Joel. He'd been working intensely with Al on being assertive, and Dr. Gross was doing well. In fact, he wasn't going to sleep over as usual; he was going right home to confront Bonnie, the accused-apparent.

"He wants to take Lisa back with him," Joel said.

Seeing my outraged face, he added, "Now don't get excited; Al will be sure to see that she's well cared for this time. He's promised. I've taught him a lot."

Al nodded agreement.

"Now, Hedda," Joel went on, "now that we've made that clear to you, the final decision is up to you. Do you think we ought to let Al take Lisa with him?"

No! I thought. *Of course not!* But then, *Joel seems to be hinting at "yes." And Al's promised to be strong and caring. Maybe I should say yes. I think that's what Joel wants me to say, and he knows best.*

"Yes," I said. "He can take her."

But, thank heavens, he didn't; Joel didn't let him. I breathed a sigh of relief and felt guilty for having said yes.

Although I didn't wonder about it then, I do now: Why had Joel asked me to make that decision in the first place? Was he testing my loyalty to him? Probably.

Later, instead of questioning Joel about the decision, I asked him why he'd made such a fuss over the haircut while ignoring everything else.

"The haircut was symbolic," Joel answered. "It stood for everything they did that they should not have. Al understood. Bonnie'll never touch Lisa again. Trust me."

And that I did, to an extremely dangerous degree. I trusted him with my mind and with my child's life.

When, at Joel's trial, I revealed that I'd seen Lisa's bruised vagina and done nothing, that I'd "left it to Joel's wisdom," I made a lot of enemies. I hope they can now see that by the time of this occurrence, my actions were no longer my own, that Joel Steinberg had already ruined my independent thinking and controlled me totally.

One odd postscript: The time spent alone with Joel had done for me exactly what he'd promised. No longer did I forget things or fall asleep at inappropriate moments. No longer did I feel like I was coming apart at the seams. But maybe that was because I had to keep myself sane to succor Lisa, who continued to act withdrawn.

Buzz

August 23, 1983. These days I can hear both sides of Joel's telephone conversations, and he can hear both sides of mine. That's because one day he and Al together installed a speaker phone, and we keep it on at all times.

Today, the third day that I'm living with a strangely altered Lisa, something I'm finding almost unbearable, we get a call from Bonnie. She says that Noah wants to talk to Lisa; so, curious to see whether she'll talk to him, we put her on the phone. Of course, their conversation is broadcast over the speaker.

Noah keeps repeating the same words over and over: "Are you a good girl, Lisa? Are you a good girl, Lisa?" This seems very strange to me.

My Lisa says, "Yes," and nothing more.

"That's a buzz!" Joel exclaims after the call is finished. "Noah kept repeating those words to buzz Lisa. Bonnie must have taught it to him."

I should explain. A buzz is a word or phrase implanted in a subject's consciousness during hypnosis. Afterwards, whenever the subject hears it, he or she will act on a hypnotic suggestion. For example, a hypnotist might have said to a hypnotized Lisa, "Whenever you hear the words, 'Are you a good girl, Lisa?' you will go into a hypnotic trance." And from then on, whenever Lisa hears those buzz words, she'll go into a trance.

In spite of Joel's theory, Lisa doesn't seem at all affected by Noah's words, nor has Joel explained how she would have reacted if she *had* been influenced by them. What was Lisa supposed to do as a result of this so-called buzz? But one thing is pretty clear—Lisa appears to be in a permanent hypnotic state.

And it's driving me nutty! Also, I can't figure out why Joel, who can solve any and every problem, hasn't done something to help her already.

So I plead with him. "Joel," I beg, "Help her. Please do something for her right now."

"Okay," he says, as simple as anything.

Then sitting up in bed, he gathers Lisa onto his lap and holds her for a few short moments. That's all I see him do, but it results in an instant transformation! Lisa begins to smile again. Her energy returns, and she begins to chatter.

What a genius he is! What magic he can work! He returned me to normal a few days ago, and now he's given my daughter back to me.

I embrace the two of them, but Joel pushes me away.

"It's not so simple as all that," he insists. "She's still in danger of being buzzed. And, in fact, those drawings she brought home, the ones you put on the refrigerator, those are sexual images meant to buzz her. They're not her drawings at all."

"She told me that she didn't draw them!" I burst out, totally amazed that Joel could know this, but also frightened for Lisa.

"What should we do?" I ask.

"Take those drawings down from the fridge and let's

put them away from Lisa's sight."

So I remove the pictures, and we put them into an envelope in a file we mark "Buzz."

Besides the drawings, Al had also brought along a satchel full of new clothes for Lisa, which I now put away, too, far in back of the closet. Since we'd packed only a few things for her stay with them, Al had explained, Bonnie had gotten tired of looking at the same pants and tops and went out and bought an entire wardrobe for our little girl from skirts and blouses to a bathing suit to night gowns.

Night gowns! Why nightgowns and not pajamas? I'm now tormented by horrible images of sexual abuse, and gather my toddler into my arms. Giving me a big kiss, my now-smiling child says, "I love you, Mommy."

False Confessions

Amazingly, Al continued to visit us. Apparently his guru had forgiven him all his sins. But I never again saw Bonnie, definitely no loss to me or Lisa.

At first, Al's presence worried me. If Lisa had been abused while at his house, wouldn't she find him a frightening reminder? Convinced, however, that Joel knew best, I never mentioned these misgivings to him, and I saw the proof of his wisdom in Lisa's behavior. She didn't seem at all uneasy when Al was around. So I breathed a sigh of relief, and life went on.

Life during Al's visits invariably consisted of long "therapy" sessions with Joel, in which we learned that his relationship with Bonnie was in trouble. But one day, October 9, 1983, to be exact, Joel suddenly decided to depart from habit: Al needed a rest from therapy; so it would be my turn. Al would sit in on my session as I often did on his.

This sounds reasonable, right? Well, when I recently came across the papers I'd written during that session, I was blown away. Totally! Remember when I said that things had started to get weirder, more freakish and frightful? Well, these papers were *weird*, all right!

They consist of four legal pad pages, hand written, in which I swear to all kinds of completely false statements—my "confessions." They contain the kinds of accusations Joel always made against me and my family. Some are based on actual incidents, but here I "confess" to Joel's interpretations of those incidents. Truth is, I created this document in order to protect Joel—

just in case. It was also a kind of protection for me because it would please my mentor. Maybe he'd raise me back to the status of our early glory days. Let me quote:

> October 9, 1983
>
> I, Hedda Nussbaum, do solemnly swear that on this date I have reviewed my conscience, and I have found before God and for the sake of my own soul, that I must make the following statement under huge emotional pain and of my own free will:

That first part of this so-called confession was definitely dictated by Joel and dutifully recorded by me as my own. As for the rest, I cannot now recall which parts he dictated and which topics he simply ordered so nothing that he felt important would be omitted. But one thing is certain: I didn't need to be coerced into writing this. I truly felt it was a necessary evil.

> Because of enormous emotional pressure from both my mother and sister, I did give them the following information they wanted specifically for the purpose of destroying Joel and getting him out of the picture so that they could control me and Joel would no longer be able to protect me. [Talk about transposing the truth! Joel certainly knew about control and about getting people out of the picture who could protect me.]

> 1. I told my sister of occasional cocaine use by Joel—yet Joel never did any.
> 2. Passed on similar information to members of my office who disliked me and were in contact with my sister.
> 3. Provided actual substance—both marijuana and cocaine—to both my sister and mother, attributing it to Joel

4. Laid out my own funds to purchase these substances specifically or their needs.

5. Introduced cocaine into this household and scattered vials around in hiding places for the sole purpose of providing evidence for them.

6. Displayed test tubes—actually cigar tubes to reproduce test tubes that could be used to cook freebase to all— mother, father, sister. Also displayed to them freebase pipes which I purchased and collected specifically for the purpose.

7. Deliberately allowed my father to catch me cooking what could have been freebase in such a tube. [Willie did actually see me cooking freebase when he visited one day. Clearly, I did *not* set this up, nor did I want him to see me doing this.]

8. Provided parents with such a tube as well as a view of a book entitled COCAINE, prominently displayed.

And all was originally induced because my sister was a heavy drug user, and I made the mistake of telling my mother about it. I also swear that Joel never used any drugs of any sort. I fostered the image of drugs for both Joel and myself by doing the following:

1. Practically starving Joel on a low-calorie diet so that he got very thin.

2. Awakening him nights so that he had little sleep.

3. Deliberately and selectively falling asleep on the telephone.

4. Falling asleep in the supermarket and the street on my feet.

5. Deliberately sounding sleepy.
6. Deliberately sounding like I have a "cold."

All of the above was for the purpose of presenting the image of drug use, creating problems for Joel and alienating people from Joel.

7. Also, I overstated my funds to my family, then deliberately exhausted my funds and let my family know, creating the impression that Joel had used up my money for drugs—to comply with their suggestion that Joel had abused my assets. In fact, Joel made all his assets continually available to me, covered my pension and other depository accounts, provided constant, supportive, loving care and emotional support tolerating enormous personality variations and misbehaviors produced by the constant stress levied upon me by my family, and because I could consistently trust the gentle, tolerant and continual love, care, patience and forgiveness, I was able to take the latitude to perform the absurd & destructive acts & abuses and presentations of feigned violence upon myself while he constantly attempted to help me care with my family's behavior and resultant emotional disarray. [This one definitely sounds like it was dictated by Joel.]

In addition, I deliberately—although primarily unconsciously—did produce bruises and other physical symptoms on my person of beatings, mostly through accidents induced by great pressure from my mother and sister. I also produced screaming that was totally unprovoked and at times occurred when no one else was in the room to sound like I was being beaten, and then prominently displayed myself to neighbors, friends, co-workers, etc.

I have reflected upon my statements and realized that my parents and sister will cause me inordinate hardships, which were the cause of my behavior in itself; but I felt that I could not maintain my self-respect without admitting at least the above few elements of their barrage which I made myself a part of and cannot fully to this moment muster the internal strength to oppose or undo because of my historical experience with their venal and destructive, persistent behavior. I sincerely regret what I have allowed myself to be manipulated into doing to other people, but I hope that this statement, albeit incomplete, will lead me from the path that they have maintained for me throughout my life.

Hedda Nussbaum

Wow! This is mind-blowing! Incredible! It is hard for the sane me of today to believe that I could have written this. And yet I did. It is also clearer and clearer as I reread this that most, if not all, of my statements are in Mr. Steinberg, Esq.'s words—certainly not mine—and, therefore, actually dictated by him.

Directly under my statement is one signed by "Alan Gross," MD:

I observed Hedda Nussbaum at her request at the time she wrote this document and signed it, and found her to be extremely stable, sincere, concerned, and pained by the realizations she had to encounter and under no duress or inducement.

I have known Hedda Nussbaum for six years both as friend and patient. I have been familiar with her struggle of conscience and have discussed her problems with family and am familiar with the facts stated above. By conversation or observation I know them to be true.

Apparently Joel had induced Al to swear falsely as well, and I have a clue as to the carrot held out for the doctor. Whatever Al's motivation, it's clear that I wasn't the only one being controlled by Joel Steinberg.

Stored in a manila envelope together with the above sworn statements are other startling papers in which I similarly "confess" to more of Joel's accusations. Those pages are undated, but I know they come from the same general time period. Suffice it to say that, in retrospect, I can see that the situation was becoming monstrous, appalling, horrible, and that it should have been frightening to me—but it wasn't because my battle for awareness was already lost; I'd been blinded by Joel Steinberg's brainwashing.

The Marathon Week

A week later, Al appeared again. As soon as he walked in the door, Joel took me aside and whispered, "Al's not aware of it yet, but he doesn't want to return to Bonnie."

I accepted this statement as fact and was surprised by it, but I wasn't amazed at all at Joel's foreknowledge (which of course turned out to be accurate) because he'd proven his powers to me so many times before.

From my current vantage point, it's clear that Al had previously told Joel his intentions, although the thought never occurred to me then. Today, however, I think that for Joel's help with creating grounds for a divorce, Al had agreed to falsely swear to my crazy "confessions" and to a lot more, as you shall see.

"This is the perfect time to work with Al therapeutically," Joel went on. "But since this is a major moment for him, I'll need some help. And Gary'll be the perfect assistant."

Joel meant Gary Balken, cocaine dealer, coke addict, charges-dismissed former client, and avid Steinberg fan, the same Gary who'd treated us to the infamous Gordon Lightfoot concert.

"I've been grooming Gary for this moment," Joel continued as he dialed Gary's number. He had "worked" with Gary and a freebase pipe numerous times.

Later that night, Gary joined us. With Lisa fast asleep in the living room,

Al's freebase-directed therapy began in the bedroom. For the next five days, the intense work with him continued, marathon style, while Bonnie made a series of frantic phone calls asking if we knew where her husband was. Joel told her he had no idea—even after she told him she'd called the police to report Al missing.

Following are samples of the kinds of therapy that took place:

Al, upon Joel's direction, acted out both his fantasies and real scenes from his life with Bonnie, although it wasn't very clear which was which. The scene that shocked me to the core was his portrayal of catching Bonnie in the act of sexually abusing Lisa in the bathtub. His pain, he said, was for not stopping it. My pain, although greatly repressed back in October 1983, was much greater. Although we all watched Al's therapeutic moment, protocol required us to remain cool and objective. That was part of our silent covenant.

Next, Al was directed to make a series of "confessions," which, like mine before him, were documented on paper. These are nothing more than a detailing of Bonnie's alleged offenses and none of his own—all of which are lurid and shocking. He has since claimed that both these and his psychodramas were inspired by Joel as a means to divorce. This may be true, but only partly, since *someone* had sexually abused Lisa. Maybe it had been Bonnie, maybe it had been Al, and maybe it had been both. In my mind, they're both responsible. The pseudonym of "Gross" is a minor expression of my intense loathing of them.

In any case, at that time, I believed that everything I saw and heard was true, and later events confirmed that Gary did, too. It's probably fortunate for Al's well-being that in 1983 my feelings were so greatly repressed. But, as you shall see, I did get an unwitting chance to express some of them.

After dinner that evening, Joel asked me to put Lisa to sleep in the bedroom and to stay there myself until he called me. Of course I complied even though this seemed rather strange to me. *Why doesn't he want me in the room with them? What's going on?* I wondered. I waited quietly for a few hours, straining to hear whatever I could coming from the living room, which was little.

At last Joel came in and told me, in a very gentle voice, that Al had said that under hypnotic influence, I'd had sex with 100 men, and he suggested that I now come into the living room. Stunned, I followed Joel.

As I entered, I saw Al alone on the couch; Gary was gone.

"Al has agreed to demonstrate how he can hypnotize you using a staring technique," Joel told me, and Al nodded in agreement.

"Is that okay? Will you let him do this?" Joel continued to use a soothing tone of voice.

"No," I answered sharply. *Apparently I've already done terrible things because of his hypnosis. I can't let this insanity go on,* I thought. "No."

"Are you sure?" Joel asked. "He can deprogram you now if you let him hypnotize you."

Al just sat there.

I felt confused, scared. And so I still refused.

"Then," Joel went on, "Al has some things to tell you."

And what "things" they were!

"One day when you and I were here alone together," Al began apologetically, "I made a pass at you. And when you rejected me, I hit you."

He and I alone together? A pass? Him hitting me? I had no memory of any of this.

"I'm really sorry I did that," Al went on. "Please forgive me."

I stood silent, totally confused, trying to take in all this new "information."

"Hedda," Joel said tenderly, putting his arm around me, "I know you're angry with Al for treating you this way. So go ahead and slap him. He's going to stand right over there in the hallway, and you just go over and slap him as many times as you'd like."

Like two puppets, Al and I walked to the hall. He just stood there waiting for my blows, and I approached and began to slap his face. Once... twice... six times... ten times... twenty times. I just kept striking him over and over, not understanding at all from whence came my robot-like fury, and he attempted no defense. It felt like someone else was acting in my body. I had no memory of the behavior for which I was purportedly angry, and because of the context presented to me, I didn't connect my actions with the abuse to Lisa described a few days earlier.

Didn't I tell you things got to be *weird*? And it's all true. Bizarre, but true. And there's more!

At one point during that last crazy night, Joel, in at attempt to "scare" but "not harm" Al, as he described it, used a technique he claimed to have learned in the military. He repeatedly stuck his fingers deep into Al's eye sockets. I recall standing and watching, a little horrified and yet captivated. Al didn't seem to be feeling any pain. I clearly recall what I saw but not why Joel did it; I accepted it as one more part of Al's renewal.

The next morning, when I went into the kitchen to make coffee, I found Al sitting up wearing two black eyes. Shocked, I realized they certainly had not come from the slaps to his cheeks, which I'd dispensed. Of course, Joel's painless pressure had done it, but I'm not sure what my conclusions were at that time.

But Al didn't seem concerned about his eyes. He had heroics on his mind: Joel had convinced him the day before to go off to rescue his son, and he was resolute. First, however, he wanted to talk to Joel. So I went into the bedroom and tried to wake him. Surprisingly, nothing I did for at least five minutes had any affect. (This became ammunition for Joel in the days ahead: He couldn't wake up, he claimed, because I'd hypnotized him so that I could have sex with Al while he was sleeping.) Frightened by Joel's total non-response, which I now believe may have been a possum game, I called in Al, who quickly succeeded.

The two men talked quietly for a bit, and then Al rose without a word and walked out of the apartment forever. Except for one phone call telling us of the surgery Al had to his crushed eye sockets, we never again saw him or Bonnie; yet Joel kept them very much part of our lives.

Amnesia

November 15, 1983. I'm so lucky to have Joel! In
spite of all the dreadful things I've done, which
have been coming out slowly, he still loves me. Most
men I'm sure would have thrown me out in a minute
after learning just a fraction of the stuff Joel has,
but he's so understanding.

He's also extremely patient with me. He's been
working with me every night since Al first revealed
what I'd done, and gradually I've been telling him
about more and more of the incidents. Of course, the
strange part is that I don't remember anything about
this stuff. What I tell him just sort of comes out
when he prompts me to talk about it. I really don't
know where it all comes from. It's so strange. But
thank goodness it's coming out; when I'm in truth
when I tell Joel about it, he rewards me by taking me
in his arms and making love to me.

At first, I was very confused about what was
happening. On the first night after Al left here, you
know, after our week with him and Gary, Joel said to
me, "Just tell me whatever names pop into your head,"

meaning those would be some of the men I had sex with. "Don't worry about what names come up. Just say them."

So I did, and the list included all our closest male friends and—this is the one that shocked me the most—Daddy! But Joel was very comforting about it, telling me not to get upset and to just let the stories about each one come out, and to save my father for the last. And I did it. I just let out whatever came into my head. Out poured sexual story after sexual story, no two the same. Very, very peculiar! It's totally baffling to me because I don't know where these stories came from.

"But Joel," I whined, "I can't remember any of these things actually happening."

"Well, you've got amnesia about all this," he explained gently. "You'd never have done any of it if it weren't for Bonnie's hypnosis, so you've blocked it out. And since I know it's not like you to be promiscuous, I'm helping you remember. All the details of what happened should come out as we continue to talk. We're actually breaking through your amnesia by having you talk about it. Soon the memories will return."

Isn't he great?

So although most of what he said made sense, I still had a sleepless night wondering how I could have done such abominable things, even with hypnosis. I know that in an hypnotic trance, people can't be forced to do something they don't want to, and I certainly didn't want to have sex with anyone but Joel. I also wondered about the amnesia. Although I've had some temporary memory lapses recently, they all concerned small things—like where I'd put one of Joel's files. I've never lost a big piece of my life or even a small piece of time. And I'd never heard of forgetting things totally unless you've been hit over the head or something.

So the very next day I went to the library right here on the corner of 10th Street and Sixth Avenue and looked up "amnesia." And guess what? There really is a kind of amnesia where, if you've done something totally abhorrent to your nature, you can block it out totally. So I guess that's what I did. I blocked out these terrible events. But at least I'm lucky enough to have a man who's not only forgiving but wise and able to help.

<><><><><>

For the next year, night after night, our "therapy" sessions focused on one thing: getting me to vent everything about my alleged sexual entanglements.

"If you can get these stories out of your system, out into the open, hopefully you'll regain your memory about them," Joel coaxed. "And even if your memory continues to fail you, just talking about it all will cleanse your soul. Remember, 'The truth will set you free.'"

And, so I'd never forget that important aphorism, Joel put a sign on the bedroom wall: "The Truth Will Set You Free."

It was the first of many such catch-phrases to adorn that wall.

"The person who risks nothing, does nothing, has nothing and is nothing. He may avoid suffering and sorrow, but he simply cannot learn, feel, change, grow, live or love." That was on the wall and was often quoted aloud by Joel, who insisted that I didn't take risks but must. Like the other maxims he favored, this one wasn't original. It came from a book by a then-popular psychologist Joel and I read aloud together.

And then there was the biblical adage Joel had been misquoting since I had met him: "If I'm not for myself, who am I? If I'm not for others, what am I? And if not now, when?" Oh, Joel loved that one, especially as instruction to me: Give me, and do it now!

But when you come down to it, "The truth will set you free" was, ironically, Joel's favorite. What a motto for a man who wouldn't recognize truth if it came up and smacked him in the eye, or smashed him in the mouth, or pounded itself deep into his instep.

Now I worked with Joel every night, and indeed it was assiduous work. I'd concentrate intently, squeezing my memory for any drop at all, but none came. So, motivated by a profound need to please Joel, stories emerged from my mouth. I called them "images" because that's what they were—mental pictures that just floated into my consciousness and out my mouth. But they never came from either memory or deliberate creation. Like Topsy, they just grew.

Over time, they expanded from tales of sex with men we knew, to how I acted as a prostitute for Bonnie, to how, instructed by Bonnie in the technique of hypnotizing by staring, I began mesmerizing others—male, female, stranger, friend, and relative—using them for my own sexual purposes. Then, as an outgrowth of all this insanity, because Joel encouraged me to give him more and more, came the many tales of me sexually abusing children (whom I'd hypnotized for the purpose, of course, while Al Gross recorded it all on videotape to sell in a friend's video store under the counter) and tales of involvement with S&M. Next tales of my supposed affair with Al [gag! vomit!] turned up, and Joel swore that I'd been planning to run off and marry him.

Of course, in spite of Joel's promises, "getting all this off my chest" never prompted any real memories. And he began to insist that I give him hard facts. For example, what were the words that could buzz each of us?

"This is critical information," he contended. "Although you're the only one who can hypnotize me because I let down my guard with you, if the Grosses ever buzzed you on the phone to forget how evil they are, you could then buzz *me* to forget, and we'd be in real trouble! So it's all up to you."

I searched and searched my memory, laboring and straining to find those buzz words. But of course I couldn't come up with any—because they didn't exist! Today I understand that fact, but then I so trusted and believed in Joel that I became the perfect dupe.

The incident prompted the appearance on the wall of another of Joel's aphorisms: "Those who don't learn from history are doomed to repeat it." And just in case Joel's frightening scenario did come to pass, I wrote myself a note, which I taped to the wall next to the others: "Lest we forget: Avoid Al and Bonnie Gross. They are dangerous. They program, brainwash, and injure."

Still Joel kept up his pressure.

"You know those buzz words, Hedda, but you refuse to tell me!" he proclaimed vehemently one day while we stood in the bedroom in front of one of the windows.

Unfortunately, no neighbors lived close enough to view what went on next. He slapped me across the face—on my left side, of course—once, twice, three times, four times, five. I'd committed the worst of all sins: lying to *him*. So he hit my face again, over and over, striking my left eye repeatedly, bashing my ear again and again, for hours. And more the next day, over and again. But, of course, none of this shook loose any buzz words; so by the time the barrage of clouts ended, my left eye was so swollen it was almost totally closed, the cheek under it was equally enlarged, and I sported the cauliflower ear that I bear to this day and will forever after.

Escaping III

By February 1984, my facial injuries had long since healed (except for the cauliflower ear, of course), but Joel's obsession with inducing me to remember continued, and I was regularly smacked, pummeled, and thrashed. To top off his memory crusade, Joel used his "magical" stick to beat my left knee. Of course, he broke it—the knee, that is, not the stick.

But since this was not a normal household, instead of visiting a doctor immediately, I simply hopped around the house to avoid putting pressure on the knee. This, however, was not to Joel's liking, and he insisted that I walk and not hop. Not surprisingly, obeying caused me severe pain and several spills onto the floor.

Unable to bear the pain any longer, I felt I had to get out. So early one morning while Joel and Lisa still slept, I left, taking with me only a pocketbook (a New Yorker's term for handbag or shoulder bag) containing my wallet, address book, hair brush, and a pen. I was sure Lisa would be in good hands with her daddy, but I could no longer stay.

In the dim light of dawn, I hobbled to a phone booth on 6th Avenue and dialed the last number I had for my old friend Risa. I hadn't seen her for about seven years, although she'd invited Lisa and me to her child's birthday party a year earlier. We hadn't gone because I'd had a black eye at the time, but certainly, I'd not told her the truth. The phone number I dialed wasn't in service, so I decided to go to the nearest homeless women's shelter about ten blocks away. I could think of no other option.

The walk was agonizing, but I kept going, stopping only once for some rest and coffee. By the time I reached the shelter, my knee was so pain-racked that I told the woman at the desk I needed to see a doctor.

"I'm sorry," she replied. "We have no doctor here. But you can go to the nearest hospital, Bellevue." She handed me bus fare and pointed down the block to a bus stop.

At Bellevue Hospital's Emergency Room at last, I could not see a doctor before I filled out routine forms. Hoping to disassociate Joel from my injuries, I gave the homeless shelter's address as my residence and explained my broken knee and ribs, swollen nose, chipped teeth, dislocated shoulder, and black eye by saying I'd fallen down a flight of stairs. When asked about the multiple old fractures detected by X-rays, I blamed them on the S&M practices of a "cult" I said I belonged to (inspired by Joel's stories of the Grosses' activities, which he'd called a cult at one point or another). This fictitious cult story definitely came back to haunt me, as you shall see.

To confirm the story, described in the hospital records as "bizarre," I told them to call Joel. Yes, *that* was bizarre, too, and no doubt I was being admitted to the right hospital—one famous for its psych ward. Well, the hospital did call Joel, and he affirmed the story. He said I'd had this problem for four years and had been treated by four or five psychiatrists for it. Bellevue's immediate diagnosis was "Psychosis."

Lying on a stretcher bed in a hallway, waiting to be admitted to a ward for those with both physical and psychiatric problems, a friend of Joel's showed up. Gloria Newman lived nearby, and Joel had telephoned her with orders to bring me home—but I didn't want to go home. When she excused herself to make a phone call, I was extremely grateful that a nurse whisked me off to my room, apparently thwarting Gloria's attempts to rescue me.

Thank goodness I'm safely out of there, I thought, as I lay sheltered in a hospital bed, resting my injured leg. But I had other thoughts too: How was Lisa doing? Did she miss me? I certainly missed her. What had Joel told the hospital when they called? What were his feelings about my leaving? How would I ever get along without the two of them?

The next day I called Joel, giving both him and myself an excuse: I just wanted to know what had transpired when Bellevue had called. He told me—in detail, of course.

And then, knowing a sure way to draw me back, he said, "Lisa really misses you."

But rather than letting me talk to her as I requested (which was probably fortunate because I'd surely have promised to be back home soon), he gabbed on about a client of his who made porn films, using another magnet to get me back: writing.

"Ya know, Chubby told me the other day he's in the market for writers. 'Why look all over?' I told him. 'Hedda's a terrific writer. You should make use of her skill.'

"Hedda, this would be a really excellent opportunity for you to use your talents again. Here, take down Chubby's number and give him a call. He said you could write under a pseudonym, so you don't have to worry about that. It could be fun. It's a great chance, really. Take the risk."

During that week, I continued to speak with Joel at least once a day. In fact, I definitely talked with him a lot more than I did with any psychiatrist. City hospitals such as Bellevue are so overloaded and understaffed that there's not much time for therapy. But Joel managed to have a half-hour-long conversation with my psychiatrist over the phone, proven by his recording of it on our answering machine.

But the hospital stay wasn't entirely wasted. I did get my broken knee strapped, and I was scheduled to have it re-broken and set (it had already started to heal incorrectly) in another hospital, one with experts on staff to perform such surgery. Meanwhile, I was given crutches and the physical therapy unit taught me how to use them.

Now able to walk around, I ventured into the occupational therapy room, filled with people who seemed truly crazy to me. One continually muttered to himself. Another stared into space. But neither of them upset me as much as the patient who had been howling all night. *What am I doing in this place?* I wondered. *What a misjudgment the hospital had made by putting me in a psych unit!*

"I'm in here by mistake," I told the on-duty nurse.

Then, with a sudden insight, I added, laughing, "I'll bet everyone says that."

However, I *really* did believe I didn't belong there. I now understand that indeed I *was* well suited to be a mental patient, but not for the reasons I'd been admitted. There was no cult and no S&M, but my mind did need quite a bit of repair.

When I finally got to speak with a doctor, he told me my injuries were inconsistent with having fallen down a flight of stairs. So I changed my story.

"I was embarrassed to tell the truth," I asserted, humbly. "I wasn't really living in the shelter. I was living on the street and was beaten up by two young men. They seemed to think it was fun, or something."

He seemed to buy this tale. Not trained in domestic violence, neither he nor the rest of the hospital staff ever considered that I'd been beaten in my own home.

On my third day in the hospital, as I passed a mirror in the hallway (there are no mirrors in the rooms in a psychiatric ward—too dangerous) I got a shock. My nose looked different. Apparently some swelling on it had gone down, revealing the distorted bump of a broken nose, which hadn't been obvious before.

That same day, Joel came into the room where I was lying in bed, scooped me up in his arms, and swung me about exuberantly. Thereafter during the visit, he was extremely affectionate and sweet. In fact, my roommate later remarked how lucky I was to have a man who loved me so much. And I suddenly *felt* lucky. So when Joel proposed talking to the doctors about getting me out, I said yes.

Two days later, after promising to get my knee repaired, absolutely intending to, I left the hospital with Joel—against doctor's advice.

I never did get my knee fixed. I searched the telephone book and selected an orthopedic doctor experienced in sports medicine, one expert at repairing knees. But do you think Joel wanted me explaining to a doctor how the knee had gotten broken? So I was prohibited from going. Of course, I could have escaped to the doctor's office anyway on a day when my jailer was in court, but I was already too much under his control to disobey. As you might expect, my knee healed improperly and is still slightly enlarged and crooked. Fortunately, though not because of any magic from Mr. Steinberg, I have only a slight imbalance in my walk as opposed to a severe limp. But the possibility of ever being a runner again was definitely out. I tried it and ended up with a knee the size of a large grapefruit.

As you might expect, there was another honeymoon period with Joel after I came home from my five days at Bellevue—a giant relief for me. But the best part of returning was being once again with my delightfully lovable toddler, Lisa. Yet to my great surprise, I found a changed child. I'd left a baby and returned to a little girl who'd been taught by her dad to brush her own hair and dress herself! *Gosh*, I thought, *I guess Lisa is better off with Joel. In less than one week without me, she's grown up so much!*

To add to my insecurity, Joel denied having broken either my knee or my nose.

"You fractured that knee because you kept falling down!" he repeatedly declared.

"But I fell down only because you insisted I walk with a broken knee!" I countered.

Guess who had the final word on that? Joel, of course. And that's not all. He also contended that my nose had been broken *after* I left the house to go to Bellevue.

"It must have happened in the hospital, or maybe even on your way there," said the wise man.

This gave me food for thought since the bump on my nose *had* appeared so suddenly. But I came to only one conclusion: no one but Joel could have conceivably broken it.

"I know nothing happened on my way to the hospital," I declared. "And what possibly could have happened IN the hospital? No patient could have walked into my room during the night and smashed it without my knowledge!"

As you can see, I still argued with Joel when I believed him to be inaccurate, even though I always lost. He hated this habit of mine and began to list it as one of my sins. A new aphorism appeared on the wall: "Arguing is *de*structive, not *con*structive."

As to my family, while I was in the hospital, my parents called our house, as did Judy. Joel announced to them that I was sick because some "terrible people in a hypnotic cult" had programmed me. You can imagine how worried Mommy was after that!

Joel asked Judy, who was working as a rehabilitation counselor, to recommend a deprogrammer. She gave him names and phone numbers, and I made an appointment with a counselor from a recommended social service agency. The visit, however, was doomed to fail because I showed up with not only Lisa, but Joel. And then I told the social worker the nonsense story I believed to be true: that I'd been programmed by the Grosses, whom I now referred to as a "cult." Since this was not the reality of the situation, the suggestions the counselor made weren't helpful, and I didn't return to follow up.

Because of the lurid tales I'd told doctors at Bellevue, the New York City Department of Special Services for Children (DSS) wanted to investigate Lisa's care, and we were once again telephoned by a social worker who requested a home visit. But a few days before the scheduled appointment, Joel again gave me a black eye and was forced to use his Mr. Charming act to postpone the visit. Of course he succeeded, so that by the time the social worker arrived, no bruise was apparent on my face. Joel and I behaved like normal, busy professional parents concerned about their child. Lisa, displaying her usual carefree manner, seemed in no danger—and I surely believed that was her true status: safe. Apparently, our household seemed normal; so as before, the case was closed.

Because of the failure of the NYCDSS to take any action both times they had visited our home, they were sued for millions by Lisa's birth mother years later, though the settlement was for a whole lot less.

Losing Judy...and Daddy

Spring 1984. I've seen Judy so rarely during the past year, but when she called the other day to ask if she and David—you know, my nephew—who's home from college, could take Lisa out for a day, Joel agreed. He said it was a good way to get Lisa out of the house while he worked with me. We have some cocaine a new client he's been hanging out with gave us a few days ago, and you know how Joel likes to use it to help my state of mind. But it's getting harder to do that with Lisa getting older, so this is a good opportunity.

I love the idea of her being with my family again, but I'm anxious about Judy and David seeing my face. They have no idea that my nose is broken, and I also have a couple of visible bruises at the moment, so of course I don't want them to see what I look like. And, naturally, neither does Joel. So when the bell rings, I'm going to stay in the bathroom and call out a greeting. Joel says he'll hand Lisa over to Judy without delay. And he also has a game plan for what to do when they return.

"You can't just hide out again," he tells me. "So

here's what we'll do. Listen carefully." And I do.

It's now 5:00 p.m., and the downstairs bell just rang. I'm standing in the hallway outside the bedroom, peeking out from behind the door. I can hear everything but no one can see me.

Joel answers the door and lets Judy in with Lisa who is so pooped from the activities of the day that she immediately plops down on our bed (Joel's and mine) and falls asleep. Judy says she's left David downstairs in the double-parked car and so can stay just a few minutes.

Meanwhile, Joel leads her into the living room and seats her at the round oak dining table with her back to the room's entrance. Then he tells her real serious-like, "You know that Hedda's had some problems lately. And because hypnotizing people by staring at them is one, her psychiatrist told her not to look directly at anyone for a while. So when she comes out, please go along with this and keep your back to her.

"I know this must seem strange, but I also know that you love Hedda, and so this is something I'm sure you'll do for her."

What else can Judy do but agree to go along with this? I sure hope she doesn't think it's too peculiar.

Now that the "no-viewing" issue is resolved, Joel signals me to walk into the living room and stand directly behind Judy's chair, which I do. Judy places her hands on her shoulders, saying, "Since I can't see you, will you at least hold my hands?"

Of course I do; they feel damp. And in this peculiar position, we have a conversation.

<> < > < > < > < >

Skipping ahead to the present time, I no longer recall anything Judy and I said. But Joel and I thought we'd pulled the wool over her eyes, so to speak—and I guess we had.

Years later, Judy told me what an eerie experience that had been. To begin with, she said, the room was dimly lit, the blinds drawn. And then our strange physical placement while we talked really gave her the creeps! She felt that something was amiss, but of course, she had no idea what it was. She didn't look upon my face again until November 1987, a full three and a half years later. And that was only after tragedy had struck.

The end of my association with her came about like this: Apparently seeing Judy as a potential danger to his safety, Joel now claimed that she was one of the people I'd both hypnotized and taught the skill. Judy knew how to buzz us! Obviously, had this been true, it would have put us in extreme jeopardy every time we so much as talked to her on the phone. And then, somehow, as always, Joel's suggestion caused full-blown tales of how it had happened to creep into my bedtime stories, confirming Joel's allegation.

Therefore, unless he was present when she called me, I was forbidden to speak with her. And when he wasn't at home, I had to tell Judy, "Sorry, I can't talk now because..." and make up whatever excuse I could think of.

Unfortunately, at that time Judy was going through the pains of divorce. And because I seemed uninterested in talking with her, she felt hurt and gave up on me. One day I received a letter from her saying, according to Joel who opened the envelope, that she didn't want to have a relationship with me anymore. I breathed a sigh of relief. One less danger to existence. And I never doubted Joel's sincerity when he kept the letter from my eyes because he said it was full of buzz words. Gosh, I might have wondered (but didn't), how the heck did he recognize those buzz words? He'd certainly never been able to pry them out of *me*.

A postscript to this event took place after several years of silence between my sister and myself. Suddenly, an envelope from her addressed to me arrived in the mail.

"You'd better not open that," Joel cautioned. "It could be dangerous, full of buzz words. I'd better read it first."

Reluctantly, I passed the letter to Joel to open. Of course, he claimed it *was* full of buzz words, and he wouldn't let me see it.

Recently, I've read Judy's copy of the letter and found that she simply said that she loved me and missed me. But Joel couldn't chance my reading that message, so the letter remained hidden from my eyes.

When Joel got Judy out of the picture, all my close family members were gone from my sight—except Daddy. As you might well anticipate, that condition did not last long. He made the unforgivable mistake of showing up at our door unannounced one day. This being a precedent Joel couldn't chance, I was directed to tell my father through the intercom to please go to the phone booth down the block and call us.

Naturally, I followed Joel's orders and said, "Daddy could you please go to the phone booth down the block and call us from there."

Daddy, in turn, followed my direction, ambled off to the specified phone booth and dialed our number. However, we'd been having some telephone problems and did not hear the phone ring. Assuming that we'd chosen not to answer, he went home feeling very hurt. For my part, I assumed he'd decided not to call and worried why not.

Naturally, I called him at home later, but he was so offended by the phone stuff that he wouldn't listen to my explanations. Daddy never came to visit again. One more down. One step closer to complete isolation.

Hypnosis by Staring

From this time on, the issue of hypnosis-by-staring came up frequently, and not only as a ploy to keep Judy from seeing my battered face. Joel talked about it more and more. The Steinberg theory was that Bonnie had taught me the technique, and I had used it on others. Descriptions of such behavior crept into the stories I told Joel in bed, stories that still amazed me when they came out of my mouth. I'd hypnotized so-and-so in order to get him/her to do the sexual acts I then described. I guess it was a turnon to Joel, who kept encouraging such tales. In fact, when my stories pleased him, I was rewarded with lovemaking; when he felt I was "out of focus" during my narration, punishment replaced the reward.

I have often wondered from whence these stories came. They certainly weren't memories, nor did I deliberately make them up. They just seemed to grow out of nowhere. The only explanation I've been able to come up with that makes any sense is as follows: I'm a writer, and whenever I've written any fiction, I've noticed that the characters take over completely. I don't decide what each of them should say; the characters speak. I don't plan what they're going to do; they simply act, all by themselves. They "tell" me what words to write. And this same creativity is what I think took over when I was pressed to come up with tales for Joel.

Apparently not pleased with the way I'd told him a pornographic tale or two one night, Joel proclaimed loudly, "You're not in truth. And since I know you've been hypnotizing me while I sleep and buzzing me, I'm sure you'll be doing that tonight! You're a danger to me, so go, take your pillow, and sleep in the bathtub."

Could I really be hypnotizing him and not know it? I wondered as I marched to the bathroom, clutching my pillow and blanket.

And the tub became my sleeping space for several weeks then, and thereafter whenever Joel became particularly paranoid. Once this banishment ended, I was commanded to sleep on the floor next to our bed. He couldn't risk having me in the same bed, he told me.

What saddens me now is that I did it. I slept on the floor every night from that day forward—except when Joel decided that I'd been relating to him well enough to stay in "his" bed for the night. I say "stay" for a reason. I still started out each night there, where, as always, we'd make love; I still saw it as that: lovemaking. Don't forget, I adored this man. The further down he took me, the more I needed his caresses, his affection, the more I relied on him to make me feel whole.

My main concern was having Lisa see me lying on the floor when she came bouncing into our room in the morning. *What can she think?* I worried. *What kind of example is this for her to grow up with?* But I never voiced that concern to Joel. I did as I was ordered.

One freebase-filled night, Joel insisted I wasn't in focus, wasn't relating to him properly, and needed to be banished even further from his presence than the bathroom. So, knowing that I'm more than a little claustrophobic, he commanded me to sleep in the hall closet. Desperate to demonstrate my honesty and compliance, as always, I curled up there after Joel had fallen asleep. Still, I felt guilty for having "cheated" because I kept the closet door ajar.

And then one day, Joel demanded, "Stop trying to buzz me!"

"But I'm not..."

"You are," he growled, approaching me. "You are!"

The next thing I knew, he had me by the throat, squeezing hard. And then the world went black.

I was out only momentarily, down on the bedroom floor. When I awoke he was standing over me, concerned.

"Are you okay?"

Blinking, I looked up at him, the memory of what just occurred rushing in on me.

"Yeah, I think so," I croaked and then tried to clear my throat.

But the croak remained—forever. My vocal cords had been damaged. Leave it to Joel to know exactly where they lay within my throat and thus be able to attack them directly.

As soon as I was up off the floor, feeling like myself again, the phone rang. After a pause to be sure I could do it and sound okay, I answered the phone.

"Hello," I said into the phone, suddenly speaking an octave lower than usual.

It was a woman of the Long Island group. You remember them, don't you? Those women who deliberately show mucho cleavage at parties. This one apparently had had a few too many drinks and began ranting.

"Why so lawn to answer the phone? I know. Cocaine. You two are too busy being cokeheads. That's wha's the matter with you."

Joel and I exchanged looks. The phone was to my ear, but he heard every word over the speaker. Suddenly, we were united against a common enemy, and he prompted me on what to say to her. After I hung up, Joel and I clucked together over the person who had attacked us. Gosh! We hadn't even known she was aware of our cocaine use!

The strangulation incident was forgotten for now. But the buzzing remained an issue for the future.

Escaping IV

There is a framed illustration of elephants that hangs on my bedroom wall today, a book cover proof, signed by the artist. Once, it hung in my office at Random House. I'd edited the nature book for which it was intended and liked the illustrator, a mature woman who seemed kind and motherly. I'll call her Diane.

When I fled from Joel again, I left surreptitiously, just after dawn while he slept. Fortunately, Joel was a very sound sleeper. My plan was to steal away to Diane's home in Connecticut.

But before I got very far that early morning, I noticed on the street a window blind that perfectly matched the one Joel had found using his "ESP" a few years before, one that now hung on one of our bedroom windows. I felt inspired. Joel would be so pleased to have this one for the second bedroom window. So I scooped it up, sneaked quietly back into the apartment, and left the shade on the floor in the entranceway. I felt exhilarated knowing that Joel would enjoy the surprise when he awoke.

"Hello?" you say, "You're escaping from prison and joyfully risk capture by bringing gifts back to your jailer?"

Yep. This was the case. More bizarre behavior.

This time I wasn't running simply to escape the abuse. I fled because Joel had convinced me that he and Lisa would be better off without me. You will recall that such feelings originated when I came home from Bellevue to find that Joel had taught Lisa to brush her own hair and dress herself. Being perceptive, Joel continued to play on the theme. "You're the cause of all the problems in this house," he repeated, time and again.

With the gift safely deposited in our apartment, I made my way to Grand Central Station, wearing the old clothes I now slept in. I'd felt that changing to more suitable attire would have been too risky to chance.

What a startling site I must have been for Diane who happily picked me up at her hometown railroad station. Accustomed to seeing me in tailored skirt and blazer, my dirty jeans and ten-year-old shirt must have come as a shock. Recalling my earlier pretty face, the now obviously-broken nose, unkempt hair, and pale face with no makeup must have made me nearly unrecognizable.

But we did connect. I spent that night with Diane and her husband, explaining my battered face by using the cult story. Big mistake! Clearly my decision-making powers had been diminished. The next morning, the artist deposited me at a social service agency and left without another word.

Once again I was questioned by a social worker. Where did I live?

"West 10th Street, in Manhattan's Greenwich Village," I replied.

Could he have a phone number to call?

"Yes," I said, and I gave it to him.

Thereafter, the man of course called Joel. Feeling that my options had been squelched, I went home on the next train. So, there I was, once again, back with good ole Joel Steinberg for another brief honeymoon period.

Escaping V

As cycles go in domestic violence, after a honeymoon period like the one we had after I returned from Connecticut, comes a slow buildup of tension and then violence once again. So we were soon due for another round of physical abuse.

Remember Joel's use of an ice-cold bath to take down the swelling during my first escape attempt? Well, since then, he'd sent me into a few more cold baths for the same purpose, and I'd clearly despised the frigid temperature. Aha! Here was motivation for another use: a means of "discipline." Joel now insisted that I sit in such baths with the cold water running until he decided that my "state of mind" had improved sufficiently. This was his ploy: the icy baths were necessary to get my out-of-focus mind back to center.

<><><><><>

September 1984. I'm in the tub again. And it's cold. So cold. Have I been in here for minutes? Hours? I can't tell. But it's been long. My fingernails are blue, I'm sure my lips are too. My teeth are starting to chatter. I used to think that was just an expression—teeth chattering; but no, it's real. When you're cold enough, they ch-chatter, fast.

These cold baths are the worst. Worse than Joel's blows to my eye. Those happen fast. One quick shock, and it's over. But this goes on and on and on.

The water keeps running. The stopper is open a little so the water can run out. Joel does it that way in our baths together. He always did it that way alone, too. But, of course, then there's hot and cold water mixed, and now there's only COLD. In both cases the space between stopper and drain keeps the water from reaching room temperature. Oh, what I'd give for room temperature now!

Joel, please look in and say I can come out. This seems like the longest bath ever. Have you forgotten about me? So absorbed in the TV that you've forgotten about me? Or don't you care if I freeze—freeze and die? Oh, please, come in.

Maybe I could add some hot water? But if Joel catches me, he'll make me stay in even longer—with only the cold water, of course—like he did last time. Is it worth it?

I don't know how much longer I can take this. Where are you, Joel? Please come in. I can't stay in here any longer. I still hear that TV. On and on it goes. He's ignoring me. I gotta get out.

I'm out! Grab my robe. Run. Quietly. Out the bathroom door. Out the apartment door. Let it close softly. Oh, I'm barefoot! So what? Gotta get out of here.

I'm down the stairs. No time for the elevator. Into the street. Scared. What if he heard me leave? What if he comes after me?

It's autumn. Drizzling. Cold. Gotta get inside somewhere.

Here's a place. It's 12½, two or three doors down from us. I'll run in here. Phew! Warmer. Dry. I'm sh-shivering.

Where do I go from here? Don't know. Just stand here in the hallway. Staring at the mailboxes—brass mailboxes.

Uh-oh. People. A man and a woman. They're looking at me strangely. I must be a sight. My eye's probably black and blue by now, too. Maybe more bruises on my face.

"Are you okay?" the woman asks.

"Uh-huh," I nod, looking down. Don't want them to see who I am.

"I'm a nurse," she says. "Do you want us to call an ambulance?"

Maybe that's the answer, I think. The hospital.

"Okay," I answer.

"My husband is going in to call the hospital now," the nurse tells me. Out of the corner of my eye, I see the two nod to each other. He goes inside.

"I'll stay here with you."

I don't want her to. I want to be alone. But I say, "Thank you."

I look at the floor, not at her. Still shivering.

Thankfully, the ambulance arrives quickly. I'm led in. Told to lie down. I do. Blankets are piled atop me and wrapped around me. Aah, warmth at last.

A thermometer is put in my mouth. 94.3°. I close my eyes and enjoy the warmth of the blankets.

Too soon we're at the hospital. St. Vincent's. Only two and a half blocks away.

Inside I lie on a gurney, alone, for a while. A man in schoolroom green approaches. Efficient.

"Name?" he asks, holding a pen to a chart.

I think, I can't tell my name. Hedda Nussbaum was here three years ago. Ruptured spleen. They'll put two and two together. Might get Joel in trouble. Can't do that to him.

"Just call me 'Heather,'" I say. "Can't tell you any more than that."

"Address?" snaps the efficient man in green.

"Can't say," I answer, thinking, *Mustn't connect Joel.*

The man looks at me oddly. Then shrugs. I am admitted to St. Vincent's.

It's the next day, and, thank goodness, I'm lying safely in a hospital bed. I'm still here anonymously, in the ward for the uninsured. But so what? That's better than snitching on Joel. Maybe I had to run from him, but I'll never hurt him in any way.

But, oh dear, what's this? Two detectives from the Sixth Precinct! They want to discuss my injuries. Well, I'm certainly not about to tell them the truth.

<> <> <> <> <>

And I didn't. I told them I was followed and beaten in the street. Amazingly, they didn't bother to ask why I'd been wearing only a robe!

Another astounding thing is that I couldn't resist calling Joel. Consciously I told myself that I didn't want him worrying about me; unconsciously, my true reason was attachment to him and Lisa. And, wow! He said it was okay for me to give my real name. I was surprised, but I did it. As long as he didn't worry about being connected, I ceased my own fretting about it.

The next day Joel visited me, and brought our little "monkey" with him. Of course, Lisa wasn't allowed into my room, but Joel turned on some of his especially bewitching charms and left her at the nursing station with some flattered young women. And I think she must have done some charming herself, because I thoroughly believe what Joel told me—that the nurses didn't want Lisa to leave!

And guess where I was the next day? Home.

Another Little Piece of My Soul
and Another And...

The year 1985 began with a New Year's Eve that Joel and I spent alone. He'd told me, "I'm always providing entertainment for you. We go out with *my* friends. I take you with me to events *my* clients have invited *me* to. But what do you do for me? You rely on me to arrange amusement for you. Well, not this New Year's Eve. This time, since none of my associates invited us to a party and we'll be staying home, *you* can make it a special evening for me, for a change. You can do it; just be creative."

What Joel failed to mention, of course, was that he'd isolated me from each and every one of my own associates, so how could we go places with them? But back then, I never realized this now-obvious fact, so I tried as hard as I could to make that New Year's Eve a very special evening, really, I did. I got out a bottle of champagne that had been stored in the fridge for years. I made hors d'oeuvres, I donned a sexy nightie given to us a couple of years before by one of Joel's sex-toy-making clients. But none of this was good enough for Joel. I hadn't made the evening sufficiently momentous, he claimed. Naturally, that meant I didn't qualify to spend this special night in "his" bed. So, as had become the routine of late, after the sexual exchange I needed desperately to feel cared about, I climbed off the bed and down to my designated spot on the floor.

The blessing of that year was that Joel put to sleep for a while the entire cult/hypnosis/sexual aberration concept—but only *after* he caused me a huge emotional trauma about it. One day, to my utter shock, he informed me that my sexual aberrations were not simply a thing of the past. No, I was still engaging in them, most particularly having sex with the owner of a neighborhood head shop right in his store window.

Left alone for a while after this "revelation," I began crying hysterically. How could I be doing such things now and not know it; how could I be losing time? And, my god, what *things* I'd been doing! I'd accepted that similar events had happened in the past; the present was a different story. *Am I totally insane?* I wondered.

Hearing my sobs, Joel came to see what was the problem. I sputtered out my concerns, still weeping profusely.

"Well, I didn't say that you were actually *doing* these things now," Joel offered, covering himself with a gigantic fib, "just that you *might* be. You know that I have to let you learn the truth for yourself, and you're getting there."

Relieved, but not totally reassured, I started to check my watch repeatedly whenever I was out of the house to be certain I hadn't lost any time. I even recorded in a notebook everything I did and the time when it began and ended. And nope, there weren't any blanks, no possible intervals when I might have stopped off somewhere to have sex on the way home from the supermarket.

Although, for reasons unknown to me, the mental abuse regarding hypnosis, programming, and sexual aberrations ceased (Phew!), but the physical indignities continued. One terrible night stands out in my mind. I remember Joel, his "magical" broomstick in hand, ordering me to lie down and spread my legs. I obeyed, and, for no apparent reason, he began beating me. He didn't even pretend to have a justification at this point. Over and over again the stick painfully pounded my genitals until the vagina became swollen and engorged with blood. In fact, my periods stopped completely for an ironic nine months.

What happened nine months later for my menses to resume? Joel "cured" the problem by giving my vagina one good, hard kick. Then I hemorrhaged into the bathtub for about an hour. If infertility had been his problem previously, he'd now made certain that it was also mine.

You already know that he often called me "pig." And then one day he insisted I wear a sign labeled, "I am a pig," crawl around on my hands and knees, and say, "Oink, oink."

"Get down on that floor now and oink like the pig you are," he demanded. "Go ahead, Pig, say 'oink, oink.'"

The most intolerable part of it (to me now) is that I did it, regardless of how humiliated I felt down there on the floor, snorting like a pig in front of four-year-old Lisa. I remember her being clearly puzzled by the scene, and I was thoroughly abashed.

But the most disgustingly humiliating indignity he subjected me to was— are you ready for this, folks?—urinating on my face. In my role as advocate, I've heard stories about husbands spitting in their wives' faces. Ha! That was nothing compared to this action!

Recall, if you will, that Joel liked to walk around the house nude, which came in very handy for him that day. For whatever his motivation, he simply knocked me to the ground and aimed right at my face, commenting with a grin, "You're lucky I'm not like you; I drink lots of water!" Of course, I kept my mouth shut at that time, but now I'll give my opinion. Joel is a PIG.

I've often wondered why Joel's abuse accelerated at this point as if on a high-speed escalator. Was it because he saw that he was getting away with it, and each step up was bringing him closer to his goal of total domination? *Ha! Ha! My control over Hedda is getting stronger and stronger, and that makes me feel great! But now I need another hit, one more taste of that power I love so much.*

Yes, maybe power is a drug like cocaine. You get a little, and you want more. Perhaps we should compare it to the image of someone doing crack, sucking harder and harder at that pipe, wanting another high as potent as the last one, needing more and more all the time to achieve that high. Pretty soon the desire is way out of control.

Power as an addiction; I like that metaphor. So power, like any addiction, can't be cured unless the junkie admits that he needs help and truly wants to change. Did the thought of change ever enter Joel Steinberg's brain? Power rehab for Joel? Nah, no way.

Instead of finding ways to change and stop abusing me, Joel continued both torturing me and lecturing me about how terrible I was. Here's a sample sermon that left me feeling totally devastated:

> You're aware that you CHOOSE to keep hurting me; you do
> it deliberately by not producing anything, not doing anything
> positive. You know EXACTLY what you're effecting; you're

causing me pain, and you're fully responsible for it. In fact, you ENJOY it. You get satisfaction from your behavior; you even get PLEASURE from it. You just love weakening me, reducing me and negating me. Because of you I can't move forward; I'm frustrated. And as long as I stay involved with you, Hedda, I can't win; you've got me by the balls. But you're also driving me away from you because I'm so deprived of candid intimacy, which I need, and you know I need it. You keep me from feeling loved and cared about. And do you know why you do this? Of course you do! To feel control and power over me. That's why. You get satisfaction from those feelings. Oh, for a while you'll give me some energy, and then you quickly revert to doing the same hurtful things again and again. You block out all you've learned from me. You get it, and then you just block it out and do the same hurtful acts again and again—or I should say non-acts—NOT producing energy, NOT giving, just taking. And you don't even recognize those acts as being bad. You continue to refuse to acknowledge that you already knew all this. And you go on fighting the same battle again and again. And then you want it all to go away—all the pain you cause me and my reactions to it. Well, it won't. You expect everything to remain status quo because you're "the good girl" and you expect to be treated as such, even though you continue to block out all the good things I've taught you.

Talk about projection! That's exactly what Joel was doing—projecting his own desire for power and control onto me. The sad part is that his words left me feeling like dirt.

Lisa

My little girl was growing. My little girl was bright. My little girl was beautiful. My little girl was talented. Yes, I know, every mother thinks her child is the best. But in this case, it was really true!

Lisa was very mature for her age and growing prettier and brighter by the day. I loved teaching her the alphabet and numbers and reading stories and nursery rhymes to her. With her quick mind, by age three, she could count up to 100 and say the alphabet perfectly. And she was *so* cute and *so* adorable when she recited nursery rhymes flawlessly, copying my exact intonation.

From the time Lisa was old enough to draw real pictures and form letters of the alphabet, she and I started a greeting-card-making tradition. At first, in 1984, Lisa would create the artwork and then tell me what she wanted to say, and I'd write it for her. Then she was able to print the words by herself as long as I spelled them for her. Of course, she continued to draw the pictures—all beautiful pictures of happy, smiling people. As the years passed, she began doing more and more of the process herself. She'd make cards to say thank you for the many toys, dolls, and clothes she received all the time, cards for birthdays, cards for Chanukah, cards for Father's Day to her Daddy and Grandpa, and cards for Mother's Day to both Grandmas. (But a certain party, who will remain nameless, never helped her make one for me!)

Lisa's 1987 drawing of herself and her brother,
Mitch, on a card to Grandma Emma.

While I always helped with the creation, Joel had final approval: only extra-neat cards—no mistakes—could be mailed. And that meant that a card labored over with much effort and love would sometimes end up in the trash, much to Lisa's dismay.

Once, when Joel felt that a thank-you card Lisa had spent an hour creating wasn't up to par, he ripped it up in front of her. I could see the anguish on her face, so I tried to ease her grief and be supportive of Joel's position at the same time.

"I know you hate to redo that card," I said. "You worked so hard on it. But you don't want to send a messy-looking card to Grandma, do you?"

I felt that a compromise statement such as that was in Lisa's best interest. I didn't want her to see her parents at odds about how to treat her. That would surely cause her to feel she could play us against each other. It's strange how I understood the effects of some parental behavior on a child but had blocked out even considering others.

New Friends

Now Lisa had a group of new friends—all of them feline. After settling a dispute between two neighbors on our block, Joel had become friendly with one of the couples—I'll call them Roseann and Terry—who lived two houses east of us on 10th Street. The couple had five cats, and when Joel visited there, Lisa loved to tag along and play with the furry creatures.

Joel, however, didn't want me to follow suit and meet his new friends. My distorted nose and awkward gait presented a problem for him. How could he explain them to strangers? Well, I say now, he should have thought of that before he assaulted me! But back in 1985, I accepted the situation and stayed away while Joel and Lisa spent much time with Roseann; Terry, on the other hand, wasn't home often. Meanwhile, Joel told Roseann I was resting up from a car accident and wasn't socializing. It was many weeks, in fact, until he allowed me to join him and Lisa in Roseann's company. But by then, my appearance could be explained with a tale of a terrible auto accident.

Together

During the first seven years of our relationship, at Joel's behest, I'd accompanied him everywhere. But not anymore. Joel was socializing more and more without me.

He, following habit, had become the friend as well as the attorney of a business client I'll call Eric. On a day when I knew that Joel was planning to visit Eric's home after they finished their business at Joel's office, I felt an intense need to be with my partner. Since my own associates had all been eliminated from my life, I wanted to maintain the tottering tradition and socialize with Joel's—imperfect face or not. So I made a sudden decision: I'd call Eric's wife and use a few of the manipulative techniques I'd learned from listening to Joel to ensure that she'd invite me to join them. And that's exactly what I did.

"Hello, this is Hedda, Joel Steinberg's wife."

Hmmm, did I say "wife?" I don't know what I called myself. Can't recall. Most of the time, I avoided terms like husband or wife or partner. I simply called Joel "Joel" when I spoke about him. But I really am a blank as to how I'd have described myself to Eric's wife. I also don't remember what skills I invoked to achieve it, but Eric's wife did indeed invite Lisa and me to hop on a train to Long Island and join the party. So I put a pretty dress on Lisa and some makeup on me, trying to pump up my own looks in spite of the distorted nose, and off we went.

Although Joel wasn't very pleased by my action that day, the ice had been broken with his new friends, and soon afterwards, Joel, Lisa, and I joined them for a weekend in Atlantic City, New Jersey. That's when Joel renewed his love for gambling. Remember Puerto Rico in 1975? Remember his amazing success shooting craps? Well, he continued to gamble big bucks and to win, and we later spent a few weekends in the New Jersey casinos, courtesy of the hotel management. Once, we even took the newly separated Roseann.

She and Terry were no longer together because he had a couple of problems that were not going away any day soon. He was both alcoholic and abusive. Since Joel was an attorney, of course Roseann consulted him on how to split from her spouse.

Joel, of course, discussed our friends' situation with me, just as he seemed to discuss everything with me.

"Ya know what Terry did to Roseann? He came home drunk as a skunk the other day and cut her leg with a knife."

"Oh, my!" I exclaimed. "How terrible for Roseann!"

"Yeah, she wants me to help her get an order of protection against him— you know, a restraining order that says that Terry is not allowed to insult her or assault her or whatever without his suffering the consequences."

"Well, it's clear that he deserves it!" I proclaimed. "I wonder why she married him in the first place?"

No, there was no connection in my mind between Terry's actions and Joel's. And certainly I wasn't inspired to treat Joel in like manner.

Normalcy

One thing most of us experience in relationships is that they don't always run in a straight line. Their pattern is more like a graph, with highs, plateaus, and low periods. This, as you've seen, was true of my life with Joel, although the highs were probably higher than normal and the lows certainly much lower.

So, between the dramatic incidents I've been describing, came periods of normalcy when abuse wasn't an issue and loving feelings pervaded. During such times, Joel and I would laugh a lot, we'd enjoy our Sunday *Times* crossword puzzling, I'd often read aloud to him the magazine articles I'd selected for his pleasure, and we'd have serious adult-to-adult discussions about raising Lisa.

Here are a couple of examples of such discussions. Lisa had a habit of flipping the channels of her personal TV. And although Joel and I repeatedly warned her not to—"You're gonna break the TV if you keep doing that."—she continued and, viola! Our prediction came true. So Joel and I had a powwow and decided that it would be okay if he—who loved to play with electronic equipment—repaired it this once. And he did, but with the warning to our daughter, "Daddy'll fix it this time; but if you ever break it again, you'll have no TV to watch." And Lisa never flipped the channels again. Lisa was like that. There was never any need to scold her. Logic and reasoning usually did the trick.

Another issue Joel and I discussed relating to Lisa was what sort of preschool to send her to. We were in agreement that she needed to be in the company of other children, and school seemed the best way to achieve that. As it was, at age four, she continued to accompany us everywhere, which meant she was spending all her time with adults.

So I made a series of phone calls and got bulletins from a variety of preschools. The deciding factor was, naturally, money. Private nursery schools were too expensive, and we finally agreed to send Lisa to two after-school programs the following September.

The Rules

"Goodnight, Lisa" I sang, this time from "Daddy's bed," as Lisa called it. I was putting Lisa to sleep there instead of the living room couch where she usually spent her nights. Joel was away on a business trip with Eric who owned oil fields in West Virginia, and it was quietly understood between Mr. Steinberg and me that I'd sleep in our big bed rather than on the floor during that time. And because I wanted to have my little girl there with me, I'd offered her the warm spot next to me—a treat for both of us.

However, lest you think Joel was becoming soft, some restrictions he'd newly devised regarding my eating stayed in force even while he was out of town. These consisted of the necessity for me to ask his permission before I ate anything. So, feeling committed to the rules, I ate nothing each day until I received Joel's call from West Virginia. He'd put me "on my honor," and I felt obliged to maintain that truthful position even while my jailer was away.

There were times, however, while Joel was at home that I found it impossible to keep to the honor system. For example, when he decided that I couldn't eat at all because I'd committed some obscure "offense," I'd occasionally get so hungry that I'd sneak a slice of bread or a spoonful of peanut butter. Although this "cheating" satisfied my hunger, I felt guilty about it. After all, I'd made a promise, and by breaking this promise, I was betraying Joel.

So what kinds of offenses had I committed to garner starvation as punishment? Here are some of the possibilities: I'd not responded immediately when he called to me, I'd argued with him, or I'd continued to be "resistant"—whatever that meant.

Joel's daughter also had to ask permission before eating between meals. Although, unlike her mother, Lisa was not a prisoner; she *was* a child and needed her actions supervised. Both Joel and I agreed on that. And although her food requests were never turned down, it's clear to me now that Joel insisted on this regulation as a means of controlling her and not of watching her nutrition as I was doing.

And since Joel said he feared that, like most kids, Lisa would choose inappropriate snacks, he indoctrinated her with the idea of eating healthy ones: peanut butter, raisins, and other fruit. Hooray for that! But, unfortunately, she eventually developed a fear of admitting she'd eaten any of the forbidden foods.

Ice cream was, however, not one of them—at least as long as Joel was the one who provided it. This is probably because Joel liked the treat so well. Therefore, just about every night, the three of us would indulge in an evening bowl of ice cream. Sometimes, however, there were only two eating the creamy dessert—when I'd been prohibited from eating at all.

Lisa the Schoolgirl

In September 1984, Lisa became a schoolgirl. We enrolled her in three classes at the Greenwich House Music School: Movement, Art, and Pre-Ballet, and in one class in an after-school visual arts program at a local public school. I'd take her to school and pick her up, often doing supermarket shopping in the interim.

Lisa excelled in everything—of course—and did so well in dance, that in the spring, we had her transferred from Pre-Ballet into Ballet with six-to-eight-year-old girls. Mature for her age, Lisa related better to the older girls than to the other three- and four-year-olds.

However, she developed a friendship with one child her own age, Julie, but only because I became friendly with the girl's mother. We met when sitting and waiting to pick up the girls from Greenwich House. After several such meetings in which we gabbed about our wonderful daughters, as mothers will, both Lisa and I were invited to our new friends' home. Interestingly, Joel didn't object to us making such visits, which I enjoyed immensely. I felt free! I guess Joel was confident that I wouldn't reveal any family secrets, and I certainly didn't.

Just for You

It was now 1985, and a new supermarket had just opened on Sixth Avenue at 13th Street, a Food Emporium—bigger, cleaner, and friendlier than the other Greenwich Village neighborhood markets. And it catered to kids like Lisa, still round-faced and slightly chubby then, not as yet having stretched out to become the lithe and svelte ballet dancer she'd become a year later.

"Kids, sign up for the Cookie Club," a sign in the store proclaimed.

"Let's sign you up, Lisa," I said as I pushed the cart with Lisa walking beside it. No longer did she sit in the little seat on the cart. Now she was a big girl.

Lisa Steinberg, I wrote on the list, and in exchange she received a big, freshly-baked chocolate-chip cookie and a Cookie Club card, entitling her to more of the same, free, every time she came into the store.

Of course, we told her Daddy all about the Cookie Club card.

"That's terrific, Lisa," he said, taking her onto his lap and giving her a big squeeze. "Did you eat that whole cookie all by yourself?"

"Yeah," Lisa answered enthusiastically, with a big smile.

"Well, from now on, whenever you get a cookie at the store, you save it to share with Mommy and Daddy. Things always taste better when they're shared. Right?"

"Okay, Daddy," said Lisa, getting a big kiss from Joel.

"Gotta teach her to share," he said to me as Lisa ran out of the room

One day, while shopping at the Food Emporium, I picked up a flyer announcing a coloring contest for kids. On the other side was the picture to be filled in with crayons by little hands. Although I don't recall what the picture was about, I do remember that I took one home for Lisa. Her coloring was neat with a good sense of tone, just one of her numerous talents; the others included singing, dancing, athletics, and learning numbers, letters, and colors quickly and easily. (What? Me prejudiced?)

So after Lisa had finished her artwork, I took it to the store, where it was entered into the contest.

A couple of weeks later, the winners were announced in the supermarket window. Lisa and I walked by that day and saw the sign.

"Lisa!" I exclaimed, "There's your name! You won the coloring contest!" And I picked her up so she could read her name.

"See, L-i-s-a S-t-e-i-n-b-e-r-g," I said, pointing to the letters of her name. "That's you. It says that you won the contest for the four year olds. That means that your picture was the best of all the kids your age who entered the contest."

We were both so happy that we hugged and kissed right there in the street. Then we went into the store to find out about Lisa's prize. It would be tickets to Rye Playland, an amusement park.

Lisa was so excited that I went home and got my camera.

"Let's take a picture of you by that sign, so that one day when you're big, we can remember this happy moment."

So we did. And although I certainly remember that "happy moment," I'm sad to say that Lisa never did get to be "big." And the only copy I have today of the picture in question is one printed in *People Weekly*, August 27, 1990—after Lisa's death—in a story about her birth mother, Michele Launders.

So, with an entire book of tickets to Rye, Playland—free tickets—we took Lisa there twice. Otherwise I'm quite certain that Joel never would have spent the money, and Lisa never would have had the opportunity to have two days of pure fun. On one of those days, we took snapshots and actually sent some to my parents—a rare treat for them. Any photos of me were taken from a distance, and I was wearing sunglasses.

Since we had no car available, whenever we wanted to get somewhere, Joel managed to either borrow an auto or ask someone who owned one to "join us" for the day. Of course, they'd then supply the transportation. One trip to Playland was with Joel's friend Frank, the same guy who traveled to Puerto Rico with us way back in 1975, and one was with Roseann. Naturally these friends got to share our tickets and fun but certainly not because of any generosity on Joel's part. It was purely a car-mooching move.

We did, of course, have a car, one that was unavailable—the silver Mercedes that still resided with Al Gross. Someday, Joel swore, when I was "ready," we'd go out to the Gross's home and get it.

In the meantime, he continued to manipulate his way into borrowing any car he could, including his mother's, which he insisted was really his. I no longer remember the litany of that oft-chanted story, but with the wisdom of distance and experience, I believe it as much as the tale of the Easter Bunny.

Gifts

It's no coincidence that I've mentioned some kind of bunny at this point in the narrative because a black Belgian dwarf rabbit that Lisa named Mr. Bunny came into our lives at right about this juncture. He was a gift to Lisa from Roseann, but we all became very fond of the furry little fellow who would never grow larger than a full-size baby bunny. Actually, Lisa took the name from Roseann's statement upon presenting him to her. She said, "Here's MISTER Bunny!"

Trying to make Lisa learn responsibility for her pet, at first I made it her job to help me clean his cage. We also shared the feeding and watering. But later, most of those tasks were hers alone with me as the overseer. Lisa's daddy, on the other hand, did not get involved in caring for any of the animals who shared our apartment, once Sasha had passed on, that is.

Skipping ahead a year to Lisa's fifth birthday, another friend of ours presented her with a second Belgian dwarf rabbit. We all wanted it to be a female and produce babies, so of course, it got a female's name: none other than "Mrs. Bunny," but Lisa also called her "Griselle," after one of Joel's clients to whom Lisa took a liking.

At first we put each rabbit into a separate large plastic see-through box, one next to the other. Since Mr. Bunny had never tried to escape from his cage, we didn't bother to cover it, or Mrs. Bunny's either. But when these two rabbits found themselves side by side, in a position to look but not touch, they definitely resented the separation. One morning when I got up to get Lisa ready for Kindergarten, lo and behold, I found that Mrs. Bunny had jumped right into Mr. Bunny's cage. The two seemed so contented in that position, that we removed the second cage and put the two food bowls and the two water bottles into Mr. Bunny's cage. In this manner, Mr. and Mrs. Bunny lived happily ever after—until one of them departed from the earth.

Since Mrs. Bunny fulfilled our wishes and turned out to be a female, our two rabbits behaved as tradition predicted: they copulated day and night. Although no baby bunnies resulted, Lisa certainly got a natural sex education.

The two rabbits were not the only gifts Lisa received from friends and/or relatives who loved her. The number of presents bestowed upon our little girl was colossal: toys, dolls, clothes, a keyboard, a bicycle, roller skates, you name it. It's true that some of these gifts were payments in kind for legal services Joel had provided. But many were given out of pure love for our daughter.

Lisa was loved by every single person who met her, and that is probably because she herself exuded that spiritual quality. There was something about our little girl that was warm and emotionally giving far beyond the level of most children. Sometimes when I felt sad because of Joel's mistreatment of me, Lisa would sense it and put her little arms around me. We'd hold each other a while and then I'd feel like smiling. Lisa's energy was loving energy. Lisa's heart was mature and her spirit advanced.

One day when Lisa couldn't have been more than a year old, she was sitting with Joel and me in Gene's Restaurant together with some friends, when a woman approached our table.

Pointing to little Lisa, she proclaimed loudly, "I'm a psychic, and this is a very special child. She talks to the angels." And then the psychic turned on her heel and walked away.

I didn't think about the incident much at the time. However, a few years after Lisa's death, I had a telephone conversation with a psychic recommended to me by a friend. The psychic, I was informed, could give a reading without being face to face and without knowing my identity. So, "blind" though she may have been, the seer told me that my daughter had "come from the angels" and "died to teach someone a lesson."

The moment the seer uttered these words, I recalled those of the earlier psychic. Could Lisa, indeed, have been an advanced soul who chose life with an abusive father to fulfill a karmic plan? Her death and all the publicity it received did, indeed, teach many lessons.

Very recently, I have had a spiritual awakening and consider the above scenario to be quite likely. I also believe that Lisa has been in my life in many incarnations and that we will be reunited again in our next lives. At the moment I became certain of this, tears of joy filled my eyes. Lisa's love will continue.

A Tortoise Taught Us

Like everyone else captivated by Lisa's spirit, Joel began doting on his daughter. Evenings she'd sit on his lap as we watched TV. Whenever he could, he'd take her with him to business lunches and even dinners. Although Joel wasn't terribly eager to take me with him to such occasions anymore, he *kvelled* when everyone made a fuss over his exceptionally bright and beautiful daughter.

So it's no surprise that he brought his little girl two other pets he'd found on the road near a construction site in West Virginia. Of course "Hyperbole" Joel made a big deal over the fact that he'd saved these gentle creatures, a pair of large brown tortoises, from certain death.

"They were just sitting there on the road, waiting to be hit by a passing truck. You know how those construction guys don't give a damn about anything but their beer. So instead of pets for Lisa, they'd have been roadkill, smashed to smithereens. Lucky for them that I happened by."

Although these tortoises never acquired names, in my heart they were more than reptiles; they were family, and although meant for Lisa, I was the one who cared for them daily and grew very attached to them.

Like the rabbits, the tortoises were a male and a female, and like the rabbits, they copulated incessantly. More sex education for our five-year-old.

These guys crawled around in the bathtub by day and by night burrowed deep into a bed of shredded newspapers inside a cardboard carton. I fed them

281

fresh lettuce and other vegetables and left the water dripping in the tub from which they'd drink when thirsty. They were fascinating to me, but no one else paid them much attention—except for the day when they "disappeared." Where could they be? Lisa and I searched the entire house and found them asleep in the laundry bin where it was dark and warm, which also explains why they burrowed into newspapers by night. In nature, tortoises become dormant in winter and burrow to hibernate. But they had no need to become torpid in the warm apartment. However, when the building's central boiler broke down during icy December, we lost both tortoises—this time to death.

To cheer Lisa, Joel made light of the situation. "We'll have turtle soup!" he joked. Meanwhile, I was left to dispose of the reptile bodies without letting Lisa see them dumped into the trash.

Being Mommy

Even though my life was miserable at times, it was full of moments that were equally joyous. Not only were the honeymoon periods with Joel full of sanity-saving happiness, but so was every day with my little girl.

One of Lisa's favorite times of day was bath time. In fact, she could've stayed in the tub for hours—if I'd have let her, that is. I assume her fondness for bathing came from copying her bath-loving daddy, whom she adored and emulated—a factor that unsettles me today. When kids try to be like an abusive parent, the results can be disastrous. Yeah, I know; the outcome was pure disaster, anyhow, even though it had nothing to do with emulation. I guess the moral of the story is: no matter how you look at it, having an abuser around the house is dangerous.

Anyway, bath time was also mother/daughter time. When Lisa bathed, I'd perch on the edge of the tub, and we'd play. She'd fill her miniature blue plastic coffeepot with bath water and pour it into the tiny matching cups. Then we'd pretend to drink, delicately, with our pinkies up.

"Mmmmm," I'd say. "Good coffee."

"Would you like another cup?"

"Certainly, thank you."

In retrospect, I see that having a coffee addict like Joel around might have also been dangerous. By emulating her dad (even though he now drank only decaf), Lisa was potentially becoming an inveterate coffee drinker.

Besides playing during bath time, Lisa and I would talk—about her preschool classes, her friends, her favorite TV shows—and then I'd shampoo her now shoulder-length strawberry blond hair.

When my sweet girl would step out of the tub, I'd wrap a large towel around her little body, lovingly rub her dry, and then she'd pop into a white, hooded terrycloth robe. Her finely textured hair wouldn't stay wet for long.

Lisa and I also spent time together doing household chores. She particularly liked to help me with two of them: vacuuming and making salad. Her "help" with the former was more of a hindrance, but I gladly let her take her turn at it. However, she was of real assistance in preparing our nightly salad, especially in tearing lettuce and scraping carrots. Sometimes I'd let her cut the cucumbers with a not-very-sharp knife that was soon dubbed "Lisa's knife." Working together, the salad-making ritual became fun.

But our sweetest moments together were still at bedtime. I'd generally read her a story, sometimes a chapter from one of the books I'd written or from a humorous little book she particularly adored that my friend and ex-business partner, Larry, had written. I'd give you its name, but, duh, I do not recall. Then I'd tuck her in, sing her *Good-Night, Lisa* song, give her a kiss, and leave her to sweet dreams. Her daddy would come in to say goodnight later, whenever the next TV commercial break gave him a moment to spare.

Sesame Street

Joel wasn't the only TV addict in the house. As you might expect, Lisa became one too. She loved to watch cartoons, which Joel eventually forbade her to view. Why? They were too violent, of course. A year later, he put rerun shows Lisa enjoyed like *I Dream of Genie* and *Bewitched* off limits. He felt the stars were bad role models because they were "manipulative women," he said. On the other hand, perhaps he didn't want Lisa to see powerful women.

But Lisa's favorite show was *Sesame Street* and had been ever since she was old enough to sit up and notice that something was moving on the TV screen. And because her friend Daniella, two years her senior, was sometimes on the show—in scenes repeated from a few years before when Daniella was four or five—Lisa had even more reason to watch it. The two girls had become friends because Daniella was the daughter of a client of Joel's at whose suburban home we'd spend time. Lisa particularly enjoyed swimming in Daniella's pool in the summer and would yell joyfully whenever Daniella's face appeared in a *Sesame Street* sequence.

"Mom, come here! It's Daniella!"

I would run in to look at Lisa's TV, no matter what else I was doing—and believe me, Joel kept me busy every moment of every day.

Knowing that Lisa would be ecstatic to be on her favorite TV show, I asked Daniella's mother if she could arrange to get Lisa on the show even once. She told me she'd try. Had that occurred, what a joy it would have been for my sweetie pie. But it never happened.

Once, when Lisa was about five, I asked her, "Aren't you bored with *Sesame Street*? You've known the alphabet and how to count since you were three."

"No," she told me. "I love *Sesame Street*, and I'm going to watch it until I'm 18!"

If only she'd been able to do that...

Regrettable Resurrection

What was it that was resurrected, and why did I lament it's renewal? The cult/hypnosis/sexual aberration concept, of course, which had sat in cold storage for far too short a time as far as I was concerned. Why would I possibly want to resuscitate nights of struggling to dredge up horrible images (that never actually happened) and that in the end brought me more punishment than reward?

"Once and for all, Hedda," Joel proclaimed now, "you've got to deal with it and remember what really did and didn't happen. You've established that Al and Bonnie put some of the images into your head with hypnosis and that others really happened. Someday you're going to know the difference, but you've got to start working at it or you'll never get to that point."

I truly didn't want to deal with that stuff anymore. The hiatus from our nightly inquisitions had been a huge relief to me. But now they were back, though only on freebase nights, a fact that gave me some small comfort.

Once again, I forced to the surface tales of S&M, child sexual abuse, and wild nights with a variety of both men and women, friends and strangers alike. But the tales didn't flow as freely as they used to, which displeased my master. So on most of those nights, I'd end up frustrated and alone on the floor.

Some of the elements Joel eventually induced me to add to the child sexual abuse stories no doubt were inspired by the McMartin Preschool scandal that had exploded onto television screens the previous year, 1984, the reports of which Joel had watched on TV daily, fascinated. There, the allegations were that the kids had been repeatedly molested by the adult staff. Charges included videotaping the sexual abuse to use as child porn. Joel expropriated this concept and transferred it to Bonnie and her friend "Clara" whom, he claimed, owned a video store.

I also recall describing personal sexual encounters in the back of this same video store, rendezvous that in reality had been nonexistent. Of course, when Joel demanded facts about Clara— Where was her store located? What was her last name?—I tried in every way I possibly could to come up with the answers, examining a map and a phonebook of Long Island for a town that rang a bell, even resorting to the use of a pendulum that's supposed to allow you to contact your subconscious mind, but obviously nothing worked because there was no way I could have acquired such information.

Today I can say that with confidence, but for years I worried whether such tales had any basis in reality. Truth and great relief came in 1988 when I talked with the District Attorney's office and learned that Clara, whom I'd actually met only once at a party at Al and Bonnie's house, didn't even own a video store.

And the Winners Are...

Of all the weird and raunchy tales that emerged from this phase of our lives, there are a few that are by far more grotesque than the others.

One was about my having sex regularly in the window of a neighborhood store, in the open for all to see, with the husband of a woman acquaintance. And what made it even more bizarre was that the store was a head shop, and the woman was the mother of a child who'd been in Patty's daycare group with Lisa.

The second exceptionally strange tale was all about how I'd murdered a man as part of a sexual turnon. Once again I'll say it: I don't know where these stories came from, but they did emerge from my innards. My motivation was clearly the demand Joel was putting on me; since I'm a writer, when pressed, I can always come up with an idea suitable to the occasion.

Probably to legitimize his claims, or else to cause trouble for Al and Bonnie, Joel reported the Grosses' "activities" to a pornography task force sponsored by the District Attorney's office—or so he claimed, anyway. In a telephone conversation made from our apartment with this so-called task force, I confirmed Joel's story, claiming to be a participant while keeping my anonymity. Asked over the phone the worst thing I'd done, I said I'd killed someone. And at that time, I truly believed that what I was telling them was true, but apparently the DA's didn't, or else the person Joel put on the phone wasn't even from the DA's office because we heard of no follow-up.

Trying to Recapture the Past

As you might imagine, the idyllic sex that Joel and I had been having was now a thing of the past. And Joel demanded that I tell him why. Blind to the obvious, that his repeated beatings and torture prevented me from trusting myself to him, I pondered the question intensely and came up with no answer. But Joel had his own answer: our sex life had been ruined, he said, because I enjoyed my perverse sexual experiences more, including an alleged homosexual relationship with Clara.

"But that's not true," I insisted, quite certain of this, either in spite of or because of my inability to remember those ostensible experiences. "So please, Joel, please give me back that ability to have phenomenal sex with you. When you did before, you know how great it was between us. Please."

"Well, you really don't deserve it, but since I do, I'll do that for you," Joel conceded.

But this time, his magic didn't work, and it was "my fault," of course.

Creative Torture

For those of you readers who have been in abusive relationships, you probably know how a guy like Joel would continue to come up with new ways of torturing me. Whether your partner is lying about an affair, taking the children somewhere and not letting you know where they are, or physically beating you, it's all torture to you.

Joel was, of course, the extreme of an abuser, and so his torment was extremist too. Here are a few of his inventive offenses.

Once, he put a needle through my tongue. This was, he said, to see whether it was true that the tongue has few nerves. If so, I'd feel nothing. I was his human guinea pig in an experiment that could have hurt like heck. Fortunately, the few-nerve theory was true, and I felt no pain.

Because the amount of water I drank wasn't to his liking—water was good for my health, he claimed—he sometimes forced me to drink an entire two-liter bottle of it. The result was and still is an aversion to drinking water. I drink herbal tea instead.

But Joel's pièce de résistance made use of an exercise bar that Roseann had given him—you know, the kind men use to build up their biceps. During the last year of our relationship, each day Joel would count up the times he was displeased with something I did or didn't do. For example, if I didn't appear in front of him the instant he called me, that would count as one. If I then explained that I hadn't heard him call, he would call me a "Liar!" and that would be two. So all day he'd keep count of these "offenses," and at night, after Lisa was asleep, he'd take the exercise bar, which he kept hanging right next to the spot in bed where he worked, ate, and slept, and smash me over the head with it once for each transgression. Blood would gush all over, and then he'd command me to clean up every drop. And I would, too.

Now, more and more often, he began demanding that I take a cold bath. You already know how this long, drawn-out torture was harder for me to bear than any swift blow. So once, but only once, I did defy his command to "Get in the tub!"

"No!" I asserted.

"Get in the tub!" he repeated, ominously, pointing his finger.

"No," I insisted.

Reiterating his order, still pointing his finger toward the bathroom, he stepped toward me; I stepped backwards. We continued this dance until he'd marched me, in reverse, into the bathroom and up to the edge of the tub. Once there, he shoved me, and I fell backwards into the bathtub; Joel then turned on the cold water. I sat in the icy bath with my wet clothes still clinging to my shivering body. It's no wonder I never again said, "No," to Joel's demand to "get in the tub."

A Baby Brother or Sister for Lisa

While all this trauma was occurring in our household, I had a child to raise, a child who desperately wanted a baby brother or sister. And although I had no thoughts of trying to conceive again, Peter Sarosi, the doctor who'd taken Mike Bergman's place after his stroke, brought the idea back into my consciousness. Peter and Joel were now friends, and Joel was Peter's financial advisor, too. He'd worked on Peter's partnership agreement and was giving him matrimonial advice—all free of charge—and now the two played racquetball together. Peter was also my gynecologist.

During the fall of 1985, he thought he'd come up with the reason for my infertility: my cycles were too short. Unasked for, he gave me advice on how to lengthen them, and in the process, he got me thinking again about conceiving.

Yes, I still wanted to have a baby—Joel's baby. I hear you saying, "Boy, she *really* must have been crazy!" And I have to admit that from my present perspective, I was then not exactly the most rational person on the planet. Certainly, this was not the kind of household you would find appropriate for a child, nor would I today. But sanity or the lack of it wasn't the only factor in my desire.

Here's my current theory about battered women and babies: Those women who are badly abused, like I was, who get assaulted often, like I did, and are pretty well isolated, as I was, are grateful for the comfort of having a baby to hold. You may have heard of the Stockholm syndrome, a name based on what happened to male hostages in Stockholm, Sweden, who developed an incongruous attachment to their captors. The theory that came from this is as follows: when someone is repeatedly traumatized and then isolated—kind of like hostages sometimes are—the person needs physical comfort. So he or she reaches out to whomever is there. And when isolated, there's no one there but the captor/abuser, so the needful person reaches out to him. And I surely did that; I needed Joel for comfort, to get that human touch.

But when there's a baby around, there *is* someone else to give comfort because that baby can be held a great deal of the time. I've done an informal study of this by talking to female survivors of domestic violence.

One told me, "My baby never cried because I never put her down."

Another said, "When my kids got to be about two or three and I couldn't hold them all the time, I wanted to have another baby."

I was like these women, wanting the comfort only a baby can give, a comfort I recalled from Lisa's infancy. On the other hand, a child of Lisa's age then was too mature to be held the way I could hold a baby. Somehow, somewhere deep inside, I knew this, and I desperately wanted another. And you also have to remember that I still felt a great deal of love for Joel and believed that he would never hurt a child. Of course, I had no idea of how a little person could be affected by seeing his or her mother abused. Thank heavens for the education about domestic violence the public has been getting these past 10 or 15 years, education we certainly did not have in the 1980's.

A Prescription for Conception

But Lisa and I weren't alone in wanting another baby around the house. Joel was another advocate, so he and I decided to try Peter's prescribed remedy.

I started taking a medication to lengthen my menstrual cycles, and Joel and I were assigned to have intercourse on my most fertile days, which we measured with an early morning thermometer. But I still didn't become pregnant.

So, Dr. Sarosi prescribed a potent fertility drug, which I took in daily injections, given at first by Peter and then by Joel. I remember Lisa watching her daddy giving her mommy in injection so that Mommy would have a baby, and I wondered if she was getting a distorted sex education: Where do babies come from? Oh, the daddy gives the mommy a needle in her tush, and then she has a baby. But wait! Not so fast. Since the daddy in this case had finally had his sperm count checked, and it was found to be low—but extremely active, we were told—the mommy had to be inseminated artificially on her most fertile days but with the daddy's treated sperm. Still, with two attempts, there were no positive results.

Of course, had I tried to think of a reason for this, I might have come up with one, i.e., that Joel had severely beaten my genitals not so long before. But amazingly I made no connection between the beating and the infertility. Or maybe it's not so amazing...

Mrs. Bunny

May 14, 1986 would be Lisa's fifth birthday, and I pleaded with Joel to let her have a birthday party, something she'd never had. But he insistently refused.

"If you don't want children coming in here," I told him, meaning our cluttered apartment, which I knew he didn't want kids messing up even more, "I'm sure Roseann will let us use her backyard. And it'll make Lisa *so* happy."

"No," he insisted, "no parties, and that's that."

So, as in the past, Lisa did without a birthday party. But she did get some terrific gifts that year, one of the best of which was, as noted earlier, a second Belgian dwarf rabbit, Mrs. Bunny.

Lisa had always liked Mr. Bunny, but the gentler Mrs. Bunny was by far her favorite. In fact, Lisa became so fond of the new baby rabbit that she would take Mrs. Bunny out of her cage and carry her around almost constantly.

One day Lisa came to me in tears, holding her bunny close to her.

"Oh, Mommy," she cried. "I dropped Mrs. Bunny, and now she's having trouble walking!"

Apparently, the fall had broken the baby rabbit's leg.

"Okay, Lisa," I said, "just calm down, and Mommy will find a vet that takes care of bunnies."

I called quite a few until I found one that cared for more than just dogs and cats. But I knew the proper procedure by then: I'd have to ask Joel before spending money on the rabbit. And I informed Lisa, "We'll have to check with Daddy before we make an appointment."

So we both waited impatiently for Joel to get home from court. But even after seeing Mrs. Bunny limping, he refused to let us take her to the vet.

"I want Lisa to learn a lesson," he explained. "Each time she looks at her rabbit, I want her to be reminded that she has to be more careful with her pets."

Mrs. Bunny limped for the rest of her short life, repeatedly upsetting me as well as Lisa. But it disturbs me even more today because I can see clearly the cruelty to both a helpless animal and the innocent child who loved her. What's also apparent, and what I didn't see then, of course, is that Joel had treated me as unkindly when my knee was broken—not to mention, of course, that it was *he* who'd broken it in the first place.

A Big Surprise

I said earlier that Mrs. Bunny was one of Lisa's best fifth birthday gifts. The absolute best was one not really intended for her, but it was something she'd asked for many times. It arrived rather suddenly and surprised us all.

On June 21, 1986, the phone rang, and I heard Peter Sarosi's voice over the speaker saying, "Joel, I have your son."

"Yes," he went on, "I've just delivered a healthy baby boy, and the mother wants to put him up for adoption. The doctor who was supposed to deliver him asked me to do the job, and I said, 'Okay, but only if I can have the baby for one of my patients.' And so, he's all yours."

I was in complete shock. I had no idea that Joel had been nudging Peter to get him a baby boy, which apparently had been the case. And suddenly, here we were, parents again, and I was thrilled beyond imagining.

As a defense for Peter, I must tell you that he had no idea what was going on in our home. He saw our household as professional and loving and Lisa as happy and well-adjusted. As to the broken nose I now wore, I'm sure Joel had given him some explanation.

Joel and I prepared as best we could for the baby's arrival the very next day. I dug out of the closet Lisa's old layette, which I'd saved—just in case. Having no cradle on hand, we emptied a large drawer, padded it with a pillow and crib bumper—also Lisa's—and I bought diapers and new nipples, having saved the old baby bottles. My only worry was lack of space, but we'd work it out, I was sure. Now we'd *have* to find larger living quarters, I thought, and would I be glad!. (*Ha!* I say now. It just goes to show you how out of touch with reality I was by that time.)

The next day, Peter's partner, Mitch Essig, delivered the little boy to us. Although the thrill couldn't possibly equal that of holding my first baby for the first time, there's no doubt that I was exhilarated. Joel seemed happy too, although the baby's presence didn't alter his behavior for more than a few days.

Mitchell Barnet Steinberg

As with Lisa, the Jewish name was easy to select. Joel's father's name had been Moishe, so of course Joel's son would be Moishe, too. But when it came to "Morris," Joel's father's English name, we three—Joel, Lisa, and myself—felt it was far too old-fashioned for our new babe. Lisa liked Mark. I liked Mitchell. Joel, for once, seemed to have no particular inclination. And when my mother called, although her presence was verboten, her opinion wasn't.

So I asked her, "What name do you like that begins with an M for Moishe?"

And when she said, "Mitchell," Joel, who'd probably already decided on that choice anyway, proclaimed, "Then Mitchell it will be," as if he'd given Mommy's opinion preeminence.

But when it came to a middle name, there was no question; it would be the same as Joel's: Barnet. Our new baby would be Mitchell Barnet Steinberg.

An Uncommon Agenda

With a new baby at home, life proceeded as per our own strange agenda. Within a day or two, Mitchell Barnet was sleeping in a baby carriage borrowed from—who else?—one of Joel's clients. He'd lost touch with the source of Lisa's cradle, her crib no longer existed, and no way was Joel going to spend money on buying things, baby or no baby.

We kept the carriage in our bedroom. Although it's normal to keep a newborn in its parents' room, how many other mothers have the opportunity to move their sleeping place from a spot on the floor beside their spouse's bed to one on the floor beside the baby's carriage as I did? I wanted to be sure that when Mitchell awoke during the night, I could pick him up quickly and without disturbing Joel. I thought I was doing the right thing and never once considered how bizarre the situation was.

Joel and I were equally determined to get a signed consent agreement for Mitchell's adoption right away rather than delay the way we had with Lisa so that we never had even that much of a legal right to her. With a consent agreement for the new baby, we felt we'd have no worries about keeping him, even though his adoption was out of the question because of Lisa's non-legal status.

Joel arranged with a lawyer local to Mitchell's birth mother, Nicole Smigiel, to have her come into his office and sign the consent agreement. This same attorney then recommended a New York City lawyer who could follow up with the adoption. But, of course, there was no way we could take it any further. So now we had two children living in our home, both of whom could never be officially ours. Although I was aware of this situation, I had no worries about losing either of them. After all, Joel knew the ins and outs of the law; our parenthood seemed secure.

Baby Mitchell had the "pleasure" of hearing my now-croaky singing voice nightly since I reinstated my old habit of singing lullabies while I held the infant in my arms and moved rhythmically in the rocking chair. But as miserable as my singing voice now seemed to me, Mitchell seemed contented with it and would fall fast asleep as I rocked him. I sang my little boy the same songs I'd sung for my little girl—all but the one to the tune of *Good Night Ladies*; that one was Lisa's exclusively.

Mitchell was rocked to sleep in another way, as well. Joel created a swing-like contrivance for use on our new sailboat. The baby seat, attached to ropes Joel hung inside the cabin, made a secure rock-a-bye-baby cradle as the boat swayed back and forth on the waves.

Sailing, Sailing

Since the seasonal docking fee had already been paid in Patchogue, across from Fire Island, that's where Joel kept the sailboat Peter Sarosi had acquired for us. Peter had said he'd sail too, though he never did; so I assume the boat was part payment for Joel's legal services. The other large part, of course, was our new baby boy.

Of course, we had no car, so getting to the boat wasn't possible without either borrowing a vehicle or inviting along a car-owning friend who'd end up being chauffeur for the three-hour trip each way. But Joel had no trouble recruiting someone every weekend to both drive and crew on the boat. Even Terry, Roseann's estranged husband, spent a sober weekend with us. Joel didn't allow any liquor or drugs on his sailboat. He was the perfect host and, for most of the time, a loving partner.

Lisa loved sailing as much as her dad did. In his "devoted father" role, Joel insisted that she wear her flotation jacket at all times and showed her how to steer. All of us, including me, had fun on the boat—except for one disastrous weekend. That time Joel had invited along a young woman whose case he'd recently concluded successfully, the Griselle after whom Lisa eventually named her bunny; and for some reason I've never fathomed, instead of playing the loving husband, he was extremely abusive verbally. Nothing I did that weekend was right. He openly criticized everything and left me feeling publicly humiliated. Yet, in the ladies room of the restaurant we stopped in on our drive back home, I fiercely defended him to his former client. His behavior came from stress, I insisted; had I made a mistake handling the boat, we all could have been in danger.

Today I wonder: what if Joel had behaved in this openly abusive manner more frequently? Would that have provoked me to take the kids and leave him once and for all? I guess I'll never know.

Roseann Exits Left

Joel and Lisa had become extremely close with Roseann, frequently spending evenings and/or Sundays in her house. However, to everyone's surprise, she made an abrupt exit from our lives.

The excuse she used was anger about an investment Joel had recommended that turned out badly. But I'm pretty sure the reason lay in her personal dreams about some sort of union with Joel Steinberg. I imagine that he'd encouraged her fantasies by telling her, as I later learned he had told others, that he was tired of me and that we'd soon split. But once we acquired a new baby, her hopes must have been shattered.

"Wait a minute," she must have said to herself, "if he's going to break it off with Hedda, why on earth are they adopting another baby?"

Whatever the true reason for Roseann's departure, the result was not only the end of her relationship with Joel but with Lisa too. And the blameless little girl, who'd become extremely attached to the affable woman, felt suddenly abandoned and hurt.

Lisa Goes to Kindergarten

As a preschooler, a book I adored was *Mumpsy Goes to Kindergarten* about a cat who went to kindergarten one day with her young owner. If a cat could do it, I'd thought, so could I. My sister had been a kindergartner then, and more than anything, I'd wanted to be one too. Because Mommy had saved that book for me, as well as another of my early favorites, *The Bouncing Bear*, I had them in my possession when I moved into my own apartment. I'd brought the two books to West 10th Street, and one day even before Lisa had been born, Joel decided to teach me some sort of lesson by ripping up both my treasured possessions. As a result, I was never able to read either of those books to my own little girl.

September, 1986. Now it was Lisa's turn to go to kindergarten. Since she had no birth certificate, something necessary for public school registration, Joel accompanied his daughter that first day all set to use his best manipulative techniques. And it came as no surprise to me that he succeeded. A little charm here, a little charisma there, and it was done.

Thereafter, I arose early each morning and got Lisa ready for school. Then, with Mitchell in tow first in the Snuggly® and then in the stroller, I accompanied her on the two-and-a-half block walk to PS 41 and up the stairs to her classroom.

When I'd get home, I'd put Mitch back into the new playpen Joel's mother had purchased for him, and he'd go back to sleep. We'd selected the playpen specifically because it could be adapted to many shapes. The silhouette we settled on was an L-shape so it fit perfectly around Joel's desk in the crowded living room where both kids now slept.

Occasionally I'd go back to sleep too, but most days, Joel's business phone began to ring at this point, and while Joel still snoozed, I'd answer his calls. He'd not awaken until, at the earliest, 10:00, no matter how often the telephone rang. Then I'd bring him his coffee, and his day would start.

Most days, unless Joel had to be in court, he'd pick Lisa up from school at three. Because both Joel and I would have work to do when our daughter got home, the big sister had the job of keeping an eye on her baby brother while she watched *Sesame Street* and other programs on TV, which gave me a break. Between 9:00 and 3:00, I had to tend to the baby as well as to both Joel's business and stomach.

Sing for Your Supper
and You'll Get Breakfast

Like all domestic abuse, Joel's continued to escalate despite the new baby at home. It now became common for him to call out at various times during the day, "No breakfast!", "No lunch!", or "No dinner!" (and very often all three at once) whenever he was displeased with something I did or didn't do. So I was left pretty hungry much of the time. As a result, I frequently began to "steal" food, as Joel termed my grabbing a slice of bread or cheese while he wasn't looking. And since I always suspected that Joel's "special powers" gave him knowledge of my trespasses, the fear of punishment constantly hung over my head.

On the other hand, since Joel loved being in the role of father confessor and doling out rewards, he'd sometimes cajole me into admitting some food transgressions. And, although I generally continued to fear his finding out that I was eating behind his back, at these times I'd get forgiveness, approval, and sometimes an extra meal for my honesty.

Up the Escalator

During the winter of 1986, Joel added, "No blanket!" to his list of penalty commands. That meant I had to sleep (on the floor, of course) without a blanket. But the cruelest step up the escalator was when on cold, wintry nights he would add, "No clothes!" This meant that on such nights, I was forced to "sleep" naked on the floor in front of an open window in a cold room. You see, Joel required that a bedroom window always be open and also that the steam heat be turned off so that he could breathe cleanly while he snoozed under his warm down quilt.

Obviously, I didn't really sleep under such circumstances, but Joel did. So, not being a total robot, when I was sure he was safely dead to the world, I'd pick myself up off the floor and crawl into bed beside him, cuddling my chilled body into that nice, warm quilt. Oddly, if the next morning he found me in "his" bed, he'd never reprimand me for it. I guess he figured he'd have had a frozen corpse on his hands had I followed his orders.

Scrounging at Midnight

One afternoon I noticed that a neighborhood supermarket had discarded about a dozen dented cans of tomatoes, the kind I used for making tomato sauce. Indoctrinated by Joel about the virtues of getting something for nothing, I felt that this was a great opportunity. So I phoned Joel to help me carry home the treasure and noticed that I'd spawned a very happy man.

Subsequently, when I discovered that each night all the local supermarkets put on the street not only dented cans, but day-old bread, fruits, and vegetables that would soon become overripe, and other still usable food, I offered to go out and bring some home. How could thrifty Joel resist my offer? So I got a chance to leave the apartment and be on my own for a half hour or more, and when I brought home the recently expired boxes of Lisa's favorite cereal, dozens of eggs, lots of fruits and veggies, etc., Joel was thrilled—enough so to make me an offer I couldn't refuse: eat as much of it as I wanted.

Thereafter, from time to time, especially when I was very hungry or needed *out* of the house, I'd go out around midnight when I was sure the discards would be on the street. Then, like the homeless men and women who scrounged with me, I'd fill as many shopping bags as I could carry and bring them proudly home. Ahhhhh! I could eat!

Out of the Mouths of Babes

Everyone adored Lisa. She had energy, intelligence, and charm, and gave others plenty of warmth and love. An angel? Well, she certainly was my angel, Joel's angel, Chubby's angel, Gary's angel, Roseann's angel, etc., etc. And how's this for coincidence: on her grave marker are words I didn't have the privilege of composing: "God's Angel." Could be.

Anyway, Lisa seemed to capture everyone's heart. A few of Joel's clients would tease her and tell her they loved her and would marry her when she grew up. One of these was Bobby, who happened to have a bad marijuana habit that caused him to be consistently late for meetings.

Wanting to impress upon Lisa the negative nature of drugs, Joel pointed out to her that marijuana caused Bobby's persistent lateness; ergo, be warned, Lisa: don't smoke dope. As with so many things, I'm sure Joel didn't see the conflict between his words and his deeds.

One day, when Joel had been waiting hours for Bobby, Lisa piped up with, "I'm not going to marry Bobby. He'd probably show up late for the wedding!"

I still *kvell* when I recall her clever expression. And I think of all the intelligence and love the world missed out on because Lisa lived only six years, five-and-a-half months.

Hiding Behind the Baby

Joel continued to smack me around—almost daily. Once, when I fell against the television set in our bedroom and it moved from its secure spot, threatening to fall, Joel shouted an accusation, "You did that deliberately!" Of course, I got an additional whack for that.

One day, while I was holding Mitch, Joel became incensed about something and raised his arm to strike me.

"Joel!" I yelled, "The baby!"

But he struck anyhow, knocking me to the floor. To protect Mitchell, I clutched him snugly to my breast, shielding him from feeling any impact. He wasn't even shook up enough to cry. But as I picked the two of us up from the floor and glared at Joel, he accused me of "hiding behind the baby."

I frequently retreated to the bathroom immediately after one of Joel's assaults, often holding Mitchell in my arms. I'd cry and talk to the infant, telling him that his daddy just didn't understand me. That was the focus of my anguish: If only Joel understood me, he wouldn't accuse me wrongly, and he'd have no reason to hit me.

One day when Mitch was about six months old, during a scene in the bathroom like the one I just described, I saw a look in his eyes that told me, *Hey, this child understands my distress. I'd better stop weeping around him like this.* And, of course, I did. But today I know that he must have registered my painful feelings all along, and I'm filled with regret for inflicting them on him. On the other hand, a psychologist who heard me say that I held Mitchell close much of the time told me it was an enormous benefit to him. I truly hope so. I tried my very best to be a good mother in spite of the conditions in our home.

Ice

When a situation arises over and over again, you get to know how to deal with it almost without thinking. That's what happened to me with regard to treating the frequent blows to my face. They were usually severe enough to cause swelling and bruising. So, I soon learned that if I acted quickly, sometimes I could prevent one or both from occurring.

Ice was the answer. As soon as I'd dry my tears, I'd run to the freezer and apply an ice cube directly to my skin; only direct contact efficiently took down the swelling. Now and then I'd even succeed in preventing a black eye by moving the ice cube around the injured area sufficiently to get the circulation going.

Since Joel's mood switched very quickly during that period from anger to sweetness, by the time I'd exit the bathroom holding the ice cube with a washcloth and rubbing the ice around and around the injured spot, Joel had often transformed into Mr. Congeniality. Thoroughly relieved to see this, my mood would change right along with his. So we'd often sit and chat pleasantly as I rubbed the ice cube on my eye just as if nothing had happened.

Joel's behavior is probably not as peculiar as it may seem at first glance since he apparently felt in complete control when controlling someone else. A man like that, I've been told, doesn't get a rise in blood pressure at such times; rather, his blood pressure goes down, and he keeps his cool. So Joel probably achieved calm so rapidly because he was never far from it.

Joel's unperturbed affect proved to be a boon to his credibility. Because he wasn't a frenzied monster, I believed the good intentions he swore motivated his actions: He was only trying to help me (although I certainly didn't think that his abuse did me any good). Today I believe that a calm and cool abuser such as Joel is diabolical. An out-of-control villain is pitiable; a thinking one is just plain evil.

Gaslighting

Remember that old Ingrid Bergman film, *Gaslight*? Her screen spouse, Charles Boyer, tries to make her think she's going crazy. One of his methods is to say, "Don't you remember doing that?" And of course she can't remember because it's something she's never really done. Well, guess who first told me about that film and the term "gaslighting" that came from it? Yeah, Joel Steinberg. Obviously he was fascinated with the subject because it was something he'd been practicing on me with the cult/hypnosis charade.

But gaslighting wasn't his only means of toying with my mind. Joel would say one thing and later insist he'd said another—when the second turned out to be true, that is. One good example of this regards Oliver North.

The first time Joel had ever heard of North, months before the Iran-Contra mess became public, he'd showed me the newspaper article he'd been reading and said, "Read about this guy. His job in intelligence is very similar to what mine was."

Wow! I thought after reading it. *Joel had all that responsibility for our country's espionage!*

Months later, after North became a household word, Joel, emphasizing his own "precognitive abilities," pointed out, "Remember when I first read about North? I told you then to watch him, that he'd become well known."

"Yeah," I agreed, though I was a bit puzzled. That's not how I recalled what Joel had said. Still, maybe I'd forgotten.

More on Lisa

Contrary to what people seemed to think after the story of Lisa's life and death hit the news, Lisa was seen by a pediatrician regularly, was very well nourished, had her own TV and videotapes, and had a mother who loved reading children's books to and singing silly songs with her daughter. Let me deal with those one at a time.

When Lisa was an infant, I'd paid for regular well-baby visits with my own money. Remember, I'd still been working then. But after I'd been fired, and with Joel so tightfisted, if Lisa had an occasional cold or fever, Dr. Sarosi would treat her *gratis*. However, once Mitch came to live with us, and since babies need recurrent medical care, Joel began to use the services of a Dr. Heiss. The pediatrician apparently "owed one," as they say, to Peter Sarosi and so treated Lisa and Mitchell for free. Making certain that the new pediatrician didn't meet his undernourished spouse with a boxer's nose, Joel kept me away from the man. So I never met him; instead, Joel took our healthy, well-nourished kids for office visits to the unsuspecting doctor.

Lisa loved to eat and, in fact, had an enormous appetite. Amazingly for a little person, she could eat more at one meal than even Joel did. Even more remarkable is the list of Lisa's favorite foods because they included broccoli and spinach. However, her love for Popeye had a lot to do with the latter.

Speaking of Popeye, we had the videotape of Robin Williams playing the role, and Lisa adored watching it over and over. That and the tape we had of

317

Snow White and the Seven Dwarfs performed live at Radio City were her favorites. I must have watched those two tapes with her 100 times each.

Although Snow White was her favorite storybook character, Lisa loved Cinderella too. When my little princess was about four, she and I used to act out the Cinderella story, alternating the roles of the heroine and the fairy godmother. I even made her a magic wand from a dowel and a cardboard star Lisa colored yellow.

Moreover, as an editor and writer of children's books, each night at bedtime, I'd read Lisa a story, and sometimes I'd read from *Plants Do Amazing Things* or *Animals Build Amazing Homes*—the books I'd written. She felt so proud of me, and brought the books to school and bragged, "My mom wrote these." It's difficult not to include here something Lisa wrote in a school composition a year later: "My mom is a book writer. She gives me books for me. They are Random House books." Lisa even knew the name of the company I'd written for, although it had been years since I'd done so.

But what Lisa and I loved doing together most of all was singing silly songs and laughing. I have the strange knack of recalling every song I ever learned during the first 25 years of my life, so I had plenty to teach Lisa, including a very silly one in which we'd add "throw it out the window" onto the end of every nursery rhyme we could think of.

But Lisa also taught me a song she learned in preschool. We'd sing it sitting face to face and eye to eye, and all the hand motions that went with it were meant for each other, especially, "I [point to yourself] love [hug yourself] you [point to each other]." Lisa, a neglected child? I don't think so.

Lost Chances

Now, at age five and in kindergarten, Lisa's class was planning to put on a play—a musical version of *The Elephant's Child* by Rudyard Kipling. Because Lisa continued to take ballet lessons, and now attended a dancing school with one of her new classmates, Enrica, she desperately wanted to play the role of a bird that got to dance solo in the play. She tried out for the part and practiced it intensely at home, certain she'd be chosen for it. I don't think I'm prejudiced when I say that my graceful little girl did a superb job, but she didn't get the role after all. At the last minute, it was given to another child, and Lisa, left feeling devastated, was in the chorus.

But her distress was nothing compared to mine when Joel insisted I stay home on the day of the performance because, in Joelspeak, my head wasn't "in the right place." That was one of his frequent excuses for controlling my actions. But he, of course, was right there in the audience *kvelling* over his daughter, even though she didn't have a starring role. The one slight compensation for me was that Joel charmed a parent with a video camera into giving him a copy of the play on tape, so at least I got to see Lisa on stage that way.

But I was totally deprived of watching my beautiful dancer in her ballet recital. I loved how she looked in her romantic blue tutu, took pictures of her wearing it with her hair pulled into a dancer's bun (guess who styled it?), and cried hysterically when I was forced to remain home during that performance because Joel had given me a black eye.

319

Beautiful Lisa, the ballet dancer.

Parents, take note: appreciate your children's talents, watch their performances with pride, and celebrate the opportunity to do so. Unfortunately, in this crazy world, it may be your last chance.

I Love Lisa

Was it a coincidence? Maybe, I don't know, but two of Lisa's closest friends—Enrica from her kindergarten and ballet classes, and Vanessa who lived down the street— were both adopted.

From day one, Joel had insisted that Lisa know of her adoptive status.

"She ought to have that knowledge as she's growing up," he declared. "It should be part of her understanding of who she is. I don't want her to find out suddenly one day when she's 18 or 19 and then feel traumatized."

I agreed, and so we always told her she was "chosen." Unfortunately, Lisa had no idea what we meant by "chosen," and regardless of our verbal commitment to telling her the truth, we were hesitant to explain the connection between "chosen" and "adopted."

One day, however, Lisa, knowing that her brother had been "adopted," asked me, "Mommy, am I adopted?"

"Why do you ask?" I queried, astute enough not to give her a yes-or-no answer.

"Because I remember coming out of your belly," was her sweet response, indicating to me that she deeply wanted to be my own. And in fact, as far as my feelings went, she very well might have come out of my belly; I couldn't have possibly felt more love for a flesh and blood child. Lisa was my own treasure, my delight.

And I'm quite sure the feelings were mutual. For example, although Joel no longer wanted to take me with him to dinners and lunches as he used to, and he took Lisa instead, she'd often plead with her daddy, "Please, can't Mommy come with us?" And she'd sometimes actually persuade him to take me along.

But even if she didn't, I would help Lisa get dressed in one of her many pretty outfits—all gifts from clients, relatives, or friends—and get vicarious pleasure from fussing over her. I'd spend time fixing her fine, flyaway hair so it would look just right. I'd brush it and then put a rubber band and/or barrettes in the appropriate places, taking motherly pride in seeing her excitement; Lisa loved to get dressed up and go out.

Fred

A few years previously, Joel had worked in an office with an attorney named Fred Caines, with whom he'd remained friendly. One day Fred offered Joel two tickets to the popular Broadway hit, *Cats*. Probably because Joel had no desire to see the show, he decided that Lisa and I should attend the performance. Wow! This was a treat for both mother and daughter.

I'll never forget the enraptured, wide-eyed look on Lisa's face as the costumed "cats" came right up to where we sat. For me, the entertainment was primarily watching Lisa watch the play.

Another time, Joel invited Fred and his domestic partner, Karen, to go out to dinner with us. Since this was the summer of 1987, and I'd not seen Fred or Karen for years, I told them the cult story to explain my changed appearance. I must assume that they believed it and did a bit of wondering about my mental state.

The next day, Fred joined us on the sailboat. Mitchell and I hadn't been on the boat since the previous summer, and my sailing skills were rather rusty. So while I tried desperately to steer the boat safely, I was continuously maligned by Joel for my ineptness, and the trip turned into a repeat of the one with Griselle a year earlier. When Fred, whispering so that Joel wouldn't hear, asked me what was going on, it should come as no surprise that I made excuses for him.

The Game Worsens

I've learned in recent years that once an abuser establishes his power and control, he needs to continue extending them, constantly stretching the boundaries. And now Joel began including Lisa in his malignant game.

Whenever he'd order me into the ever-more-frequent cold baths, instead of checking on me himself, he'd send Lisa to do his dirty work. She'd take one peek at me shivering in the tub and run back with her report, which would always be the same: "Mommy's ready to come out now."

But Joel, who usually lay in bed watching TV, invariably sent her back at least once on some pretext before releasing me from my icy torture.

What was going through my little girl's mind? How was she making sense of this? My imaginings are horrible, but I'll never really know.

Even worse was the time when he asked Lisa, "Should I hit Mommy?" What an obnoxious thing to do! And, although Joel had always told her "Daddy's helping Mommy" whenever she'd seen him abuse me, and I'd always confirmed it to ease any possible anguish she might feel, she replied, "No," to that question. "No, don't hit Mommy."

Once, after emerging from the bathroom tearstained with some new bruises showing, I complained bitterly to Lisa.

"But Daddy's helping you," she said, probably with some question in the statement.

Her words jolted me into reality: what I'd just done was totally

324

inappropriate. I couldn't inflict my sorrow on this little girl. Joel had forced her to play a part in his violent behavior, and I felt helpless to stop that. The least I could do was to shield her from my grievances.

But it wasn't just Joel's involving Lisa that indicated an advance to another level. His assaults on me continued to become worse and more frequent. Although he sometimes beat my head against the wall until it bled profusely, his preferred instrument of torture was the exercise bar. You remember that exercise bar Roseann had given him, the one he kept hanging against the wall molding behind the bed and used to strike me over the head once for every "transgression" I'd allegedly made that day? Whenever Joel picked up that exercise bar, terror would fill my heart. If I made any noise when he struck, I got an extra blow for that. So I tried my best not to cry out. I'd learned that if I stayed calm and made eye contact with him, once in a while he'd call off the assault. And, by this point, trying to avert an attack was all I even considered doing.

Only once did I succeed in using my wits to do just that. He'd just hung up the phone after talking with his friend Sam Altman and announced that he was about to mete out some "help."

"If you're doing so much good by hitting me, why don't you tell Sam about it?" I queried. I didn't dare say it as a challenge, just a quiet question.

That made Joel stop and think, and he put away the bar. Unfortunately, I didn't get an opportunity to stop him again, or if I did, I never recognized it.

A Losing Game

Sometimes, pre-attack, Joel would chase me around the bedroom. Although I knew exactly what was coming, I also knew that short of a miracle, my running was totally useless; there was no way I could escape. Joel was big, about 200 pounds then, strong, trained in karate, and better nourished than I was; I weighed about 100 pounds and was slowly starving. I never attempted to hit back.

Once, Joel smashed my mouth repeatedly and hard enough to split open my top lip. Then, playing the concerned spouse, each night—if I asked him nicely—he'd replace the tape I used to hold my lip together so it would heal. And it did. But about two months later, his blows reopened the gash in my lip. This time the injured tissue didn't heal, and I was left with a permanently split lip. But all I felt about that was sadness and not anger toward the man who had caused the injury.

Because my normally straight, tall body was now hunched over, Joel continually barked at me, "Stand up straight!"

And I'd try, but I could no longer straighten out. One day he pulled me over to the full-length mirror in the bedroom, saying disgustedly, "Look at you! Look at what you've done to yourself!"

I looked, I saw, and I cried, blaming it all on myself.

One evening, Joel painfully thrashed both my legs with his "magical" stick. It was just another incident to add to the hoards of others. I had no idea it would nearly kill me.

But did I want to leave Joel? Not anymore. Repeatedly, he told me, "You can't survive without me."

"You'd never make it on your own."

"You need me."

And I was convinced he was right. I needed him: he was my guru, my teacher, my guide, my support; I would kill myself if I was forced to be without him. Only when Joel brought it up did I consider leaving.

"Get out! Go!" he'd holler, sometimes even handing me a few dollars to tide me over.

The first few times I obediently put on my jacket and walked to the door, though I certainly didn't want to go. But Joel physically stood in front of the doorway and blocked my exit, so I learned that the order was just bluster. He used it to make me feel more of a need to stay. So from then on, I knowingly played the game—donning my jacket, taking my toothbrush and comb, etc.— aware that he'd never let me out that door.

Love and Protect

When he wasn't throwing me out, Joel was telling me how much he loved me and ascertaining that I still loved him. During one of our baths, we had a conversation that went something like this:

Joel: "If we were crossing the street, and I saw that a truck was about to hit you, you know that I'd jump right in front of you. I'd protect you and never let anything hurt you."

Then a pause to let it sink in before he continued with: "You'd do the same for me, wouldn't you?"

And of course, I had to say, "Yes, absolutely, I would." And in fact, I probably would have!

My Sweet Babies

I needed a lot of comfort, and my sweet little children became my constant source of solace and peace. My little one, Mitchell, was just a babe, so holding and coddling him was normal, appropriate, and welcomed by both of us. As a result, Mitch became spoiled in many ways. For one, he became so accustomed to going to sleep in my arms at night that he wouldn't nod off unless I was holding him. Occasionally, if I was out shopping at his bedtime, Joel's were the arms he lay in. But there was no spiritual contact between father and son because Joel would be busy watching TV. Mitchell, therefore, wouldn't close his eyes until I came home eager to rock him to sleep and share my love. He and I needed each other equally to survive, both physically and emotionally.

As Mitch began getting bigger, he loved another form of rocking. Having natural agility and balance, he would stand, not sit, on Lisa's rocking horse and joyfully move to and fro, no hands. The first time I saw this I panicked. But he was as sure and steady as a professional, and when I could watch him carefully, I didn't stop his delight.

Mitch also loved to talk on the telephone, both the real one and his plastic toy, perhaps in imitation of Joel, who was on the phone for hours during the day. I cringe now at the thought of my innocent boy copying his abusive dad. However, Mitchell's mirroring at that time was harmless enough. When family or dear friends called, and Joel, Lisa, and I took turns talking, Mitchell wanted his turn too. He wasn't verbal yet, but he'd get on and babble and babble. He was unstoppable. If we tried to remove the phone from his grasp, he'd yell ferociously. He also loved to talk on his toy phone, and the two of us played a ritualized game with it.

"Ring, ring," I'd say and pick up the receiver. "Mitchell, it's for you. It's Grandma."

Grinning, he'd take the phone, and start to jabber. Although babies aren't supposed to have much of an attention span, he'd happily chatter away on the pretend phone for ten or fifteen minutes.

The comfort I got from Lisa was, obviously, of a different nature. My little girl and I shared laughter, singing, storybooks, hugs, and bedtime kisses. Gone were the days of my holding her in the rocking chair and singing lullabies.

But I continued to tuck Lisa in every night, culminating with a big hug, a kiss, and her own "Goodnight, Lisa" song. Joel, who always watched television in the evening, gave her a kiss as well—during the next commercial break. His TV viewing couldn't be interrupted, even for the daughter for whom he proclaimed immeasurable love.

And "love" was also the reason he gave for getting on Lisa's case about water, as he'd been getting on mine for some time.

"Did you drink enough water today?" he'd hector.

Perhaps it was a feeble attempt at resistance, but I rarely drank the amount Joel required. Since Lisa seemed to be following in my footsteps, I felt responsible for his nagging her about it.

But Lisa did some nagging of her own. Her most persistent dream was a trip to Disney World, and she repeatedly begged Joel for a chance to go.

"Please, Daddy, can't we go? Please."

"Lisa," Joel replied with a chuckle each time his daughter, who was the perfect age to enjoy Disney World, appealed this issue to him. "You're too young for Disney World. When you're seven, you'll be old enough to appreciate it. But not yet."

So Joel saved his pennies, and Lisa lost out.

Strange Things Begin to Happen

August 1987. Lisa and I are packing so that she and her daddy can spend the weekend on the sailboat. This has become a weekly ritual ever since the early summer.

"Mommy," Lisa says, "don't forget Daddy's tooth glue," which is Lisa's name for the adhesive Joel has been using for his new dental bridge.

But there is no reason for her to fret about the tooth glue. Mommy will never forget that or any other item Lisa or her daddy might need on the sailboat. Mommy is exceedingly diligent about seeing that they'll never feel a lack of anything while away from home—that is, all except one thing: herself.

Although I really want to go along, I don't even ask anymore. I know that Joel isn't about to take me anywhere. So I settle for the vicarious pleasure of seeing my family well accommodated for their trip.

<><><><><>

A month later, in September, after Lisa had started first grade, the two

331

were still sailing every weekend and usually taking along a boat guest. Almost anyone at all would do (except you-know-who), and one momentous weekend the lucky person chosen was a neighbor on the block named David, a man Joel scarcely knew.

As soon as I laid eyes on my daughter that Sunday night after my two weary sailors arrived home, it became quite apparent that there was a large chunk of hair missing from the crown of Lisa's head.

"What happened, Lisa?" I inquired.

"Oh," she replied, "I was chewing bubble gum, some got in my hair, and David cut it off."

This is very odd, I thought, and couldn't imagine why the man might have done such an obviously botched-up job. I mean, Lisa's hair was virtually ruined.

Not so surprisingly, back then in 1987, I had no sense at all that Lisa might have any reason to hide the truth, despite the fact that Joel was sitting right beside her when she recited the anecdote. However, today I have an awful image of Joel getting enraged at Lisa for getting gum in her hair and furiously chopping it off.

This was by far not the last of the strange happenings that fall. In fact, there had already been an incident right before Labor Day. During that holiday weekend, I had seen Lisa trot off happily to the zoo with a new friend (a little Black girl whose name I don't recall) and her parents, and the next day, they all joined Joel and Lisa on the sailboat.

I believe, based on photos in one of the many scrapbooks I've put together since November 1987, that prior to that weekend, Joel may have done some injury to Lisa. It was reported (with pictures taken by the family Lisa was with that day) by *The New York Post* on November 23, 1987, a few weeks after Lisa's death, that "A bruised Lisa (right) cavorts joyfully at Bronx Zoo with new friend…" I now believe the bruising was probably so, even though the photos aren't clear enough to show any, nor do I have any memory of seeing black and blue marks on her that Labor Day weekend. Additionally, I can't get any help from the newspaper text because on that date, so close to Lisa's death, all I'd wanted from that article was to possess the photos of my child. Who cared about the text!

Mitch

Fortunately, there was nothing strange connected with Mitchell. He was a bright, energetic, and curious 15-month-old little boy who had recently discovered how to get out of his playpen/crib. He'd simply lift the mesh at one side and crawl under it. Although I enjoyed my son's ingenuity, I realized that I could no longer leave him playing in there alone, not for even one minute; while he napped, I had to check on him frequently. If he found himself alone in the room upon awakening, he'd crawl out and get into anything and everything. Once, I found him pulling out papers from a cabinet. What a mess! Another time when I entered the room, he was swishing his arm around in one of the aquariums Gary had given us. But his favorite place was the rabbit's cage.

Mitchell had suddenly become aware of Mr. Bunny and fallen in love. When we'd first shown him the rabbit, he'd pulled its ears; so I told him to stroke the bunny, demonstrating and saying, "Nice, Mr. Bunny, nice." And that lesson surely took hold. One day, I was in the bedroom working with Joel as Mitchell napped. Suddenly, there stood Mitch, holding Mr. Bunny in his two little hands. The rabbit sat there calmly; they'd obviously become friends.

This seemed very sweet until one day I found my boy sitting inside the rabbit's cage, right on top of all the droppings. He'd gotten onto the couch, up to the table on which the cage sat, pulled off the grating on top, and climbed

333

right in. His behavior was becoming dangerous. The solution: a toddler harness.

Joel, however, Mr. Penurious himself, wasn't about to buy one. Instead, he suggested that I make one, which I did. In fact, I made two so that when Mitch got one wet, I'd have a replacement. For each I tied together two long sashes, put a hook at one end, and tied the other end around Mitch's waist. Then I clipped the sash to the top of the playpen/crib, and he had plenty of room to move around safely.

My boy was also beginning to say a few words. His first word, just as Lisa's had been, was "Mama." His next was "Dada." Pretty soon he'd added three others to his vocabulary: "hi," "bye," and "nye."

"Nye," meant "nice," something he'd learned petting Mr. Bunny. But now he used it exclusively with me. Sometimes he'd climb on my lap and begin to stroke my head gently, saying, "Nye, nye." Our love was mutual.

Sibling Love

Lisa was now in first grade and, as in kindergarten, loving every minute of it. So when her morning behavior changed, I should have had a clue that something was amiss. Instead of getting dressed and ready with alacrity as before, now she dawdled, causing her frequent lateness. But I never realized that the increasingly difficult situation at home might be the cause. So I simply started waking Lisa a few minutes earlier; that, indeed, worked in getting her to school on time.

As soon as Mitch heard me wake Lisa, he'd be up and raring to go. So I'd get both of them ready for the day, and together we'd all walk over to PS 41.

Lisa adored her little brother. So, she kindly volunteered to relinquish the little, antique wooden chair with an attached tray (the low chair) at which she'd been eating her dinners in "Daddy's room" in front of the TV every evening for years. Within a week of Mitchell's vigorous use, it was broken, as was the miniature rocking chair that Lisa had used gently for years. What a difference between the temperaments of those two children! The broken furniture was added to the clutter already in the living room, waiting until Joel could find time to repair it.

Forays for Food

By now my nighttime forays to pick up supermarket discards had become frequent. Since Joel was allowing me out of the house less and less and starving me more and more, trash picking became my only sure means to get both food and time outside the house.

Lisa, now six years old, naturally noticed that food suddenly and mysteriously appeared in the kitchen, and she asked her daddy about it.

Joel's response was, "Mommy goes on adventures." It's sad to think that she found this quite exciting, but not knowing the truth, it's natural that she did. So often when we said our goodnights, she'd inquire if I'd be going on an adventure.

Lisa especially relished it when I brought back boxes of cereal, which she adored—probably because of all the TV ads for cereal on children's shows. Once I brought home an entire case of Rice Krispies a few days past its expiration date. My little girl was ecstatic.

One night, coming home with a case of Haagen Daz ice cream, I bumped into my next door neighbor.

"Oh!" she exclaimed, eyeing the ice cream. "Are you having a party?"

Not knowing what to say, I stammered, "Sort of," and was glad she didn't question me further. Imagine my mortification had she discovered my secret!

Endogenous Opioids

About mid-September, a bruise suddenly appeared on Lisa's face. I knew immediately that Joel had inflicted it because I heard him tell her what to say if anyone asked about it: that her brother had hit her. But instead of instantly grabbing my kids and taking off the moment I heard that, which is what I'd do today, I had absolutely no reaction—zero. You see, in September 1987, I was a chronically beaten woman, deliberately numbed by my own brain—not to mention sleepless nights caused by Joel and freebase. So there was no way I'd have reacted like the normal Hedda Nussbaum.

I now know, through the words of Dr. Bessel van der Kolk, a Harvard Medical School professor and expert on trauma of battered women, abused children, hostages, and concentration camp victims, whom I mentioned earlier in this book, that my brain secreted substances to deaden the pain and calm the terror of Joel's repeated assaults. He talked about such substances when he testified in a 1994 hearing in my civil case against Joel.

He said that when a person is repeatedly traumatized, the brain secretes endogenous opioids specifically to reduce the victim's terror and ease his/her suffering. Now we all know what opioids do: they make you numb. Endogenous opioids aren't selective about which parts of you they numb. Yes, they numb the pain and the fear, but they also numb the rest of you. Ergo, one of the results of my being repeatedly traumatized by Joel was that I became numb in body and mind. Add to that my smoking freebase with Joel and lack of sleep, and you end up with a completely zombie-like creature—me.

337

No Mandatory Arrest

On October 6th, 1987, although I think that the noise that emanated from our house while Joel was beating me was nothing unusual, a neighbor called the police—the second time anyone had ever bothered to do that. At first, Joel refused to let the officers in, but they wouldn't leave, and he reluctantly opened the door. As always, I disclaimed any abuse, stating that we'd simply had an argument. But my battered appearance, which was now the norm, caused one of the policemen to call me aside in the kitchen, out of Joel's hearing. I imagine he thought that there I might make a complaint. But he was wrong; I wouldn't betray my mahatma, and the police left empty handed.

Tragically, back then there was no such thing as mandatory arrest for domestic violence. The very first time I heard about this phenomenon in the early 1990's from a videotape distributed by Quincy, Massachusetts, where such a mandatory arrest was first tried, I began to wail loudly. I suddenly saw how Lisa's life might have been saved had Joel been arrested that day. But he wasn't, and Lisa's been dead now far longer than she was ever alive. During these past 17 years since Lisa's death, the world has learned much about dealing with abusive spouses and parents—too late for Lisa.

Cocaine Paranoia?

JOEL: You're staring at me again! You're trying to hypnotize me.

ME: No, I'm not! I wasn't even looking at you!

JOEL: Don't lie to me. I know when you're doing it. In fact, I've seen the way Mitch stares at me; you've been teaching both those kids to hypnotize me, too.

Of course, I knew I'd never tried to hypnotize Joel, nor had I taught Lisa and Mitchell to stare at him. It was all a crazy idea! Yet, like some years before, I began to doubt myself. Could I be doing these things without realizing it?

And then, to get their advice, he claimed, Joel called both his mother and my parents to tell them I'd been staring again. Although he very rarely spoke to either my mother or father anymore, for this "critical" news, he made an exception.

The reactions of these three senior citizens *are* interesting. Joel's mother spoke directly to me regarding the issue.

"You know what your problem is," she told me observantly. "You don't get out of the house enough."

My parents, on the other hand, responded superstitiously by sending me a locket Mommy had worn for years with pictures of her two little girls inside. Now, however, Daddy had inserted a prayer a rabbi had given him many years before. He'd been sick, and he believed the prayer had helped him recover. My loving parents sent it to me for the same purpose: the staring was apparently a sickness, and wearing the prayer close to my body would cure me. Joel was a very convincing man.

The Catastrophic Kilo

I was fortunate in that I didn't have much desire for cocaine, except of course to keep Joel happy, but the drug surely had its hold on Mr. Steinberg. Although the particulars escape me today, I recall that as a way to obtain the powdery white substance, Joel arranged for his old client/buddy Gary Balken, who was still dealing drugs, to take delivery of a kilogram of the stuff. Then Joel graciously volunteered to keep it in our apartment. Not suspecting Joel's designs on the coke and happy to escape the risk of possession, Gary of course agreed.

So here we had an entire kilogram of coke hidden in one of Joel's file cabinets. Do you know how much white powder there is in a kilo? Since it's equivalent to about 2.2 pounds, picture a two-pound box of powdered sugar. That doesn't seem like much until you think of it in the following way: The kilogram is made up of 1,000 grams. Joel would usually acquire one gram at a time, which would last the two of us two or three nights. Just imagine how long 1,000 grams would last. Whoooeeee! Joel must have been thrilled. And he told me that because we'd assumed the danger of possessing the drug, Gary had told him we could use as much of it as we liked. Naturally, I believed him.

Now completely out of control, Joel wanted to smoke every night, which we did; we stayed up all night each and every night during the entire month of October. How did we function without sleep, you ask? Joel did just fine.

Since we continued in the morning-after pattern we'd already established, Joel obtained sufficient z's. We'd crash at about 6:30 a.m., and he'd sleep until about 2:00 p.m. when I'd awaken him. But I, on the other hand, got only forty winks between 6:30 and 7:00 a.m. after which I arose to get Lisa ready for school.

Since Mitchell was growing, he no longer went back to sleep after we returned from our walk to PS 41 as he'd done habitually in the past. So with him awake and active, I had to be too, meaning I could no longer indulge in a nap before Joel's business phone began to ring.

For a week or maybe two, I managed to function on this schedule. By the end of two weeks, I began falling asleep during the day.

"Whenever you see Mommy falling asleep," Joel instructed Lisa, "throw water on her so she'll wake up."

Lisa, of course, never complied. But Joel did it once. He saw me beginning to nod, and splash! I was doused with water.

I decided that as a precaution, I should have a little cocaine put aside as a wake-me-up. While both Joel and Lisa were out of the house, I put a small amount of powder from the kilo into a vial, which I then stashed and quickly forgot; so I continued to nod off.

By the third week, Joel forbade me to sit down mornings while he was still asleep. "If Mitch is on your lap," he announced, "the boy might fall off and get hurt."

Since I wanted to protect my kids as well as I could from any harm, I actually adhered to Joel's demand—as hard as that was to do. Too bad I wasn't swift enough to modify the requirement by saying, "Well, then if I'm NOT holding Mitch on my lap, there's no harm in my sitting down."

And so, with almost no rest, I continued to take care of the kids, get Lisa off to school on time, wash clothes by hand, iron, cook meals, serve them, and go out scavenging at night. But what shape do you think I was in by the time November rolled around? Remember, I had no sleep, which means no dreams to keep me rational and very little energy to exert. And then there were those endogenous opioids...

Now, for the first time, Joel began to smoke freebase during the day as well as after Lisa was asleep. When she was home, he'd retreat to the bathroom and actually close the door—a first. But so he wouldn't have to put himself in this uncomfortably confined position, he'd encourage Lisa to go out after school to play and to stay out as late as possible.

Her friend Vanessa, who conveniently lived on our block, loved to roller skate, just as Lisa did. So almost daily our girl would lace up the white professional-looking roller skates that Gary had bought her and skate over to Vanessa's without ever having to cross a street. When Vanessa's mother called to ask if Lisa could stay for dinner, Joel more than willingly gave his permission. Hooray! A few more hours for him to smoke without hiding since he had no problem smoking in front of Mitch. Our son's 16-month-old eyes had too little experience to understand what his daddy was doing.

Lisa and Mitchell, Mother's Day 1987.

Even More Madness

They say that overindulging in cocaine makes one paranoid. Not being a scientist, I'd say it does even more damage: it makes one crazy. Anyway, it certainly increased Joel's bizarre and violent behaviors. I sat in cold baths more often, ate less than ever, and was struck by both Joel's hands and his exercise bar more and more frequently.

And he began telling me strange, new stories. Didn't I remember my mother telling us that for generations my whole family had been hypnotizing people by staring? Didn't I recall that when we visited my relatives in California, one of them had told us about the family pact never to use hypnosis again? Well, they'd kept to it, he said, that is, until I had started doing it. Now they'd all gone back to it, and it was completely my fault. Guilt! Guilt! Guilt!

In case you have any doubts, I certainly did not remember those things occurring because they never had. But, as usual, I assumed Joel's words were true. I even believed him when he swore that my parents had told us I'd been adopted from a poor European family during World War II.

Worst of all, during the second week of continual freebasing, Joel got angry with Lisa, grabbed her by the shoulders, and started to shake her. It's bad enough that there was no real cause for his anger but to actually see him lay hands on her was a shock to me. I watched, horror-stricken but silent, as he threw her to the floor. Following the pattern she'd observed at home too often, Lisa said nothing and simply got up. But Joel wasn't through. He repeated the violence, shaking and then throwing her once again.

Oh, if only the Hedda who observed that scene was the Hedda who sits here today. I'd step in front of my child and block Joel's attack; I'd grab the exercise bar and smash him over the head; I'd run to the kitchen, get a knife, and say, "Get away from her NOW or I'll use this on you;" and I'd grab the phone and call the police. But I wouldn't just stand silently and do nothing.

Well, maybe I did do something, although unconsciously. Joel barked at me to be sure Lisa wore long sleeves to school the next day to hide the bruises left on her arms from his firm grasp. But, somehow, I forgot; I dressed Lisa in a short sleeve blouse. Those bruises were seen and reported by the student teacher in her class. But sadly, no one stepped in. In 1987, people weren't as attuned to child abuse as they are today.

But who am I to protest? I was the one who could have made a meaningful difference. Yet, I was paralyzed again later that week when, upon return from the supermarket, I found Lisa in the tub putting cold water on her body with the shower massage. I knew what that *had* to mean, but my only reaction was relief that Joel hadn't made her sit in a tub full of the icy water. Later, neither Lisa nor I discussed the incident, and I held my tongue with Joel. As in most abusive households, silence reigned.

Lisa and the Toll Taker

As usual of late, when Joel went on a business trip, I stayed home, and Lisa went along. On the evening of October 23, 1987, the two left for a drive to Albany, NY, where Joel was to appear in court for his client, Charles Scannepieco. I wouldn't learn of it until a year later at Joel's murder trial, but while Lisa slept on Scannepieco's lap in the car, Joel suddenly slapped her across the face, claiming that she was staring at him.

Ignorant of this occurrence, I sat at home planning what I'd accomplish in the apartment while they were gone. With no one to distract me and the potential to get a good night's sleep for a change, I intended to do a thorough cleaning in the morning. *The house sure can use it!* I thought, observing dust bunnies in all the corners.

But, unbeknownst to me, deep under the skin on my right leg, something potentially deadly was brewing: cellulitis, an infection akin to gangrene. A few weeks earlier, Joel and his magic stick had done a number on that leg, beating it severely in several places. Nothing had appeared on the surface except a few scabs where Joel had broken the skin. But now, suddenly, on the morning of October 24th, the leg turned an intensely hot red and hurt like heck. Walking on it was extremely painful. I could do nothing but stay in bed all day, rising only to get food and diaper changes for Mitch who stayed with me in the bedroom. Such a good little boy, he either sat on my lap as we watched TV and cuddled, or he played on the floor attached to his toddler harness. He

346

never complained about the restriction.

Toward evening, I received a frightening call from a police officer in upstate New York.

"Is this Mrs. Steinberg?" he queried.

"Yes."

"This is Officer Whatever from State Police Barracks. I have your daughter here with me."

"My god!" I gasped, while all kinds of frightening images went through my mind. Lisa was lost. Something had happened to Joel (I knew he was driving them home since Scannepieco was remaining in Albany). They'd been in a car accident.

But then the officer put Joel on the phone who calmly told me the following story: A number of children had been kidnapped in the area recently, so when a toll taker on the Thruway thought she saw Lisa crying, she called the police—just in case. But Lisa hadn't been crying, and it was all a mistake.

Then Lisa, who'd learned too well how to be untruthful, got on the phone.

"We're fine, Mom," she told me, cheerily.

I breathed a sigh of relief and was glad when she added that they were stopping at Grandma Charlotte's on the way home. *Maybe they'll stay the night,* I hoped, thinking, *I'd really like to do at least a little of that cleaning I planned.*

But they didn't, and I didn't. When they returned around 9:30 or 10:00 p.m., Lisa assured me that she hadn't been crying in the car; the toll taker had made a mistake. I had no reason to doubt her words and never even considered the possibility that Joel had prompted her. In fact, the whole idea of Lisa crying seemed ludicrous; tears were not a part of her *modus operandi.*

Head to Toe

Although I was still in agonizing pain the next day, I dutifully hobbled around serving Joel as he sat propped up in bed watching the New York Giants Sunday football game. On Monday, the skin on my right shin suddenly burst open, releasing thick yellow pus that kept flowing. And when that evening, Joel pushed me and I fell to the floor, a second spot—near my knee—opened and began to run. With the release of all that pus, apparently some pressure was relieved and I was in less pain. So I convinced myself that the leg was healing.

Today, I am amazed at this conclusion. I'd been to college; I knew that pus means infection. But thinking clearly was apparently beyond me by then. However, at least I realized that I should bandage these wounds, but there were no bandages to be found in the house. Because I sported a black eye, I couldn't go out to buy any. Rather than ask Joel to do me the favor, I simply wrapped my leg in paper towels.

Oh, I was a sight to see—a mess from head to toe. Around my eyes two blister-like protuberances had suddenly appeared, caused, I later learned, by Joel frequently jabbing his fingers into the corners of my eyes—because, he claimed, I was staring at him.

And although I didn't know it then, the finger poking had also crushed one of my tear ducts.

But since "sufficient unto the day is the evil thereof" was not one of Joel's favorite aphorisms, he continued to assault me. One day that week, he (weighing over 200 pounds) picked me up by one arm and one leg and bounced me (a mere 100 pounds by then) on the floor. A huge bruise on my buttock was the result.

Nor was my leg getting any better, so Joel promised to heal it for me—if, during a freebasing session (still occurring every night), I was in focus and related to him exactly as he expected. So because I truly believed in him, I tried especially hard. However, in *his* opinion, of course, I didn't succeed. So he had an excuse for not healing my leg. However, what he *did* do that week was give me a second black eye.

On Monday Lisa Stayed Home

That Sunday night had been seriously frustrating for me, as were all freebase nights around that time. I put out every effort to please Joel, failed, got no sleep, and no help with my oozing leg—nor, if you will recall, was I allowed to sit down all morning because I "might fall asleep while holding Mitch." Then, on top of it all, Joel refused to take Lisa to school on Monday, telling her while glaring at me, "I can't take you because Mommy kept me up all night. So, Lisa, you'll have to stay home." My little girl focused her big blue eyes on my battered face and understood why only Daddy could take her. I sadly noted her long face, indicating that school was where she wanted to be.

Once out of the bedroom where Joel sat drinking his coffee, I attempted to cheer Lisa.

"You'll have a vacation day," I offered. "All the kids'll envy you." In that was also a hope that she wouldn't blame me for the circumstances.

So even though Lisa was affectionate toward me that day, I wondered if her warmth was offered for the wrong reasons. Joel had often told her, "Mommy has problems," "Mommy's sick," and Lisa's tender heart rendered her sympathetic.

The concept of having an invalid for a mother was nothing new to Lisa. She'd once told Vanessa's mom, via Joel's instructions, of course, that I'd been ill when Linda asked why she never saw me anymore. Joel had also told Lisa, repeatedly and definitively, that she didn't have to speak the truth to people outside the family.

"No one has to know what goes on inside your house." Reckoning that Lisa would comply was Joel's safety net.

But I wonder now, what was Lisa's true understanding of the situation? Did she think I was sick, or did she understand that Mommy couldn't go outside because Daddy had given her a black eye?

Anyway, on Monday Lisa stayed home. That night and every night through Thursday there was no difference: We were still awake past dawn, Joel blamed our lack of sleep on me, and neither of us walked Lisa to school in the morning. Instead, on Tuesday Joel decided that she could walk the two blocks by herself.

"Remember to look both ways before you cross our street," I urged repeatedly until Lisa gave me that, *I know, Mom*, look, and I realized she'd gotten the message.

Fortunately, the only other street on her route had a crossing guard at the corner. But still, I worried and blamed myself for Joel's inability to take her.

The Brown Puddle

Because Joel was in court on Wednesday, he couldn't pick Lisa up from school, something he continued to do every day—sleep or no sleep. So he asked Peter Sarosi to do it. I was nervous about Peter's coming to the house while I looked like—well, like a battered woman. When I heard the downstairs doorbell, I buzzed them in and opened our door. While the elevator was bringing them to the third floor, I carefully placed myself at a distance from the doorway in our unlit hall near the bathroom.

"Please," I beseeched the heavens, "please let the darkness hide my bruises from Peter."

In they came. Peter stood by the door, and I hoped he didn't feel insulted because I didn't invite him to sit down and have a cup of coffee or something. I simply made a little awkward small talk while Lisa scooted into the kitchen. Boy, was I glad when Peter left.

Later, I discovered a brown puddle on the kitchen floor near some bottles of soda. *I guess one of these bottles must have a leak*, I thought to myself. Yeah, right! How naive I was! Never did I suspect the truth: Lisa had hidden a cup of chocolate ice cream behind those bottles, ice cream that Peter had bought her. Because Joel's rule was *no sweets without permission*, my dear little girl had been afraid to tell me that Peter had given her ice cream. Apparently she saw me as Joel's standard bearer and enforcer, and with good reason. She knew who held the power in our household and knew that as much as I loved her, I wasn't able to take her part against him, that I was powerless to help her.

Mousetraps in the Walls

Thursday, October 30, 1987. Lisa hadn't been sleeping much since Sunday night. Whenever I walked in to check on her, there she was, eyes wide open, staring into space. A few soft words and a kiss didn't seem to help because the next time I checked, she was still awake.

"Is anything bothering you?" I asked.

"No," she replied.

"Are you sure?"

"No, I'm fine."

Naturally after the second night, I told Joel about it.

"Let's try some soothing music for her," Joel suggested.

Since I agreed that sounded like a good idea, that night, Tuesday, Joel put on a soft, classical LP. But that didn't seem to help a bit. There lay Lisa, awake.

Then, on Wednesday, Joel had another idea—or three, actually.

"It must be the noises from the fish tank pump keeping her up. Have you ever noticed the tiny sound that pump makes? I've explained to you how that works, haven't I? The pump..."

"Yeah, you did; you explained it. Do you really think that could be it?"

"Since Lisa's so sensitive, I'm sure she's aware of that sound. Or maybe it's simply noises coming in from Vicky's apartment next door. I sometimes hear stuff when I walk into the living room at night...Or, I KNOW! I'll bet

Vicky's put mousetraps in the walls. You know, those electronic mousetraps that make sounds most of us can't hear, but mice do. But their subtle vibrations could affect a very sensitive person. Yes, vibrations from the mousetraps. That's got to be it! Let's go in and see."

So I followed Joel into the living room where he moved around it slowly, seeing if he could sense the vibrations, and I trailed behind him, listening as hard as I could. But I couldn't hear a thing.

Back here in the real world, I'm sure we all know what was keeping Lisa awake—and clearly, so did Joel, despite his absurd charade. I'm sickened now remembering myself, an impotent dupe, following Joel around the living room like a robot. Yes, today I know what was keeping Lisa awake: terror, dread. Her beloved father had become her enemy. He'd attacked her while she slept, so slumber was now something to fear. It tears me apart to imagine my precious little girl lying awake, staring into the darkness, knowing that no one could help her.

Halloween

On Friday, October 30th, the day before Halloween, Lisa's class was having a party. I now assume Lisa was too upset to think much about costumes because she failed to mention that the kids were allowed to wear them that day. I, in turn, was too numb and spaced out by lack of sleep to think of inquiring about it; so Lisa's Roadrunner outfit remained in the closet.

The next day, after watching the same Saturday morning TV programs as per usual, Lisa spent a few hours with Vanessa but came home pouting.

"Vanessa said I had to leave," she whined, a tone quite unusual for Lisa. "Her sister's having a party tonight, and she said they had to get the house ready.

"Why wasn't I invited, Mom? We're friends too, and I'm only a few years younger than she is."

"Maybe she prefers to have kids her own age at the party. You're Vanessa's friend, and Vanessa's even younger than you are."

"I don't know," said Lisa, continuing to brood. "I thought she'd invite me."

Because I was troubled by Lisa's peculiar state of mind, I decided to telephone Linda and get an explanation that might smooth over my little girl's pain. But each time I dialed, all I got was a busy signal. Apparently, that household didn't want to be disturbed.

Fortunately, Lisa's gloom didn't last long. She was excited about the annual Greenwich Village Halloween Parade scheduled for the next evening. She and her entire class from PS 41 would be marching in it; then, of course, Lisa would be wearing her costume. Since Joel didn't spend his money on non-necessities, Roseann, while still Lisa's bosom buddy the previous year, had bought the costume for her. Happily, Lisa didn't seem to mind that it was the same one she'd worn for Halloween 1986.

Guess who took Lisa to the parade? That wasn't hard, was it? Of course Joel took her, and I stayed home with Mitchell. But I could clearly remember the previous Halloween Parade. Joel and I had stood in front of our brownstone, Lisa in her costume and Mitch in his stroller, with Roseann joining us as the paraders marched right across 10th Street. Their variety had been incredible. The outfits had ranged from ordinary (the school kids) to wild (the adults) to bizarre (the gays). Everyone had laughed and clapped and had a grand time.

Although I wasn't there in '87 to see Lisa march, I can imagine the kids from her first grade class greeting her, "Hi, Elisabeth!"

Recently, she'd started to prefer using her full name to the diminutive, Lisa. It must have seemed more sophisticated now that she was six.

Before leaving for the parade, Joel had instructed me to empty his entire file cabinet and shake out every file in case there was coke inside. You see, there'd been a spill—some of the coke from the kilo had fallen into the drawer. Okay, so why bother with that when there was so much more? Oh, did I fail to mention that Gary had stopped by earlier that day to pick up his stash? Of course, I'd gathered up as much of the wayward coke as possible to return to him.

Still, Joel was hoping that maybe enough was left for a decent high that night. But he would be in for a disappointment because, although I took all the files out of the cabinet and searched to its bones, I found very little and was forced to cook up the lone gram we'd removed from Gary's stash before returning it. Since Joel had made it clear that I was to cook up whatever coke I could find and have some freebase waiting for him when he arrived home, I hadn't time to put away the files, and they sat piled on the bedroom floor.

Once Lisa had been put to bed, Joel and I began to smoke—or rather, I should say, Joel began to smoke because I refrained that night but for one, lone hit. My leg was still very painful and oozing pus, and Joel—again playing the concerned spouse—suggested that I abstain from smoking that night. Since I knew as well as he that cocaine interferes with the body's circulation, I agreed, not comprehending Joel's true motivation: to have all the coke to himself. And indeed that night he consumed the rest of that gram.

The End Is Near

Sunday, November 1st, began much as any other day. The kids awoke about the same time Joel went to sleep—meaning that rather than getting any shut-eye, I got busy feeding them breakfast. I recall watching some TV with Lisa—but only while standing up, as instructed—and then ironing some of her blouses and Joel's shirts.

Although his favorite team wasn't playing that day, I woke Joel in time for the football game anyway. He enjoyed watching Sunday football even when the Giants had a day off, albeit without the same obsessiveness.

As he drank his coffee, Joel inquired, "Did you drink enough water today?"

"No," I replied, answering honestly as always.

"And you, Lisa?" Joel questioned.

"No."

"Make sure you do. I'm going to ask both of you again later."

That was a warning—one that went unheeded.

Because Joel wasn't really absorbed in the Giantless game that day, at about 3:00, he joined Lisa and me in the kitchen where we'd just begun making a big pot of vegetable soup. With the sounds of football in the background, Joel cheerfully chopped the carrots, turnips, and other solid vegetables; Lisa, using her own little kitchen knife with a blunted blade, cut the softer potatoes; I transferred the vegetables to the bubbling pot and added herbs and spices; and Mitchell watched all from his seat in the entranceway. We talked and laughed as we worked. Apart from my battered face and oozing leg, we might have been any normal, happy family.

By the time the soup was finished and each of us had eaten some along with the spare ribs I'd cooked, it was already dark outside. Joel then repeated his question about water: Had Lisa and I had enough? Once again, we each said no. The time had come to pay the consequences.

Joel marched us to the refrigerator where he pulled out a hot red pepper. Cutting a large piece for me and a smaller one for Lisa, he instructed us to eat. Of course, he was quite aware that although he loved hot peppers, I couldn't bear the sharp bite, and Lisa's virgin mouth would be even more sensitive to it. But we did as we were told, with the desired result: eagerness to drink water.

Letting the cold water run, each of us filled and drank glass after glass of tap water while Joel watched with callous amusement.

"You'd better keep drinking, or I'm not going to take you with me tonight, Lisa," proclaimed Joel as he exited the kitchen to begin getting dressed for that occasion.

Lisa's eyes opened wide with concern. She was scheduled to join Joel for a business dinner at Gene's Restaurant, and she loved stepping out with her dad.

She and I continued to down lots more water until Lisa complained that her stomach hurt.

"Do you think Daddy's going to take me tonight?" she added then.

"He said if you kept drinking water he would," I replied, "and I guess you've had enough to satisfy him."

Joel had never left her home when she'd wanted to go, so I assumed this time would be no different—water or no water.

"Ask him for me!" Lisa urged, a request I now understand was based on the distrust caused by the previous week's incident. But then, I hadn't a clue.

"Go in and ask him yourself," I answered encouragingly, using a thoroughly outdated state of mind. My policy with Lisa had always been— unlike my mother's, who'd babied me—never do for your child what she can do for herself.

How many times since have I replayed that scene and said, "Okay, Lisa, I'll go in and ask him." But Joel's behavior hadn't been at all menacing that day; he'd been laughing and joking. I had no sense of impending danger, helped, no doubt, by my continued denial of what I *did* know—that he'd been abusing Lisa for the past month and a half.

Lisa put down her water glass and walked into the bedroom to talk to Joel. I resumed drinking until my bladder beckoned me to the bathroom.

Pump, Pull

The phone rang and Joel picked it up. I heard his voice, then Lisa's, then nothing. And suddenly, Joel stood in the bathroom doorway, still only half dressed in a shirt and undershorts, holding Lisa, limp and unmoving in his arms.

Stunned, I exclaimed, "What happened?"

"What's the difference what happened?" he replied. "This is your child. Hasn't this gone far enough?"

I had no idea what he was talking about, though it was obvious he was blaming me.

I stood up then, and he handed Lisa to me. Still in shock, I just stood there holding her.

"Flush the toilet!" Joel commanded, his senses offended.

With his help, I laid Lisa on the bathroom floor and then flushed the toilet, after which I immediately bent down to my child. I lifted her closed eyelids, though I didn't know what I was looking for. I checked her breathing and neck pulse just as I'd learned when I'd studied CPR several years earlier. Her breathing was raspy; her pulse normal.

I could imagine only one scenario that might have caused this: Joel, feeling that Lisa hadn't had enough water, had poured some down her throat and nose, and she was drowning. With a minimal knowledge of first aid and a fading memory of CPR, which doesn't include reviving the drowning anyway, I began giving her the best version of artificial respiration I could: I pressed on her back to pump her chest.

Joel, playing the concerned and helpful father, suggested a better way. He'd been a lifeguard and knew how to give artificial respiration properly.

As I write this, rage overtakes me. Joel knew very well what had happened to his child and that she certainly wasn't drowning. He knew quite well that artificial respiration not only would do no good, but that the time being wasted might do substantial harm. Still, he gave instructions—quietly and sensitively—giving me more reason to believe he was certain they would help; I followed them. Rhythmically, I pushed on her back and pulled her elbows up and back.

My entire concentration was focused on trying to revive Lisa, but the only change I saw was that her breathing seemed more regular when I pumped her back. She still appeared to be unconscious. So from time to time, I lightly slapped her cheeks, trying to get a response; when I got none, I continued to pump.

Joel, whose dinner appointment was at 7:00, went into the bedroom to continue dressing, though occasionally he walked over to the bathroom and gave advice.

"Relax," he counseled, buckling the belt on his camel-colored slacks. "Just go with her; stay in harmony with her." Psychobabble I'd heard so often before. If I were on Lisa's wavelength, he implied, my resuscitation efforts would be successful. So I tried to do that, to feel her essence and move with it.

When her condition remained unchanged, I pleaded desperately, "But she's not waking up."

"Let her sleep," he answered, issuing her death sentence. "She hasn't been getting much sleep lately. Just let her sleep."

Because I knew she wasn't simply sleeping, I ignored Joel's latest suggestion and continued my resuscitation efforts. Still, I tried to take comfort in his casual attitude. After all, Joel knew more about medical matters than I did. He loved Lisa intensely; he'd never be so relaxed if she were in danger.

Then Joel was ready to leave the house. But just before departing, he told me, "I've closed the bedroom window so Lisa won't get a chill." That was what Joel Steinberg did to help the child he claimed he adored, the child I eventually learned he'd knocked unconscious.

"I'll call in about half an hour," he added. "And don't worry so much. I'll get her up when I get home. Just go with her, relax, stay in harmony."

And with that, he walked out the door.

I felt somewhat relieved; Joel had said he'd get Lisa up, and that meant he'd heal her. She'd be okay.

And so, with intense concentration on staying in tune with her body, I continued giving her artificial respiration: pump, pull; pump, pull. Over and over and over. From time to time, some water and undigested food came out of Lisa's mouth. I wiped it up and proceeded compulsively with my task.

The bathroom telephone caught my eye for a moment.

Should I call 911? I pondered. *Should I call Dr. Heiss?* He was our pediatrician. *No,* I finally decided. *Joel said he'd get her up when he got home, so he will for certain; I know that. Why, then, have him think I don't trust his word? Why show disloyalty?*

Yes, loyalty was a big issue with Joel Steinberg. Why would I indicate I wasn't loyal to him, when I *was,* when I trusted him 100%? I believed Joel's word was beyond question; there was no need to call for outside help. Joel would heal Lisa, and everything would be fine.

Then for the first time I realized that Lisa was lying on the bare tile floor and wearing nothing but underpants (apparently, she, too, had started getting dressed to go out to dinner).

This won't do, I thought and put a towel under and a blanket over her. While doing that, I noticed that she'd soiled her underpants, so I removed and washed them. Then, once again, I checked her pulse and breathing. Nothing had changed.

Suddenly, I heard a toddler crying; Mitch had awakened from his nap. Once out of the playpen and on the floor, he immediately ran over to Lisa. Fearing that he'd poke at her or hurt her in some other innocent way, or that he'd become frightened when she didn't respond, I whisked him off the floor and into his little seat near the kitchen. Automatically, I started to prepare his dinner.

The phone rang; it was Joel checking on Lisa's condition.

"It hasn't changed," I moaned.

When he didn't say anything in response, I told him I was preparing Mitchell's dinner.

"You can eat something, too," he told me—as if expecting me to have an appetite—and hung up the phone without indicating when he'd be home.

Oh, please let it be soon, I implored the spirit world. Though an agnostic, at times like this, I automatically reverted to prayer. The sooner Joel arrived home, the sooner he'd get Lisa up as promised.

Meantime, I finished feeding Mitch. Then I diapered him and put him back to bed. Since he'd never gone back to sleep after a long nap, I talked to him, hoping he'd comprehend.

"Your sister's very sick, Mitch, and I'm very upset. I'd like you to go back to sleep. Okay, Sweetie?"

Whether or not he understood the words, he must have picked up something from my tone because, amazingly, he fell asleep right away. *Thank heavens!*

Of course, I then went back and checked Lisa's vital signs again and tried a little more artificial respiration, but her condition stayed the same—not conscious, breathing stable. That's when I realized that nothing I did seemed to make any difference. So I decided that checking on her periodically would be sufficient until Joel returned and got her up.

What to do in the meantime? What might keep me busy without needing much thought? The file folders! They were still there on the floor where I'd left them the previous day. I seized upon them as a means to occupy myself. One by one I put each client's file back in the metal drawer, trying to make the task fill the time, checking on Lisa every so often.

Joel Returns

It was 10:00 by the time Joel returned. Oh, what joy I felt hearing his key in the lock. In he came and walked right to the bathroom where Lisa lay. He simply glanced at her, however, and said that before doing anything else, he would bring a file downstairs to his dinner partner.

The few short minutes he was gone seemed like forever, and when he was back, I said, "Okay, you said you'd get Lisa up, now get her up!" I'm sure there was pleading in my voice.

"No," he responded, "we have to be relating when she gets up. So let's smoke."

Smoking, of course, meant freebasing. Eager to please him so he'd feel ready and willing to help Lisa, that small amount of cocaine I'd put away the week before came to mind. Praising my good fortune that I'd never used it, I cooked the coke to Joel's appreciation.

Pleased that we were off to a good start, I hoped he would soon feel we were communicating well enough to help his daughter. But, of course, that wasn't about to happen quickly. No, what I should say is that it wasn't about to happen—period.

In his customary style, Joel talked on and on for hours while he smoked. But one thing he said during that monologue will stay with me forever.

"I knocked her down, and she didn't want to get up again. That staring business has gotten to be too much for her."

At the time, it was as hard for me to believe that he'd actually knocked her down as it was to believe that she didn't want to get up again. The fact that he'd hit Lisa hard enough to render her unconscious didn't sink in at all. I heard the words then, but not their meaning.

I remember, too, another statement Joel made that night: "She was talking negatives. She was always telling you to talk positives, and yet she was talking negatives."

He'd taught Lisa the same concepts and maxims he'd taught me, and one was to state things positively. Was that what had triggered him, I wonder now? Did Lisa say, "You don't want to take me with you tonight," a negative, instead of "I want to go with you," a positive? Did she provoke his fury by using the "wrong" words? Of course, anything at that point might have had the same effect: the wrong words, the wrong tone, an imagined stare.

Aside from the few moments when Joel's dramatic words pierced my brain, I heard little of what he said. I was alternately worrying about Lisa, checking on her condition, and nodding off. Also, I fretted because I knew that Joel wouldn't consider such behavior adequate communication, and it made me feel I was the cause of his failure to revive Lisa.

But suddenly I had a realization: whatever the level of our communication, Joel *had* to revive Lisa anyway—so why wait any longer? And, disgusted with his inaction, I said, "This is ridiculous!" got up, and walked to the bathroom.

"Let's communicate by working together on Lisa," I submitted.

For once, Joel followed me, and when he reached the bathroom, he gathered Lisa into his arms. At the same time, he ordered, "Clear off everything from the bed!"

That referred to the papers, magazines, and files he kept piled on the half that had been mine. I did, tossing them onto the floor, relieved that at last he was taking action.

But instead of reviving her, Joel placed Lisa in the bed and sat beside her with his arm across her chest. As long as his body made contact with hers, her breathing, which had been ragged when he'd carried her in, remained regular. That alone fulfilled my expectation of magic, though it surely fell short of my hopes.

It must have been 2:00 a.m. by then. Lisa had been unconscious for about eight hours. Of the next four I remember little, though I do recall pulling out a trauma book from Joel's legal collection to see if I could discover a possible cause for her condition. I looked up "unconscious," but I bypassed "coma" as something far too immutable to be the problem. In spite of Joel's earlier confession, *"I knocked her down, and she didn't want to get up again,"* it still hadn't penetrated my brain that the cause of my child's plight was sitting there in front of me with his arm stretched across her. I also recall Joel saying that he was going to sleep—but he didn't. He joined me in my continued vigil.

At about 6:00 a.m., I paid a visit to the bathroom. Suddenly, Joel called to me frantically. I ran to the bedroom to find him in a panic, trying to revive Lisa by alternately pounding on her chest and blowing air into her mouth, quite haphazardly.

"She's stopped breathing," he gasped.

"Should I call 911?" I asked, so used to having Joel direct everything that even now, I wouldn't go to the phone without his permission.

"No, not yet," he answered. "Give me a chance first." And he continued his frenzied resuscitation attempts.

"What CAN I do to help?" I pleaded.

Apparently frightened, he finally conceded, "Call 911."

Good-bye Lisa

The doorbell rings, and I dashed as fast as my leg would allow to let in the Emergency Medical Service workers, forgetting completely about my black eyes and split lip. My mind was singular: get help for Lisa—now.

As Joel emerged from the bedroom, carrying her, he snapped quietly, "Get back inside."

Oops, my injuries. I forgot all about them.

I retreated to the bedroom door that opened onto the hallway where Joel had laid Lisa on the floor, the EMS workers immediately bending over her. The light switch in the hall had been broken for weeks, but Joel hadn't gotten around to fixing it. His freebasing/sleeping agenda didn't allow for repairing things, I'm afraid. Darkness, and the people surrounding Lisa, prevented me from seeing what was going on, even after Joel retrieved from the closet an emergency light with a long yellow cord and focused it on her. I kept straining to see what was happening, not thinking, only watching and listening intently.

Then, minutes later, Joel brushed by me, going into the bedroom to put on his shoes. He was going in the ambulance to the hospital. But, of course, with my injuries apparent, I couldn't go too. So the last I saw of Lisa in the gloomy light was one small, limp arm hanging over the edge of the stretcher as the EMS workers carried her out the door.

Today, so many years later, that scene stands out vividly in my mind's eye.

Or does it? Would Lisa's arm really have been hanging down from the stretcher? Wouldn't the EMS workers have wrapped her securely in blankets? Perhaps imagination has dramatized this last view of Lisa because I know now that it was a final moment. But back then, I hadn't the slightest inkling that I'd never see her again.

And back then, just as the door closed, Mitchell began to cry from his playpen in the living room where he'd been sleeping. I picked him up, stroked him, and carried him to the kitchen to refill his empty bottle. It felt so good to hold him, though I wished he were still asleep. I felt shaken to my roots by the events of the last 13 or 14 hours. I was actually feeling dazed, unsteady on my feet, and I didn't want to handle Mitch in this state. *At least*, I reflected with relief, *now Lisa's in good hands at the hospital.*

Mitch's diaper was wet, but I really didn't feel up to changing it right then; I was so glad he was not complaining about it.

"Sorry, Mitch," I said, giving him a kiss on the cheek. "My good little boy, you can wait this one time."

Usually I changed him immediately, but not this time.

Back in the playpen, Mitchell finished his bottle and, amazingly, as if he knew I needed some peace, fell back to sleep—again!

But soon I heard the downstairs buzzer. *Groan*, and I pulled myself up from the bed where I'd been lying and staring at the ceiling and asked who was at the door.

"The police."

This time I was not in such a hurry, and so I remembered to quickly apply cover makeup to my black and blue eyes before opening the door.

Two police officers entered. They seemed friendly and congenial and told me of Joel's report: Lisa had choked on vegetables and vomited; was there any of the meal left that could be tested? I went to the refrigerator and gave them the container of leftovers.

One officer, bending over Mitch in the playpen, began to chat with me about babies; he had a 10-month-old child of his own, he said. He noted that Mitchell's diaper was wet.

I responded with, "I know," but I didn't have the energy to explain.

The police left, and I was glad because I'd realized that no matter what else was going on, I *had* to change Mitchell's diaper; he must have been drenched by now.

There, it was done, and his wet sheet and blanket were in the bathroom sink, soaking. *Okay, now I'll feed Mitch breakfast. I wonder if I'll be taking unfair advantage of the situation if I also eat a piece of bread and butter— since it's without Joel's permission.*

Well, I ate it, and then, amazingly, Mitch was asleep again and I was back on the bed studying the ceiling. But I heard the door opening. It was Joel!

"How's Lisa?" I asked immediately, sitting up, expecting him to say that the doctors had revived her. Why else would he be back so soon?

"She's still unconscious," he said, kicking off his shoes and lying down on the bed beside me.

"I'm afraid she might be brain-damaged because no oxygen was going to her brain when she stopped breathing," he added, putting his arm around me and holding me close.

Oh, no! I thought, and a terrible sorrow swept over me. But feeling Joel's protective arm eased my pain; I felt secure. *Somehow Joel'll make it all okay; Lisa will be all right.*

Good-bye Mitch

Our moment of synthesis was interrupted by the telephone, which I answered immediately. It was one of the doctors from St. Vincent's: Could they have permission to drill a hole in Lisa's skull to relieve the pressure on her brain? At that moment the words meant little to my own numbed brain. Since Joel had heard the question over the speaker phone, I looked to him for an answer. He nodded approval, and robot like, I intoned, "yes."

That'll do the trick, I supposed. *For sure she'll come to after they relieve the pressure.*

While I was still on the phone, the doorbell sounded again, and Joel roused himself to answer it. Two officers, one male and one female, had arrived with a detective. I could hear their voices, but I didn't see their faces until they summoned me to join them in the living room.

Someone from the Bureau of Child Welfare arrived soon thereafter, but I scarcely noticed. Everything was happening now as if in a dream. I was aware that the detective was asking questions. As I stood quietly, watching, listening, unthinking, Joel explained that Lisa had choked on some vegetables and thrown up. When the policeman turned to me, I automatically repeated Joel's version of events.

Then Joel fell into his name-dropping act.

"I represent Officer Marrow," he boasted. The cop worked in their precinct. "And I've been friends with Officer Moltan forever." That was our

370

friend Frank who'd worked for the 6th Precinct for years. But Joel's performance seemed to have no effect on these officers. Instead of responding, the detective asked if we'd come to the station for further questioning. Joel knew we had no choice, and asked boldly, "Are we under arrest?"

"Of course not," the detective replied. "We just prefer to question you in the precinct. We really don't have the proper facilities for it here."

Then someone said that they were going to take Mitchell to be examined at St. Vincent's. That seemed logical, so I wasn't at all alarmed; I gave the female officer, Irma Rivera, a diaper, clothes, and shoes for him. I observed as she began to dress him with a tender touch, and I felt relieved that she seemed to be a caring person. *At least my little boy won't become unduly upset by all this.* In a journal, a year later, I wrote: "I keep seeing Irma's eyes—those sweet, loving eyes. I remember them well now. They were comforting."

But I too had to get dressed, and I selected some of the only decent clothes I had left (I hadn't shopped for clothes since leaving Random House more than five years earlier): the jeans Chubby had bought me when, feeling appreciative of work well done, he'd gratefully showered Joel with gifts, including a few for me; a turtleneck and blouse given similarly by a client in the shirt business; and a jacket left behind by another client's girlfriend.

As we started out the door, Joel whispered sternly, "Put on a hat." That was actually an order to cover the bald spots on my head (left after Joel had pulled out handfuls of hair), for beneath them were the scabs left by his exercise bar assaults. And Joel surely didn't want the police to notice *those.*

Going back inside for a scarf while everyone else went down the elevator, I thought, *Gee, Mitchell might be away from home for a few hours.* So I stole a few extra minutes to prepare a fresh bottle of milk for him; when I got downstairs, I gave it to Officer Rivera who was carrying him. My little boy was stony faced and silent and remained so while I got into the police car. Joel and I, at his insistence, rode in one car, Mitchell, Rivera, and the social worker in the other. Joel certainly wasn't about to take a chance of having me out of his sight at that moment!

As I entered the 6th Precinct, just a few blocks away, the first thing I saw was Mitchell being held by a strange policewoman. My boy was still silent, and though he gazed at me, his eyes seemed to look right through me. He looked confused, almost in shock.

"Please bring him to see me before he goes to the hospital," I pleaded, knowing that this situation was becoming traumatic for him.

"Of course," the officer answered.

But she was lying, and that's the last time I saw Mitchell. In retrospect, I think, had I realized that, I would have grabbed him and run. Or maybe that's only my fantasy. In reality we wouldn't have gotten very far, anyway. But, in any case, I didn't run; I trusted the police. And now, after more than 17 years, I've yet to see my little boy again.

The Questions

The police procedures we see on TV shows like *NYPD Blue* are accurate. Upstairs at the 6th Precinct, I was brought into a small room and questioned. When I didn't provide appropriate responses, the interrogating officers walked out and left me alone for what seemed like forever—I presume that was to give me time to think. And I did. I thought that Lisa would be fine; it was just taking longer than I'd expected. I thought that there was no way they could get me to betray my man. Why tell tales when soon all would be back to normal? So when a police officer finally returned to the room, my answers remained the same: Lisa had choked on some vegetables and stopped breathing. The bruises on her body had come from falling down roller skating. My own injuries were due to being clumsy.

A man I considered extremely disturbing kept popping into the room and saying, "We'll find out the truth at the autopsy."

I was outraged. *Lisa's not going to die! He's just trying to trick me into talking against Joel!* No way would that ruse work on Hedda Nussbaum!

Whenever I had the opportunity to talk with Officer Rivera, I asked her to call the hospital to check on Lisa's condition. Each time her report was the same: "There's been no change." I was truly amazed, stymied.

Eventually, one officer advised me, "We want to photograph you, just so we can prove that you came in here looking this way—that we didn't do this to you." It seemed reasonable, so I agreed. Had I understood that the pictures would be used against Joel, there was no way they could have convinced me to cooperate.

I was taken into another room and videotaped, a sequence that later shocked the nation; a sequence that is stunning even to me now for it's portrait of a bruised, debilitated, dazed, undernourished woman. I had no idea that's what I'd become. The videotape clearly shows the bald spots on my head with scabs peeking through my sparse gray hair; a split lip; the leg wrapped in paper towels, leaking bright yellow pus; numerous scars on my rounded back; and a huge black and blue mark on my buttock.

When the taping was done, a police officer not present earlier walked into the room. Looking closely, I saw that it was Joel's old friend Tim, an NYPD sergeant whom I'd not seen for several years—not since he'd gotten disgusted with Joel's style of friendship. Because Tim had once given his then-buddy a policeman's shield with his ID on it, one that Joel still carried in his wallet—flashing it to impress people—the 6th Precinct had called upon Tim to come down and talk to me. They must have figured, maybe *he* could get me to open up.

"My god, Hedda!" he exclaimed when he saw me. "What happened to you?"

Of course, I wasn't about to tell him the truth either. But he continued trying to get me to talk about my injuries, or Lisa's.

"When Jan [Tim's old girlfriend] saw you last she suspected Joel was hitting you."

A noble attempt on his part, but my answer served my own agenda.

"He would never hurt a child, and that's the issue here."

Determined to continue protecting Joel, I thought I was handling Tim's questions pretty well. In fact, he left without having made one bit of progress. Thus far agreeing to let the police make the videotape of me had been my only crumb of cooperation.

At about 7:00 p.m., after Officer Rivera had brought me a welcome sandwich (I'd not eaten since early that morning), I was led back into the interrogation room where the questioning continued. Probably feeling quite frustrated with my non-cooperation, one police officer finally suggested we go to the District Attorney's office, which prompted me to say, "Then read me my rights."

And so they did, and I was officially under arrest.

The Second Videotape

Both Joel and I were fingerprinted and photographed. Then after each of us had spoken with a criminal lawyer Joel knew—Bob Kalina—we were led downstairs in handcuffs to be taken out of the station house to Central Booking. That's in midtown where we'd enter the New York criminal justice system. As we entered the precinct lobby, a sea of reporters and flashbulbs assaulted my eyes and voices my ears. But I never heard what they said. I was absolutely in shock. If you watch me in the videotape taken at that moment, the one that was shown repeatedly on the TV news and is still played from time to time, you can see me shaking my head from side to side in disbelief. I recall thinking, *Why are they making all this fuss, just because my daughter's in the hospital?* Yes, I was out of touch with reality.

I also had no idea that a story of a Jewish lawyer and his apparently battered live-in companion, also Jewish and a former book editor, both arrested for assaulting their six-year-old daughter, might be big news. I didn't realize that back then in 1987 people believed that the only families who encountered domestic violence were poor, uneducated, Black, Hispanic, or so-called White Trash. Professional Jewish men were assumed never to assault their wives, girlfriends, or children. The case of *People v. Joel Steinberg* would open the eyes of the world to the truth about battering: no one is exempt. Domestic violence occurs in every country of the world, in every socioeconomic, racial, and religious community. The sad truth is this: until all children are brought up to consider men and women truly equal, every boy will grow up to be a potential batterer, every girl a potential victim.

375

Booked

Joel and I were escorted into separate police cars and whisked off to midtown to be booked. Entering Central Booking at the same time as me, Joel, who'd been there many times before to counsel a newly arrested client, turned to me and whispered, "I never thought I'd be here THIS way."

Then we were swept off in different directions by the officers leading us—I to the women's section and Joel presumably to the men's. That was the last time I'd see him until his murder trial more than a year later.

Then I was hurried away to a large prison cell, relieved of my shoelaces and scarf, and put inside with eight or nine other women.

Jail

My god, this is all so strange. Look at those women! Indifferent eyes, sad eyes, a dirty face. And that skinny one definitely looks like a hooker.

I sat observing from a long wooden bench beside another woman or two on one side of the otherwise bare cell. The only other object in it was a twin of that bench on the opposite side. It also held a few unfortunate women. A couple more sat on the floor.

I wish I could reproduce even a little of the dialogue that took place in that cell; it held me fascinated. But lack of sleep had gotten to me by then, and so most of what transpired slid through my brain. I *do* recall that one my cellmates described herself as pregnant and another talked about her experiences as a shoplifter. I'm certain that when I was asked why I was there, I said it was too sad to talk about. That was true. But I also didn't want to say it aloud: *attempted murder, endangering the welfare of a child.* Those were the charges against me.

Sitting there on the floor for four hours, listening but not talking, I learned that you could request temporary transfer to a hospital.

Yes, a hospital. I should get my bandages changed. That's what went through my mind: clean bandages instead of those paper towels I'd put on so many hours before. And, I admit, a hospital environment was more appealing to me than a jail cell.

So I made the request, and after a brief stint in a tiny cell by myself (did they think the other women might assault me because I was charged with harming a child?), I ended up at Bellevue an hour later with my hands cuffed behind my back.

Bellevue

Sometime during the early morning hours of November 3, still without sleep and still handcuffed, I found myself waiting on a long line at Bellevue Hospital. When I finally reached the front and asked to have my leg bandaged, I was summarily sent back to the prisoners' waiting room with these words: "Wait until morning." Leg bandaging was apparently a minor need compared to the gunshot wounds and lacerations of others.

Looking around the room full of prisoners and cops, I saw a policeman reading a copy of the *New York Daily News*. The front page bore a picture of Joel and me taken at the 6th Precinct. The headline shrieked *TOT TORTURE*. I felt people staring in my direction. All I could do was close my eyes and lean my head back against the wall.

Suddenly I felt something slap onto my lap. I opened my eyes and saw an elderly man tossing sandwiches at the waiting prisoners. I stared at the sandwich sitting there on my leg; it was exactly what my too-often empty belly longed for. But how could I possibly eat it with my hands cuffed behind my back?

"Need a hand?" said a smiling young man sitting next to me, enjoying his pun.

His offer, however, was in earnest, so he held the snack in his front-cuffed hands, while I leaned my face forward and took bites. We must have been a comical sight to anyone glancing our way, but there was nothing funny about it to me. It was the only way I could get some food into my malnourished body. In this peculiar manner, I managed to eat the entire sandwich, which activity held my concentration and kept me from thinking about Lisa for a few minutes.

Hours later I finally saw a doctor and learned that I really shouldn't have been kept waiting all that time.

"Much longer and you'd have lost your leg," he said. At that moment, sleepless and dazed, he could have told me that the moon was made of purple spinach, and I'd have simply nodded in agreement. His statement had absolutely no impact—not then.

A year later at Joel's trial, when the very same doctor testified that I would have died of blood poisoning had I continued without treatment for another week or two, I finally realized how serious my injuries had been.

Handcuffed to the Bed

By six o'clock p.m. November 3, I was admitted to Elmhurst Hospital in Queens, where women prisoners needing medical care are hospitalized. Handcuffed to my bed in the small emergency room cubicle, receiving intravenous antibiotics, I felt relieved and somehow safe: my needs were being taken care of for a change. And I felt hopeful: doctors would heal my injuries, Lisa would be okay, and Joel would be out on bail soon. Everything would be all right.

"We'll find out at the autopsy."

I tried to shove those words aside. She wasn't going to die. I was sure of it.

My eyes were closed when a voice beside my bed startled me. A young doctor raised the white sheet above my right knee and removed the bandages put on earlier.

"Mrs. Steinberg," he said (I'd registered at the hospital as Hedda Steinberg), "I'm going to inject Demerol into your IV while I clean and scrape your wounds. The procedure is called debreeding.

"Even with the drug, it might be painful," he warned. "The ulcerations are deep and close to the nerve."

I'd always been an obedient patient. As children, when my sister and I had injections, she would scream as the doctor chased her around the room, and I'd cooperate quietly—but not this time. When the doctor began, it was more than I could bear. So I yelled. I roared. It was the worst pain I'd ever experienced.

And out of my mouth came a cry: "Lisa, Lisa."

Apparently, feeling the doctor's scalpel—or simply *feeling*—allowed me to release for the first time the deep grief inside me.

When the debreeding was over, my body relaxed, but my mind remained troubled by images: Mitchell in a strange policewoman's arms…Lisa, lying still on the bathroom floor… the phone nearby…her small, pale arm, suspended from the stretcher. I didn't know it then, but soon Lisa would be dead.

Family

November 4, 1987. So here I am in a large room all by myself on the locked floor where mental prisoners are kept. There are bars on the window and a 24-hour guard outside the door. They tell me that's all for my own safety. Nothing from outside is allowed in my room—not even a newspaper, so I've not seen what's in today's papers about us. But I've asked for a TV so I can watch the news, and I think I'm getting one. Then, when Lisa wakes up, I can hear the good news immediately. Oh, yes, and I'm handcuffed to *this* bed, too, but not for my own safety, I'm sure.

The events today have been so weird. First a nurse came in and told me that my sister was here to see me.

"Tell her I don't want to see her," I responded quickly. I can't take the risk that she'll buzz me or hurt me in some other way, for gosh sakes.

But then Mommy and Daddy showed up with Uncle Natie and Aunt Virginia who just happened to be in New York! I hadn't seen Mommy and Daddy for four years—not since Lisa's second birthday! But here they were. Ya know, it actually felt good to see them. And I was

383

sure glad to see Natie and Virginia. I hadn't seen *them* since Joel and I were in California maybe eight years ago.

Anyway, when Mommy and Daddy started talking about getting me a lawyer, I told them that Joel's lawyer is also representing me. But Uncle Natie said he thought it would be a good idea for me to get one of my own. So, since I respect and trust Uncle Natie and don't have to worry about his trying to hurt me—like *some* people—I decided to listen to him.

"And I know a really good New York attorney," he said. "Why don't I call him?"

"Sure," I said. "Go ahead."

So they all left for a while. And that's when the nurse told me that Judy wanted to come in for just a minute. And knowing that everything in my life had changed, I figured, *Oh, well, I guess I'll have to see her soon anyway, so I may as well start now.* So I agreed to let her in, but I made sure I structured the conversation so I'd keep control of it. And you know what? By the time she left, I was thinking, *Gee, she really doesn't seem so bad, after all.*

And now, Uncle Natie's coming back in by himself. I wonder where the others are.

"I want to talk to you, just the two of us," he says.

I wait to hear what he has to say.

"Lisa's dead," he says.

"She is?" I say and just stare at him.

Lisa's Dead

At the moment Uncle Natie told me that Lisa was dead, it just didn't sink in. The experts say that when a person learns of a close family member's death, it often doesn't penetrate right away; the person is unable to face reality, especially if the death is sudden, the way Lisa's was. Add to that my already numbed state, and my reaction was nil.

The actual circumstances of my child's death were these: she'd been declared brain-dead on November 4th, but the hospital disconnected her life support the next day—the day of my arraignment.

What did I feel when the judge at the arraignment declared Lisa dead? Nothing. It was as if I were dead too and watching the events from above. I saw myself being arraigned for the second-degree murder of my own beautiful daughter: me, the defendant, sitting in a wheelchair in a makeshift courtroom with intravenous tubes attached to my arm, wearing a hospital gown, hospital robe, and handcuffs. Though I sat alone, two lawyers were there for me: Bob Kalina, the attorney Joel had summoned for us, and my own new lawyer, Barry Scheck. Mommy and Daddy were there too as were a slew of reporters. I saw them all and heard the judge pronounce the charges against me, now upped to murder. But there was no reaction. All emotions were asleep.

Shackles

After the arraignment, I was transferred to the custody of New York City's Department of Corrections who preferred a foot shackle to handcuffs, and I was shackled to my bed. Worried that the circulation in my leg might be affected, Mommy complained to a doctor about it. So when a few days later, the shackle was removed, I assumed the doctor had effectuated the change. But I was wrong. An editorial in *The New York Times* on Thursday, November 12, 1987 described my situation:

> New York City's Department of Corrections has stationed two officers outside Hedda Nussbaum's private room to guard her 24 hours a day. Has it really been necessary also to shackle and chain her by one leg to her hospital bed?"

It then asserted that only women prisoners in medical wards are treated thusly, but not men, and finally:

> The public may feel conflicted about Hedda Nussbaum, charged with complicity in the beatings of a little girl. But she is also a victim. Shackles and chains inflict a kind of battering— for no good reason. Shackling is prohibited by state prison officials. The city's Correction Department now says that it will

386

no longer shackle women, and will stop shackling men in general population wards within a week. When it does, it will not be a day too soon.

Behind the Scenes

Judy later told me that when my parents had seen the news broadcast about Lisa's condition and Joel's and my arrest, they'd been stunned and horrified. But when they'd seen the pictures of me leaving the police station a battered mess, my father had actually cried. Never, in all the 45 years I'd known Daddy, had I seen him shed a tear.

As soon as they'd learned that I was at Elmhurst Hospital in Queens, they'd gotten in their car together with my California relatives who'd just coincidentally shown up, and had driven to see me. When they'd arrived, they'd found a woman from STEPS to End Family Violence waiting for them in the lobby. STEPS is an organization that helps incarcerated victims of domestic violence, and it was this woman whom they'd asked to recommend a lawyer. She'd suggested Michael Dowd, Esq., who had recently won a highly publicized case for a woman who'd killed her abusive husband. Judy called Mr. Dowd, who was out of town, and his office recommended Barry Scheck.

Mommy, Daddy, and Judy were perceptive enough to realize that I'd not take a recommendation from any of them, so they had asked Uncle Natie to say that he knew of Barry Scheck and recommended him highly. Fortunately for me, Natie took their advice and I took his because in the end, Barry turned out to be a godsend. To this day, Judy considers the fortuity of Uncle Natie being in town that day a near miracle—and so do I.

Barry Scheck

Today he's known positively for the Innocence Project—using DNA to free the wrongfully convicted—and not so positively for his representation of O.J. Simpson, a man who beat his wife and then beat the rap for her murder. But when Barry Scheck entered my room at Elmhurst Hospital on November 4, 1987, his name and face were completely unknown to me.

The only reason I even talked to Barry was Uncle Natie's recommendation. During my years with Joel, I'd been exposed to myriad criminal attorneys, and I'd found most to be either incompetent or unscrupulous. But Barry seemed thorough, knowledgeable, and caring, and I hired him on the spot. As you can see, my intellect was still intact though my critical faculties and emotions weren't. Of course, since I had no money to pay Barry, he got himself appointed by the court to represent me *pro bono*— for the good—for free.

In spite of my opinion of my new attorney, I told him the same story I'd told the police: Lisa had been throwing up vegetables, and I had no idea what had caused her coma. The next day, however, after being arraigned and hearing Lisa declared officially dead, I felt I simply *had* to get the true story off my chest. Barry not only had attorney-client privilege, but I could sense that he was a gentle and sympathetic person. So, after opening with, "I thought I'd never tell this to anyone," I presented the abbreviated version of Joel Steinberg's Abuse 101 and then I told him all the awful events of

389

November first and second.

As an odd followup to this, both Barry and I had to talk to Joel on the phone to make funeral arrangements. Not surprisingly, when I heard Joel's voice, everything I'd just told Barry flew from my mind, and I worried about his feelings of loss as Lisa's daddy. We spent some time consoling each other, and then Joel expressed anger at the authorities for removing the life support equipment without asking us first—once again shifting the onus from himself.

We did, however, also discuss funeral arrangements, not knowing that we'd be denied the privilege of burying our daughter. My parents had volunteered our family plot, but Joel said Lisa had told him she wanted to lie next to Grandma Charlotte, Joel's mother. *Suuure, she had,* I say today sarcastically. Doesn't every six-year-old think about where she wants to be buried? The absurdity of this latest manipulation by Joel B. Steinberg went right over my head back then. And when Barry contacted Joel's mother about this matter, she told him there was room in their plot only for herself and Joel. So much for Steinberg loving kindness.

The Little White Coffin

November 18, 1987. Visiting hours were over, and there I sat, alone in my bed, watching the story of Lisa Steinberg's funeral on the TV news. Numbly I watched a little white coffin being carried from a chapel into a hearse—the little white coffin holding the little body of my precious daughter. For the first time in two weeks, more than just a few tears fell from my eyes. The reality of my loss suddenly hit me, but only for a moment. A month and a half passed before I allowed a permanent chink in the armor of denial that was permitting me to go on.

Today, although many years have passed since that funeral, I still cannot look at a photograph of that little white coffin. Whenever I'm reviewing a 1987 magazine for information relating to this book and I come across such a photo, I shudder and quickly turn the page.

The little white coffin.
Credit: Ricki Rosen/Redux Pictures

As Jewish readers probably realize from the white coffin and the two-week delay before burial, Lisa's funeral was Catholic, not Jewish. You see, during the two week interval, Lisa's birth mother, Michele Launders, had come forward, and a judge had awarded her the right to bury our child—hers and mine. So Lisa was buried in a Catholic cemetery. But as a concession to her Jewish upbringing, the funeral services were interdenominational. Urged by Barry, who knew it would be good for my frame of mind, I wrote a eulogy, but he never submitted it, knowing that it would be unwelcome. To all but a few, I was considered one of Lisa's murderers.

On the morning of the funeral, my parents arrived at my bedside. To say that I was shocked would be a gross understatement.

"Why aren't you at the funeral?" I gasped.

Apparently trying to protect me from a truth that might hurt—*they were scared to show up at the funeral*—my father told me, "Oh, I'd never find a parking space around there."

This "white lie" was much more wounding than the truth would have been. But once I understood Daddy's motive, I forgave both him and Mommy. Covering up the truth in order to protect me was an old habit of theirs, and in spite of all my Joel-induced efforts to get them to "go on the line," they still clung to their old way.

Worries

Intellectually I knew that Lisa was dead, but the truth hadn't sunk in at all. So instead of feeling despair, I worried. Oh, not about myself. Oddly, even though I had murder charges against me, I trusted the system. Since I felt innocent of any wrongdoing, I wasn't worried about being convicted. No, I was worried about others who'd been affected by this tragedy.

"Please call Charlotte," I begged my mother, concerned about Joel's mother's feelings. She dearly loved both Joel and Lisa, and, I fretted, the news must have torn her apart.

I tormented myself over Mitchell's sudden separation from his mother, father, and sister. How badly would that trauma touch him? After all, I'd been permanently affected by Baba's technical abandonment of me, which was certainly a lot less severe than what Mitch was suffering. He needed to be with his mother now, not in foster care. I longed for the day when we'd be back together and prayed that it would be soon enough to prevent any permanent damage to his psyche.

I also worried about Gary Balken. He adored Lisa and looked up to Joel. He was already using too much cocaine and alcohol. Would current events deepen his addiction? Would he survive?

Michele Launders' pain was also on my mind. She'd never known her child, but I realized that the feeling of responsibility for abandoning Lisa must be weighing massively on her. I wished that I could comfort her and wondered how she felt about me.

Contact with Joel

Both Barry and my appointed family court attorney, David Lansner, who would handle my fight for Mitchell, cautioned me to disassociate myself from Joel.

"It's not a good idea for you to talk to or have any contact at all with Joel," Barry advised. "And I'd warn you to stop using the name 'Steinberg.' You really have to separate yourself from him unless you want to be held responsible for Lisa's death along with him."

If you will recall, I'd been admitted to Elmhurst Hospital under the name Hedda Steinberg and liked being called "Mrs. Steinberg." Although I understood Barry's words, I simply couldn't grasp the logic behind avoiding contact with the man I loved, and I insisted on writing to him. However, I conceded to having Barry read them to Joel's lawyer over the phone rather than mailing them.

One day when I returned from having whirlpool therapy for my leg, there was a message waiting for me, and to my surprise and pleasure, it was from Joel. Of course I couldn't resist returning the call, even though I knew my attorneys would be furious. Wait a minute. How could Joel, a prisoner, get phone calls at Rikers? Leave it to Joel Steinberg. In those days, before he'd gotten a reputation as a child killer, he was able to charm just about anyone and convince that person of anything his little heart desired. So he'd apparently befriended the prison law library attendant and arranged to get and

395

receive phone calls there. Not bad!

Anyway, I was escorted into a room with a phone and reluctantly suffered the presence of an aide while I conversed with my lover. After exchanging "I love you," and "Are you all right?" both ways, I told him I was going to Columbia Presbyterian Hospital in a few days. Barry had arranged to have me transferred there instead of to Rikers. Upon hearing that, Joel immediately cautioned me.

"Keep your eyes open at that hospital. It's full of hypnotizing doctors," he warned.

Did Joel actually believe the hypnosis-by-staring story he'd created? Or was this more Steinberg manipulation? Who knows! Not me.

Joel then emphasized that we had to work with and see each other in court whenever possible—"to get Mitch back,"and "to be together."

"I just want to see you," he said. "I miss you. What else is there?" Still blinded to Joel's ruse, I agreed, thinking that we had nothing left now but each other.

Then he informed me that the autopsy report said Lisa's death was caused by a subdural hematoma—a brain injury.

"But we both know she didn't have any head injuries," he added indignantly.

"Well," I responded naively, "I assumed she must have hit her head at some point."

I still didn't realize that everything Joel said was an attempt to both cover his ass and influence my thinking.

Then, to top it all off, Joel tried to convince me that Barry Scheck was "worse than incompetent," and that I should fire him.

But I told Joel, "Next to you, Barry's the best attorney I've ever met." And amazingly, Joel didn't try to dissuade me from that point of view. If he had, I'm sure I'd have acceded to his demand and let him choose an attorney for me, which is what he wanted to do.

Instead, he simply said, "You've got to let me monitor everything Barry does. Understand?"

Of course I did.

"And I want to keep talking to you—even if Barry insists on listening, I MUST talk to you."

But that never happened—the talking, I mean. We never again spoke, and in fact, the only time I had any contact with Joel after that day was a full year later when I appeared as a witness at his murder trial.

Neuro 12

As I'd informed Joel, Barry had arranged for me to go from one hospital to another—from Elmhurst to Columbia Presbyterian—instead of to Rikers Island Prison. Phew! What a relief that had been. However, I felt a bit uncomfortable with the idea that I was slated for the psych ward.

"It's so they can evaluate you," Barry informed me, "give you tests."

That sounded okay.

Actually, I'd already had one battery of psychological tests by a forensic psychiatrist. Both he and the hospital social worker, after hearing my talk about Joel being a better parent than I, about his magical healing abilities, and about hypnosis though staring, agreed with Barry that I had "mental problems." But wisely, none of them mentioned this opinion to me.

When I arrived at Columbia Presbyterian Hospital, I was put into a tiny, locked unit (designated Neuro 12 because it was on the 12th floor of the Neurological Institute) with 14 other patients. Because of the murder charges pending against me, when the others went out on passes or group walks, I had to stay inside. All my phone calls were supervised (just in case I got the urge to call Joel) and my visitors restricted. Although I wasn't in jail, I was definitely a prisoner. Still, I was glad to be there rather than at Rikers.

Five days a week I talked with Louis Opler, my assigned psychiatrist, the unit head. He was direct but gentle, and I had no problem opening up to him. Obviously I was ready to listen to his logic because little by little I began to realize that Joel had no special powers; he'd simply created that image of himself. And because no one was able to find any hypnotizing, child-molesting group on Long Island, I realized that Joel had created that apparition too, along with my so-called hypnotic powers and my family's alleged evil designs.

Such realizations would have been earthshakingly painful but for the continued numbed state of my consciousness. So I maintained my deep devotion to Joel Steinberg, feeling as intensely in love as ever. The knowledge of how horribly he'd used and controlled me was still far beyond my understanding, nor had it sunk in that he was the only reason I was a prisoner and a hospital patient. Even the intellectual knowledge of Lisa's death (though not the emotional comprehension) hadn't altered my feelings for Joel. It would take time for my eyes to open fully to the truth about my messiah. However, I began to think that he was a very sick man—a small bit of progress, anyway, although not accurate.

Since that time, I've learned that most abusers aren't sick and they aren't crazy. They make rational choices, which means they're quite sane. They choose to abuse their spouses, sweethearts, and children—but not their boss or the grocery clerk. The latter two would result in too many consequences. As to Joel, he was a charmer in public and chose never to strike me with people around—an obvious sign of rationality.

But back in 1987, I knew nothing of this, and I still longed for contact with Joel. So although I realized that mailing letters to him was forbidden, writing letters addressed "Dear Joel" felt better than simply recording my thoughts in a journal. So I penned such epistles daily for a while—including one letter 11 pages long!—and deposited them with Dr. Opler instead of in a mailbox.

The Most Painful
Decision of My Life

Although I'd now given two people (Barry Scheck and Louis Opler) detailed descriptions of what had happened on the night of November 1st, I still couldn't take in the reality of Lisa's death. I often spoke about her in the present tense, while I frequently spoke of Mitchell in the past tense. I suppose it was easier to accept the reality of Mitchell being gone, since there was still hope of being reunited with him, than it was to accept the finality of Lisa's death.

But soon all hope for a reunion with my surviving child disappeared. Shortly after I arrived at Columbia Presbyterian, Nicole Smigiel, Mitchell's natural mother, came forward: she wanted her son back.

A judge awarded her temporary custody, and I sat in the common room with other patients silently staring at the TV, eyes filled with tears, as she lovingly carried him, renamed Travis Christian, into her home. Suddenly the newspapers were full of photos of my adorable little boy with his blonde hair and smiling face. Viewing those pictures today of little Mitchell/Travis wearing a spanking new sailor suit and mischievous grin, my heart is torn open. Back then, however, although I couldn't feel the pain as intensely, I *did* want those photographs.

Until then, having been trained to give deference to authority figures, I'd never dared to cut out an article from Neuro 12's newspapers; after all, they didn't belong to me. But I coveted those pictures of Mitchell desperately enough to ask permission to take them at day's end. It was granted, and I began clipping everything about the case and saving it in a scrapbook. I wanted to hold close everything written about those I loved: Lisa, Mitchell, and Joel.

Then Barry Scheck came to me and said, "Now that his birth mother has Mitchell, you know that the public will be on her side. They'll want you to give him up to her, to stop fighting to keep him."

"But he's my baby! How can I give him up?" I replied, distressed. The possibility of losing Mitch as well as Lisa caused powerful feelings to seep through my emotional paralysis.

"Take the next few days and think about it; then make a decision."

I wrestled with this notion for two torturous days. It was the most agonizing decision I'd ever faced. I *really* wanted to be reunited with my little boy; I missed him terribly. The thought of never seeing him again was simply too much to bear. But in the end, I came to a decision, not for me or my case as Barry had advised, but for my son: I had to think of him first. The following is the limping statement I wrote—the best I could do at that juncture:

> I have just made the most difficult decision of my life, and that is to stop fighting for Mitchell and to give up my rights to him. It was so difficult because I truly love Mitchell and have held him both in my arms for 16 months and in my heart for 17 now, and will continue to forever. Both he and Lisa will always be an important part of me, and I miss them both terribly.
>
> Because of my love for Mitchell, I want what is best for him. I fought to keep my rights to him because of my hope that I will one day be well enough to take care of him again. I knew nothing about Nicole Smigiel. But when I saw Mitchell on TV Thursday and Friday nights in Nicole's arms, from behind my tears I could see him smiling and her beaming with joy. And I was now glad he was no longer in foster care but with his natural mother who, it seems, will give him plenty of love.
>
> I believe that it will be a long time before I completely recover from both my physical ailments and the psychological suffering I've been going through. By the time I might be ready

to care for him, he would have been in Nicole's custody for many months and would have formed a strong love attachment to her. It would be very painful for him to be subjected to a custody battle or to be taken from her then. One painful separation is enough in a child's life.

Also, as I said, I now think that Nicole will give Mitchell plenty of love. So to spare Mitchell any more anguish or disruption, I have made this decision.

I know the joy that Nicole has now, and will have for years to come. I had that same joy for 16 months. I do not begrudge Nicole her new-found love; I do envy her. But I wish her the best for Mitchell...or Travis. I can only hope that one day Nicole will allow me to see him again.

When I read this aloud to my three lawyers, Barry, David Lansner, and a young woman who worked with him, tears streaming down my face, they wept too. Barry took the statement, released it to the press, and Mitchell was no longer mine. Even now, writing this, I find it hard to control the tears. As of the day I wrote the statement, both my children were gone forever.

Healing

While I concerned myself with matters of the heart, those around me dealt with various other parts: my nose, eye, lip, brain, and psyche. I was given tests, hoards of them—a series of neuro-psychological tests and three kinds of brain scans came first—to see if I were brain-damaged. I was, but it was confined to my word memory; somehow, it manifested itself by my forgetting people's names, even those I'd known for many years. (I sometimes think this may have been more psychological than physiological—in spite of what the tests showed—because the names I blanked on all belonged to people I'd met during my years with Joel.) Eye tests resulted in a recommendation for immediate surgery on my crushed tear duct—or else I'd get eye infections, an ophthalmologist warned. My hearing was also tested, and I learned that Joel had damaged that, too; I had a 30% loss in my left ear. A plastic surgeon recommended sewing up my lip and using cartilage from my right ear to fix my badly broken nose. My psyche would probably recover from being delusional (which is how I was diagnosed—though erroneously), but slowly. For the time being, I was given the psychotropic drug, Trilofon, to clarify my thinking, and pills to help me sleep.

Perhaps because I was still somewhat benumbed, none of these medical findings upset me very much. Of course all of this was enormously expensive, so I was profoundly grateful to Peter Sarosi for having included our family in his office insurance policy. Then I learned that the insurer claimed I wasn't a legal member of the group (after all, Joel wasn't one of Peter's employees—even though he did do work for the doctor) and wasn't certain it would pay. But I knew I couldn't worry about money then. Somehow it would work out.

At the end of December, I was operated on, twice in three days, and I spent New Year's Eve 1988 alone in the surgical ward. Though I was feeling somewhat sad and lonely, endogenous opioids and denial kept me going.

Pains

Returning to Neuro 12, I read the special end-of-year section published by the *Daily News* Magazine that another patient had saved for me. The full-page "Story of the Year" was about Lisa, and reading that—its final words were, "Goodnight, Lisa,"—I broke down, and for the first time, wept. The entire unit could hear my wailing. For a few moments, I allowed reality to penetrate my protective armor: Lisa was really dead.

The feelings of pain and loss that article brought up prompted me to tell Barry, though hesitantly, that I'd testify against Joel—for Lisa's sake. Although I felt I still loved Joel and was unable to resent him for what he'd done to me, I knew that he had to pay for what he'd done to our little girl.

Before any arrangements to testify could be made, however, the ADA's on the case had to learn more about me to decide, first, whether they could believe what I'd say and, second, whether a jury would. Besides talking to Barry about me, they came to Columbia Presbyterian to meet with Dr. Opler. But I wouldn't talk with the prosecutors myself for another four months.

For Christmas/Chanukah, the Neuro 12 staff bought a gift for each of the patients, and mine was, appropriately, a journal; that rekindled the tradition from my high school and college days of writing down my thoughts every day. The first few months' entries indicate to me how shut down and out of touch with reality I still was. I wrote about what I ate, how I slept, what the temperature of the unit was, how one day I called Bingo in two languages

(English and Spanish), when I first put on makeup again, when I got reading glasses for the first time, and so on. Feelings rarely made an appearance in the journal.

Although I'd already agreed to testify against Joel, I still felt an enormous attachment to him and wrote him one more letter dated January 8, 1988, which apparently never got into my psychiatrist's possession; I still have it. Here are a couple of quotes from it:

"This is a pretend letter to you. I know you won't get it."

"It's funny, I've been keeping a diary, but I don't feel right unless I write to you. It's different."

"So how are you bearing up under all this pressure? Living at Rikers must be horrible."

The letter also included news about my surgeries, medication and medical insurance, and a meeting between Barry, the prosecution's psychiatrist, Dr. Opler and the two ADA's on our case.

At the end of January 1988, I was allowed to go out of the building accompanied by hospital staff or someone from my lawyer's office, and about once a week I had lunch at a coffee shop two blocks away with Peggy and Rebecca, two law students working on my case. As dull as that may sound to you, to me it was thrilling; finally I had a chance to get off Neuro 12.

One day when Dr. Monte Keen, my plastic surgeon, was on my unit, he motioned to me to look out the small glass pane in the unit door. I did and immediately burst out crying hysterically. The proud smile Dr. Keen wore wasn't enough to prepare me for what I saw outside that door: his wife, holding in her arms a smiling little girl, just about Mitchell's age. It brought home to me, graphically, my own loss: I'd never again hold Lisa or Mitchell in my arms.

Yet I also suffered physically. Because I was now allowed off the unit when accompanied, I was able to go on group walks. On one such walk, the leader was moving so fast we were practically trotting; this set off severe pains in my lower back. Similar but much milder back pains had appeared suddenly while I had been at Elmhurst Hospital. Then I'd blamed it on the hospital bed, but now the condition was diagnosed as arthritis. Walking became exceedingly difficult for me. Previously, I'd been participating in and even conducting exercise classes on the unit. But now I could hardly move; I hobbled with my back hunched over like an aged woman.

This, unfortunately, occurred at the same time as I was told I'd "just have to live with" the poor vision I'd been experiencing since my tear duct surgery. The new eyeglasses prescribed for me didn't help at all (the difficulty, I later realized, was due to tears interfering with my vision), and I was unable to read. The confluence of these two events put my spirits way down in the dumps; self- pity prevailed. Would I be blind and crippled as well as childless? And how would I ever be an editor again if I couldn't even read! But then I said to myself, *I've been through so much and have kept going; I'm not going to give up now.*

So rather than curl up and die, I kept fighting to survive—a characteristic of mine that has served me exceedingly well. And sure enough, although I couldn't have guessed it then, by the time I left Columbia Presbyterian, physical rehabilitation had begun to improve my back and further surgery, my vision.

Money Becomes an Issue

Soon after learning of my arthritis and eye problems, money worries also became inescapable. After debating the issue for three months, the insurance company decided they would *not* cover my expenses—more than $100,000 in hospital and doctor bills. Aaaargh!

Although Joel had transferred about $20,000 to my checking account (a little money laundering attempt), it was being held in escrow for eventual payment of legal and medical bills. The court was paying Barry (as criminal attorney) and had paid David Lansner (as civil attorney), but I'd since hired another lawyer in Lansner's place, Betty Levinson, a former criminal attorney who understood the implications of my civil cases on the criminal. She wouldn't be covered by the court, and I didn't realize that Betty'd be totally satisfied with a pittance from the escrow and never charge me another dime.

Legal bills aside, I was now jobless and without assets. Although the Nussbaum family had never had much money to spare, I'd never before been indigent. Yet I couldn't go on public assistance because I still had assets— even if they were in escrow.

And, perhaps worst of all, Neuro 12 said I had to leave. It was considered a short-term unit, and the average stay at that time was six weeks. I'd already been there more than three months. Because of my legal status, I couldn't go home—and wasn't sure I'd want to return to the memories in that apartment, anyway—and I couldn't afford another hospital. Still, a social worker was trying, unsuccessfully, to find one that would take me without insurance, personal funds, or public assistance. Not that I looked forward to her prevailing over such odds. After spending so much time in a small, locked ward, I dreaded the idea of staying a whole year in another such place, and a year was predicted.

Another option was a battered women's shelter. But there are children in such shelters, and the experience with Dr. Keen's daughter made me realize how much pain the sight of them caused me. Also, a shelter could house me for only a limited amount of time.

On top of all this, after three months, I'd become quite attached to Dr. Opler, and I didn't want to leave him. I was frightened of the unknown. However, in the end, a hospital called Four Winds in Katonah, New York, said they would take me—free of charge.

Four Winds

Apparently, an administrative debate had taken place at Four Winds before admitting me. Was I an immoral person who didn't deserve the hospital's free care, or was I, like my dead child, a victim of Joel Steinberg? Those with the latter opinion prevailed, but three patients on my unit felt differently and gave me a cool welcome. On one of my first days, one of them even removed himself from the lunch table when I sat down. I'd not yet been exposed to such attitudes, and I was stunned.

Sam Klagsbrun, the director of Four Winds, had decided he would be my doctor, though, as head administrator, he rarely took on patients anymore. The first time I met him, I was favorably impressed, noting in my journal: "He said he'll be direct and expects me to be so, too. I like that." I felt that Sam, as everyone called him, was, in fact, a lot like Dr. Opler.

Wanting to begin by gaining my confidence, Sam first discussed my childhood with me and slowly got to Joel and Lisa. He's told me that he tried very hard not to take on the guru role. And we both think he succeeded even though I have great admiration and respect for him. We even became adversaries at times, especially regarding Joel. Quite early on, Sam came down heavily against my former lover, comparing him to Hitler and calling him evil. Still feeling much in love with Joel and not taking in the full impact of all the atrocities he'd committed, I was enormously defensive. But when Sam told me that he believed I wasn't delusional, as I'd been diagnosed at

Columbia Presbyterian, but "influenced"—which I now see as a polite term for "brainwashed"—I felt he was right on target. And because of his conclusion, Sam took me off the Trilofon to no ill effects. Obviously I'd never needed the drug in the first place.

More about Four Winds

At Four Winds I had a great deal more therapy than simply private sessions with Sam. Just as in college students have a schedule of classes, each patient had a schedule of groups to attend: art therapy, psychodrama, conventional talk therapy groups, assertiveness training, arts and crafts workshops, and physical activities consisting of groups walks or sports. We also had visual journals in which to draw feelings whenever they came up, something I used extensively, talks each day with one or another of the staff, and I had individual art therapy because it was an effective vehicle of expression for me.

Four Winds had several units, each in a different unlocked cottage. There was no gate and no guard at the entrance, though, of course, patients were obligated to stay on the grounds. The hospital's more than 20 buildings were located on a beautiful estate, said to be formerly owned by P.T. Barnum. Instead of concrete, I was surrounded by grass, trees, and flowers that changed with the seasons.

This was a place where I could and did grow, where I came to understand what had happened to me, to mourn my losses, to stop loving Joel. Here my artistic abilities, somewhat developed before I met him but which had lain dormant during my twelve-and-a-half years with Joel, resurfaced. I'd always wanted to throw pots on a potter's wheel, and when I saw the Four Winds art workshop had such wheels, I worked hard at mastering the technique and got individualized instruction at it. And although I had done a bit of darkroom photography in the past, I'd never studied it. Now I did, and, in fact, I eventually sold some of my work.

At Four Winds, I thoroughly renewed my relationship with my parents and sister who visited me weekly and telephoned often. To this warm place came old friends who wanted to show their support and love for me. Slowly, I started to come back to life.

Facing My Loss

When reading my journals from Four Winds, I see a human being beginning to reemerge and starting to deal with reality. Now I frequently had to handle the pain of seeing other children visiting their parents.

Today there are several children visitors around—little girls. I wished my little girl could be visiting me. If only she could— somehow if I could turn time back. Then I would save her.
and
Sundays always make me sad. A lot of children come to visit, and they always make me wish my children could... I feel bereft.

And then one day, about a month after I'd arrived, I dealt head on with my pain about Lisa's death. In psychodrama, in which patients act out past, future, or imaginary events as a therapeutic tool, I was given the opportunity to say good-bye to Lisa, something I'd never gotten a chance to do.

At first I hesitated doing the psychodrama, saying, "I don't want to say good-bye to Lisa. I want her to come back."

But when I went through with it, weeping the whole time, it was a great catharsis and a big step in my healing process. I chose a small, slender young woman to play Lisa's part, and when I hugged her, she felt like Lisa; it was almost like holding my little girl in my arms again. Oh, how the tears flowed.

The tears, however, weren't confined to me. Because saying good-bye to a departed loved one touched everyone in that room in some personal way, as I wept, so did everyone else. One of the psychodrama instructors later told me that she'll never forget that remarkable day, as I certainly will not.

Ready to Fight

Everyone said the same thing—TV reporters, newspaper columnists, magazine writers, and even Barry Scheck—Joel is going to lie and say that Hedda killed Lisa. *No way!* I thought at first. *He'd never do that to me. Never!* I was sure of it—until I heard Joel's attorney, Ira London, say in a radio interview, "HE didn't kill Lisa." That's when the truth hit me like a stone from a slingshot, and I wrote:

> You know what that means. There's no more guessing
> and wondering to do. He's going to say I did it...I
> can't believe he'd betray me like that, but he is going to.
> What will I do? It won't be easy. Joel is now my enemy.

The evidence to support that theory kept popping up. The magazine *Vanity Fair* published an article called "Joel Steinberg's Version," by Maury Terry. Joel's rendition was that he'd never hit me, and he wasn't even at home when Lisa was fatally injured. Man oh man, was I now ready to fight! I wasn't going to let Joel blame me for *his* crime.

> I've been fantasizing about testifying at Joel's trial, telling
> the truth, telling the jury that I'll tell the truth even where it's
> not favorable to me because I'm committed to the truth now.
> I won't lie for Joel anymore.

415

And yet, as amazing as it may seem to an outsider who's never been brainwashed or had Stockholm syndrome, I still maintained my love for him and ached to be with him—although certainly *not* at Rikers.

So shortly thereafter when Barry urged me to sue Joel for assault, I agreed, even though I'd refused when Betty had suggested the same months before. Now I was ready to do it.

My sister, Judy, was also ready to fight. A second article, "What Lisa Knew," by Joyce Johnson, in that same alarming issue of *Vanity Fair*, was full of lies about and condemnation of me. When Judy read that, she was enraged and was almost desperate to find a way to help me. But what could she do? She felt she needed to speak with a feminist who knew the media, someone she could assume was on my side. So, on the spur of the moment, she called *Ms. Magazine* and left a message for the well-known feminist, Gloria Steinem. To Judy's great surprise, Ms. Steinem called her back, and they had several long conversations. She advised Judy to write a letter to the editor of *Vanity Fair* and to inform the magazine that it would be coming so that they'd reserve space for it in the next issue, all of which Judy did. Her letter pointed out the distortions in Ms. Johnson's article and defended her sister to the max. Judy then brought the letter by hand to *Vanity Fair's* office, and it was printed in the next issue.

I Talk to the ADA's

By the time the two Assistant District Attorneys on the case, John McCusker and Peter Casolaro, came to see me on May 5th—already convinced by Barry that I was innocent—I was well-equipped to assert why I'd be able to testify in front of Joel, a jury, and the public:

> Joel blamed everything that went wrong on me, but I won't let him do it this time. He's taken so much from me—my children, my beauty. He has to pay for it.

Two days later, the two ADA's announced that they were recommending that the charges against me be dropped. Naturally, the press grabbed the story and told the world that I planned to testify against Joel. Knowing that he'd be reading about this, I felt a huge conflict and wrote:

> I wonder what Joel's thinking. I hope he realizes that he blew it when he gave that *Vanity Fair* interview. It has given me an excuse to testify on my own behalf. He threw the first stone. But even so, I feel a little disloyal. It's absurd! But I do…I have tears in my eyes. Maybe I'm saved, but Joel's doomed.

In these confused words, I see growth, progress. At least I realized the absurdity of feeling disloyal to Joel, although I didn't recognize that the first stone had been thrown back in 1978—the very first time Joel hit me.

The *New York Post* Comes A-snooping

Thursday, September 1, 1988, 6:56 p.m. I was just accosted by a reporter who apparently took my picture with a telephoto lens as I walked out of the dining room. As I approached, he said, "Miss Nussbaum?"

"Yes," I answered, thinking he was the psychologist who'd done the psych testing on me. That's when he introduced himself, saying he was a reporter from the *New York Post*.

"Will you answer a few questions?"

"No," I responded and kept on walking, but he started to chat.

"You look really good."

"Thank you."

"I see you have some papers there." I was carrying some negatives and contact prints from the photo workshop.

"Photography," I answered; I shouldn't have.

"Oh, you've been doing that here? Now can I ask you

the big question? Everyone wants to know, will you testify at the trial?"

"You can ask me," I said, "but I won't answer." I guess that was a little wise-ass. But he deserved it.

Suddenly Larry Arpino (one of the Four Winds staff) grabbed me, saying, "He has a camera!"

But it was too late. He'd taken a picture from afar before he talked to me. Pam (a sister resident) had seen him and run to get Security.

Well, it's exciting anyway. However, I don't want anyone to know at what level I'm functioning. This guy does. There's been so much speculation about my brain-damage and whether or not I'm capable of testifying. I should have said nothing to him after my first, "No." But these reporters are sneaky and catch you off guard.

12:00 midnight. Sam saved the day. I got a message that he was on the phone for hours with lawyers and finally with the *Post*. He has conveyed to them that if they print the story, Four Winds will sue them for trespassing. So that may stop them and other papers.

Friday, September 2, 12:25 p.m. Well, I made the front page of the *New York Post* again. That guy took more pictures of me than we'd realized. The one on the front page has me walking with Pam after lunch. I don't know how she's going to react to that. Pam hasn't let anyone know she's in a psych hospital.

They quote me as saying stuff I never said, but nothing bad.

"I feel good. I'm healthy."

"They're good to me here. The people are nice, and I do my photography."

And then after I'm asked about testifying, "'I can't talk about any of that yet. I'm sorry,' she said. After a brief pause, she added, 'But I hope everything works out.'"

They flatter Four Winds by describing the surroundings as "lush," with "dormitory-like quarters," while never mentioning the hospital's name. I'm sure they're hoping that flattery will prevent a suit.

Still, everyone here is freaked about the article. In Large Group they expressed their fear: loss of confidentiality. And it's all my fault. I told them how I feel—that I ought to leave the hospital so they won't be in danger. They all jumped in with nos. People said lovely things to me about caring about me, loving me, feeling like I'm a sister, my being more important than their confidentiality, etc. That's so kind, so loving, and I'm truly moved. Getting to know me caused them to change from hostility to love and caring. On the other hand, I'd better buy a wig to wear whenever I go out from now on!

<> <> <> <> <> <>

Update: Here's the outcome of what happened with the *New York Post*. Four Winds sued them for trespassing and won. What did the *Post* have to pay? Not money; instead, Four Winds won their only demand—that the *Post* never again be allowed to enter the hospital grounds.

As to Pam, I had a difficult time convincing her to sue as well, but I succeeded. Unfortunately, she lost after several years of legal delays. Freedom of the press won over the right of privacy.

What about Joel?

I wasn't the only one pursued by the press. Joel was in the newspapers every day, too; I avidly read as many reports about him as possible. He unsuccessfully sought a case dismissal based on the press hype in November, he was disbarred because it was discovered that he'd gotten an improper exemption from the New York bar exam—based on one of his well-executed bullshit stories, and Joel's friend Peter Sarosi pleaded guilty to charges of illegally placing Mitchell for adoption. Ira London said that if disclosures about Joel's character and habits were made, they would deprive him of a fair trial; the judge disagreed, the disclosures were made, and the papers were full of articles about Joel's cocaine addiction and tax dodging. And then Joel was denied bail.

Still fascinated by the man who had captivated my heart and soul for so long, I studied not only the newspaper stories of Joel but also the photos. I was stymied by his always being shown wearing eyeglasses: in the past, he'd worn them only for reading. But apparently he now wore them all the time. Everything was changing.

The newspapers also gave me some new insights, especially the news about his disbarment. I now realized that Joel hadn't told me the truth about much of his past. I'd naturally assumed he'd taken the bar exam. He'd often told me about missing his college graduation to go into the air force, and that, too, was apparently untrue. I was stunned and found it all hard to believe. I wrote that I was upset about being

> ...duped so badly by Joel. My whole world—
> the world I'd built around Joel—is crushed. How
> could I have so misperceived him?

Sam compared me to a concentration camp victim who comes to identify with his torturer. He was concerned about getting me to put myself—not my torturer—first. During a chat, one of the staff members suggested I talk in a group about some of the worst things Joel ever did to me so it would no longer be "a little secret" between us. I decided to try it, and I did, although it was extremely difficult to say aloud such horrible things about my mahatma. Progress was slow.

And then one "historic day," as I phrased it in my journal, I felt angry with Joel. At the time, I thought it was my first anger experience ever. I'd repressed all anger for so many years that I'd actually forgotten that I'd ever known how to feel it—that is until I recalled becoming furious with my roommate Risa on a trip to Greece. Wow! I was normal!

The next step in my progress was the following fantasy about Joel, which I recorded in my journal:

> ...his love for me caused him to do what I
> requested, and he told the truth [at the upcoming
> trial]. Now that's switching it to my power over
> him instead of his over me.

I was getting there.

Mental and Physical Health

Feeling good again, I wanted to get back into my old habit of running. But after several sessions of jogging around and around the softball diamond, my left knee—the one Joel had broken—swelled to the size of a grapefruit. I tried bandaging the knee before running, I tried ice, I tried everything, but eventually I had to realize that I'd never be able to run again, and that Joel Steinberg was the cause.

And then two things happened. First, I began to obsess about Mitchell. I wanted to see him. I wanted him back. I was sorry I'd given him up. Then I began to have flashes of slitting my wrists whenever I thought about him or Lisa. "What good is life without them?" I wrote.

I began drawing the wrist-cutting images in my visual journal—graphic, bloody pictures. So I was suicidal, you say. Not so fast. I knew I wasn't; I definitely wanted to live. But why such images? Eventually I realized that the blood stood for my pain. Whenever I felt that pain, I drew a picture of myself bleeding or even cutting myself. Somehow drawing the image worked as a substitute for acting on the feelings. The art therapist convinced me to show the drawings to the other patients in our group. They reacted with shock because I certainly didn't seem suicidal.

"I'm not," I replied. "You see, by putting my feelings on paper, I don't have to act on them."

This was an excellent lesson for all.

By drawing it, I didn't have to act on it.

At the same time, visitors commented on how much straighter and taller I was looking. All the therapy and lots of walking at Four Winds had done my posture good. Joel's assaults and the restraints he'd put on me had caused me, literally, to hunch over in a posture both protective and demoralized. Now that I was freeing myself from his subjugation, reclaiming my body, I could walk tall again. And because I walked so much at Four Winds, I could move faster without pain from my arthritis.

Educating the DA's

As the summer of 1988 progressed, the ADA's and I signed an agreement. Contrary to what the press continually reported, I did *not* agree to testify against Joel in exchange for having charges against me dropped. The agreement stated that if I told the truth, and if the DA's office found no new evidence that proved my culpability, they would drop the charges against me. I agreed to testify, *if* asked; testifying was not a condition for dropping the charges. It was based, instead, on their belief in my story and in my inability to have committed the crime. In fact, to be sure the public understood this, the DA's office dropped the charges against me *before* I testified—not after, as it were some sort of reward.

This preceded a long series of meetings—totaling about 200 hours—with the two ADA's on the case and a detective, Angela Amato, sometimes together and sometimes separately. Although Amato was familiar with domestic violence, McCusker and Casolaro weren't, and they truly got an education from my recital of life with Joel Steinberg. I told them detailed stories of his abuse, how it had gradually become the norm, why I loved and trusted him so much, and of my great love for Lisa and Mitchell. And from the ADA's I gleaned tidbits about Joel's reactions to things and what they'd learned about him from documents. I was floored by the number of lies Joel had told me. He'd embellished not only on his grades in school and the work he'd done in the DIA, but even on the way his father had died! I began to wonder if he'd ever told me the truth about anything. I invented a character in my visual journal called "The Ugly Green Lie Monster," and drawing pictures of him eased my pain.

The ugly green lie monster holds Miss Truth and Innocence in his grasp. She does not recognize him. But it's not too late. 7/25

I pictured Joel as the Ugly Green Lie Monster.

Visiting Lisa's Grave

Lisa lay buried less than half an hour from Four Winds Hospital. I'd often thought about visiting, but I'd not felt strong enough to take such a large step. But now I did.

A local rabbi had been a good friend to me, and I asked if he'd accompany me to the cemetery. At first, as I looked at the tiny marker deluged by sympathetic visitors with flowers and toys, and at the words, "Elizabeth Launders (Lisa)," I didn't feel Lisa's presence. This was just a spot in a cemetery; Lisa was in my heart, not here.

But then after the rabbi said some prayers, I asked him for a few solitary moments at the grave. Once alone, I bent down on my knees and began to sing:

> Good-night, Lisa,
> Good-night, Lisa,

And then I felt the power of my loss. Tears streamed down my face as I sang to my child one last time.

> Good-night, Lisa,
> It's time to go to sleep.

Since that time I've been paying a visit to Lisa's grave several times a year. I like to go there around her birthday and bring her a gift—usually artificial flowers because I can't bear to leave flowers that die. Also, at Halloween time I carve a jack-o-lantern and leave it for her—symbolic of the ones her Daddy was too cheap to allow her to have while alive, and also in memory of her last conscious day on earth.

The Day My Eyes Opened

I still maintained an image of Lisa as an always happy little girl (at least until her last few months). I wasn't yet willing to acknowledge the pain she must have felt because of the regular abuse her daddy inflicted on her mommy, nor of being pulled into the conflict between us, of being deprived of seeing her grandparents, of the fear she must have felt of what was happening around her. I couldn't even see, as yet, that she might have felt deprived by not having her own room or a real bed.

But during two sessions with the ADA's and Barry in Manhattan, they all hammered at these kinds of issues. In fact, during the second such meeting, Barry repeatedly badgered me with statements like these:

"Do you think a little girl could be happy not having a real bedroom fixed up just for her?"

"And what Jewish girl doesn't even go clothes shopping with her mother?"

Feeling defensive, I became so angry that I actually threw my handbag at him. I felt shocked and embarrassed by my behavior. Until that point, I'd not been able to demonstrate the few angry feelings I'd experienced toward Joel, and here I was, taking them out on Barry. So I worried, would my outburst prompt the DA's to think I was, after all, capable of killing Lisa? But fortunately, they seemed to understand.

On the way back to Katonah in a car driven by a law student, we passed

Gate of Heaven Cemetery where Lisa is buried, and I was overwhelmed with painful thoughts of my sweet little girl's suffering. When I got back to Four Winds Hospital, friends there tried to comfort me, but I didn't want to be touched. That night I slept fitfully and awoke before 5:00 a.m. Grabbing my robe and two journals—visual and writing—I tiptoed into a public room where I copied a picture of Joel from a newspaper. And as I did so, the truth I'd blinded myself to for so long suddenly hit me, and my "eyes" opened wide.

> I once was lost,
> But now I'm found.
> Was blind,
> But now I see.

I saw my own responsibility for not realizing the truth about Joel until it was too late to save Lisa. For that truth, I hated Joel, and although curse words were not my wont in those days, full of passion, I wrote beside the drawing of him:

> You lousy fuckin' sonofabitch! Look what you did to me! You humiliated me. You kept me a prisoner. You beat me. And all in front of our child. You tortured her, too, by doing that. You sick piece of shit! And you're so cheap that you deprived her of the normal pleasures of childhood! I thought you gave her so much love it more than outweighed all the other factors. Well I was wrong! It didn't! You controlled her, too. She had to be secretly terrified. There were no mousetraps in the wall, you sick shit! It was your vibes keeping her awake. You had hit her. She had to see her life turning into what mine was. Beatings upon beatings. Bruises, blood, horror. My poor baby. Poor Lisa. Why didn't I see it? Why didn't I stop it? I'm learning now. "A lesson too late for the learning."

And on the next page, I wrote, with tears pouring from my eyes as I wailed audibly:

> I'm sorry, Lisa. I'm sorry. I didn't see. I'm sorry. It's too late to see now, Lisa. But maybe we can help others. Maybe we can

save another child's life. That's not enough for us. But it's all we have, Lisa. Lisa, Lisa—I'm sorry. God forgive me. I'm sorry.

From that moment forward, I no longer felt in love with Joel. From that moment forward, I was committed to helping other victims of domestic violence—a promise I've been fulfilling ever since. In fact, it's the principal reason I'm writing this book.

Feelings

During the summer and fall of 1988, I'd get strong surges of anger toward Joel, like the day I drew a picture of my hand squashing him between thumb and forefinger. But then the angry feelings would disappear. Sam thought that as long as I maintained any positive feelings at all toward Joel, it was possible that I'd choose another abusive man someday. God forbid!

In a second meaningful psychodrama, I hit "Joel" over the head with throw pillows, grabbed "Lisa" and ran out of the room with her. "Too late," I wrote afterwards.

Autumn leaves filled me with a sad longing for Lisa, thinking of the red and orange ones she and I had collected together. Any Halloween reminders such as a pumpkin, which brought up thoughts of Lisa's last night as a functioning human being, were unendurable then. But in recent years I'm proud to say I've turned that painful concept on its head. Instead of avoiding Halloween symbols, I celebrate them with Lisa by carving a jack-o-lantern and placing it at her graveside.

A Letter and a Letter

On September 9, 1988, my visual journal once again became a place for words instead of drawings when I entered into it two letters—one to Mitchell and one to Lisa.

Dear Mitchell,

My very dear little boy, I miss you. However, I'm writing this to tell you that I now realize what a horrendous situation you were living in. Yes, you got acres of love from me. And I didn't see how you were saved by returning to Nicole; I only thought about my own loss and yours. What a tragedy for you to suddenly lose your mother, your father, and your sister all at once—the people you saw every day, the people who loved you, played with you, fed you. Yes, your mother particularly, who not only fed you, changed your diapers and clothes, bathed you, spoiled you so that you wouldn't go to sleep anyplace, at night, but in my arms. But now I see, dear Mitchell, that you've been saved from trauma and, who knows, possible death yourself. Yes, I miss you, and there's a large hold in my heart from whence you've been snatched; but I'm happy for your safety and thank God for it because I love you so much. Oh, Mitchell, (You'll always be Mitchell to me.) I miss you so much. I want to sit in the rocking chair and hold you in my arms and rock you to sleep.

You were saved from tragedy last November, but now I am sane again and strong again and more than capable of giving you a good life. But this is one of the prices I must pay for my blindness, deafness, and dumbness—loss of you, my baby.

Goodbye, Mitchell. Goodbye. May you have love, as much as I would have given you; understanding; comfort; peace; wholeness; and happiness, whatever that is. Know this, that my love for you will always be there, and I will always be there for you if you ever need a mother's love.

Goodbye, Mitchell.

I love you.

Mommy

* * * * * *

Lisa, Lisa. I don't have to say, "Dear Lisa," because all I need to do is think, and my thoughts will be absorbed by my surroundings—the air; and from there they will float to you. Your essence is. You are not.

How can I say I'm sorry, Lisa? If only I could undo what is done, but I cannot. If only I could be at 14 West 10th Street with today's mind and turn back time to a year ago, then I would see, I would hear, I would speak; I would save you. And we would still be together, you, me, and Mitchell. No, it wouldn't be easy. I guess a year ago would be too late for us all to stay together. But at least I could save your life. I care what the world thinks, but I care most about you. You're the one I want to say "I'm sorry, Lisa," to. I'm sorry, Lisa. I'm sorry. No matter what I do, I can never make it right again. I'll help battered women and abused children, I'll dedicate books to you, I'll do and do, but one thing I can't do is to bring you back. My dear little girl. You were beautiful and loving and giving. There's nothing I can do now. I didn't perceive. I didn't know your terror. I didn't hear your cry for help. I didn't see your bruises. I didn't tell the police the truth. Maybe if I had last October…Maybe, maybe, maybe. "What is done cannot be undone. Once the moment passes it never comes again." I lived with my own truth. You died for it. I don't want your forgiveness; I want your life back.

Getting the Charges Dropped

September 28, 1988. Even though Joel is in jail and I'm living relatively free at Four Winds Hospital, I still have charges pending against me—murder charges. Today's the day they're scheduled to be dropped. Phew! Even though I've never worried about being convicted, knowing the charges have been liquidated will be a relief.

So here I am waiting in the Criminal Courts building in Manhattan, and I've been anxiously twiddling my thumbs for hours. Here's why. A Long Island convict suddenly declared he can produce pornographic videotapes of me and Lisa. So of course the DA's office is giving him a chance to do so. Aargh! What if he can really do it? I've recently ruled out all that sex stuff, but who knows? I've never been absolutely positive about it.

So here I sit in Angela Amato's office waiting for the Suffolk County "honcho" to make contact with this prisoner. Now they tell me that he may be some nut who always gives the DA's crazy leads, a convict who regularly comes up with weird stories just to get a day out of jail and a meal outside. So we're waiting to see if it's him. I sure hope it is.

Yes, it's him! Hooray! But we're still not going to court today; the charges won't be dropped after all. Suffolk County still wants to talk to this lunatic and maybe investigate. They don't know him the way the Manhattan DA's do. So the case has been adjourned til next Wednesday. I sure hope it all gets straightened out. What a tiring, stressful, disappointing day this has been.

<>< >< >< >< >

Update: As you might well have guessed, Suffolk County's nutty prisoner never came up with any tapes. But the next day, another character jumped on the bandwagon, declaring that *he* had such tapes. At that point, the DA's office decided to do a thorough investigation in case the issue came up at trial. The inquiry proved that the tapes, and their supposed content, were simply a product of Joel's sick mind.

Finally, on October 26th, a day after the opening statements had been made in Joel's trial, all criminal charges against me were dropped. As I walked down the courthouse hallway to the courtroom with a policewoman holding each arm as if I were a prisoner, Barry Scheck appeared, took me by the hand, led me away from the two officers, and walked into the courtroom still holding my hand. My hero! I was overwhelmed by his demonstration of caring and respect for my dignity. The proceedings lasted exactly 22 seconds, and then, technically, I was a free woman, although I still needed to remain at Four Winds to get me through the trial and beyond.

A Mother's Tears

On the first anniversary of the loss of both my children, I wrote the following poem, entitled "A Mother's Tears."

An empty lap,
An empty heart,
I cry and cry for you.
I see your smiles,
Hear your laugh.
My memories are sweet.
A scrapbook of pictures
And ruined dreams.
These are left for me.
One is dead.
One is gone.
My tears won't go away.

The Talented Ms. Steinberg

One day, at the ADA's office, Angela, the detective with whom I spent a great many hours, said she had something to show me. It was a story Lisa had written in school, brought to the prosecutor's office by Ms. Weiss, the student teacher who'd already testified at Joel's trial.

> My Mom is a book writer. She gives me
> books for me. They are Random House books.

Wow! I knew my little girl was proud of my book writing, but to see her actual words moved me to tears; I was *so* impressed that she actually knew the name of my publisher and how to use chapters. This piece about her mom was the first chapter. There was also a "Chapter To" about her brother, a "Chapter 3" about her sailboat, and a "Chapter 4" about her aunt. But what a shame that her teacher had collected all the stories Lisa had written, and so I'd never seen any of them.

Months after the trial, I asked Peter Casolaro to send me copies of all the stories the school had given him, and he did it! So I now have those selected few, all of which are spelled phonetically—more or less. This was how Lisa was being taught to write in first grade. Spelling would come later—had there been a "later." In fact, here's the exact way she wrote the above chapter:

My Mom is a book rater She gevs me
books for me They aer Randan hoess books.

My parents also gave me every card Lisa had created for them, which they'd saved and treasured. But being parents, their own child's happiness came first, and they relinquished the cards to me. Having in my hands Lisa's words and drawings was like getting back a small piece of my little girl. Even today, I'm filled with joy and pride every time I look at them. In fact, a friend has put onto a computer disk an incredible painting Lisa did, one that shows a talent far beyond her years. From that came glossy prints, which I've hung—and even have pins and magnets of—all of which light up my life.

The Trial

Now *New York v. Joel Steinberg,* a trial for second-degree homicide and first-degree manslaughter, was in full swing, and for the first time ever, cameras were allowed in a New York courtroom—as a test. So of course all TV news programs had trial tape, which was shown as the first item every day. Newspaper reporters seemed to enjoy the ugly material they dealt with:

> *The New York Post*—Joel Steinberg was depicted yesterday as
> a domineering and brutal murderer by prosecutors who said he
> beat his illegally-adopted daughter to death—and so terrified
> his lover that she did nothing to save the child.
> But defense lawyers immediately counterattacked—accusing
> Steinberg's lover, Hedda Nussbaum, of being mentally ill and
> dabbling in Satanism, sado-masochism and pornography.

I'm certain you can imagine my pain when reading such lies about me. My parents and Judy were also agonized by this. In an effort to improve my image, they gave interviews to the press, talking about the beautiful and virtuous person they knew me to be and how they supported me totally. Reporters opportunistically grabbed at the chance to speak with my family, rang their doorbell at all hours, showed up at the senior center where my parents spent a lot of time, and generally invaded their privacy. But Mommy,

Daddy, and Judy never shirked from doing whatever they could to help me. In spite of their efforts, the distorted viewpoint of the press dominated the news. Regardless of the content, I followed the news obsessively. When I first heard that the judge in the trial would be Harold J. Rothwax, I was pleased. I recalled that Joel had always held him in respect for being an honest and tough judge. However, since those qualities wouldn't serve Joel's purposes at this time, he repeatedly tried to get Justice Rothwax replaced—without success.

In Peter Casolaro's opening statement, he said of Lisa, "Prompt medical care would have saved her." *But,* I wondered, *would she have been severely brain-damaged? Would life in that state have been worse than no life at all? And, finally, were these thoughts ways of avoiding my own responsibility for not summoning help immediately?* I was torn between that thought and my knowledge of how Joel's brainwashing had affected my reasoning powers. I didn't yet realize how the repeated traumas I'd suffered at Joel's hands had numbed me, and that the full responsibility fell directly on him, not me.

Early testimony indicated that on November 2, 1987, Joel had been told at St. Vincent's that Lisa might be brain-dead. I'd never learned of this before, and I was horrified. When Joel had come home from the hospital, he'd said he thought Lisa could have been brain-damaged due to lack of oxygen while she wasn't breathing. Might he have misunderstood the nurse's words? That was the first thought to enter my programmed brain. But I questioned it. Why then did he leave the hospital so suddenly after hearing those words?

I especially couldn't wait until the student teacher from Lisa's class, Stacy Weiss, got on the stand and, I hoped, talked about some of the things that made me so proud of my child: her intelligence, her caring for others, her teacher's-dream behavior. But that didn't happen until November 17th, more than two weeks into the trial. And in addition to the wonderful things I'd hoped to hear, Ms. Weiss testified about seeing bruises all over Lisa's legs, one on her lower back that showed when she lifted her arms in a short shirt, a black eye, and a bruise on her forehead. She said Lisa's clothes were dirty, her hair unkempt, and that she had a patch of missing hair. I understood the missing hair as a result of that incident on Joel's sailboat, but was shocked at the rest. I never saw any leg bruises or the back bruise. And I apparently didn't recall the forehead bruise, which I now remember Joel had urged Lisa to claim had been inflicted by her brother. I did recall a slight discoloration that might be called a black eye, but not when Lisa had it nor how she'd gotten it. Dirty and unkempt? I'd washed Lisa's clothes daily, and the photos taken at school showed her in neat and clean attire. I was extremely distressed. Had I simply not been seeing things accurately at that time or had I blocked these terrible circumstances from memory?

The next day in Art Workshop drew a picture I described in my journal like this:

> I drew three me's: Hear no evil, see no evil, speak no evil. I didn't see Lisa's bruises. Didn't perceive that she was in a coma. She'd be all right. I didn't hear Joel's lies. I believed truth was his credo. I didn't speak the truth to the hospitals and the police. I was protecting Joel—and my own shame [at being battered—another new realization].

But now I saw, I heard, and I was ready to speak.

The Trial Continues

One dramatic piece of evidence from the prosecution was the videotape taken of me at the 6th Precinct the day I was arrested. The newspapers reported that the jury members seemed shocked and disturbed by my condition, and I certainly understand why; it's a chilling view of the depths to which a battered woman can sink.

Although I'd stopped watching the TV news because it upset me tremendously, I was in the room that night when this disturbing videotape suddenly appeared on the TV screen. There I was, debilitated, dazed, bruised, broken, with yellow pus oozing from my leg. Like the jury, I was shocked at my appearance. I'd not realized how wretched I had looked then and how poorly I must have been functioning in that state.

The next time I saw Peter and John, the ADA's, they told me how the medical testimony had demolished each and every one of Joel's previous defenses: that Lisa's injuries came from the EMS or from a fall, that she'd died of Reye's Syndrome, etc. Joel had come up with a host of such creations—a new one each time an earlier one was proven impossible. Now, I was informed, there was no defense left but to blame me. I felt ready to handle it.

When a *New York Times* story contained a photograph of former Detective Foster William Lachenmeyer on the stand holding Joel's exercise bar, the same bar Joel had used to beat in my head time after time, I shuddered and couldn't look. I felt as though the exercise bar were the culprit—not Joel. And in spite of all my realizations about him, I still didn't have the same kind of terror-filled, repellent emotions when I looked at *his* picture.

Another photo in that same *New York Times* story had a similar effect; I had to quickly turn the page. It was a picture of Lisa in the hospital, showing bruises on her back and an injury to her head. However, the worst photo of all for me, next to that of the little white coffin, was one I saw of Lisa in the hospital, comatose, with breathing tubes taped to her face. I became so distraught, Four Winds put me on suicide watch for the rest of that day.

Last Minute Desperation

As the day approached when I'd mount the stand to testify, Joel made some last-minute attempts to influence me, the first in a letter to a *Newsday* reporter:

> My feelings for Lisa are almost inexpressible. She was the world to me. Just once, look at her smile in one of those photographs and you will understand my feelings. My sadness and sense of loss are more than I can bear at times.
>
> Regarding Hedda, I must tell you that I loved her very much. All that has occurred since, has not changed the feelings I held for her. I can only hope that she is capable of the truth in relating the events of Lisa's life and the events of Lisa's last night with us. Given what I have read, I fear Hedda may no longer be the person I knew and loved.
>
> The message I would like to give to Hedda is—Please speak the truth to my jury.

And that's exactly what I did, although I'm sure Joel's subliminal message to me was, *Remember our love and please* don't *tell the truth.*

The day after publication of that letter, an interview Joel granted with a TV reporter was aired across the country. After seeing it, I wrote in my journal:

"Well, I saw the interview. Joel directed most of it at me. He said I'm a beautiful person, he loves me, etc. He said whenever I see pictures of Mitchell on television he knows I smile. No, I cry. Anyway, I wasn't moved by him, but by pictures of Lisa.

Barry responded to Joel's interview with, 'This is a Svengali-type maneuver to manipulate Hedda and resurrect the power he once had over her...a last ditch attempt to discourage Hedda from testifying against him.'"

But it didn't work, and I *did* testify.

I hoped and prayed that my testimony would demolish Joel's lies.

I Testify

Thursday, December 1, 1988—5:30 p.m. I did it! I testified about all the events of November 1st and 2nd of last year—exactly as they occurred. Joel knows that I told the truth, the whole truth, and nothing but the truth.

I was very nervous at first, and I couldn't think clearly. But it got easier. One of the things that helped was making sure I didn't look at Joel. I sat so that the judge's banc blocked my view of him. Only when the lawyers had sidebar discussions did I change seats; then I couldn't avoid seeing him. But I felt nothing for him—even when he looked right at me, although he *did* look handsome in person. Photos of Joel never were flattering.

After I testified, I spoke on the phone with Mommy and Daddy who'd, of course, watched me on TV. I'm so impressed with Mommy. I'd been awfully worried about what she'd think when she heard my story. But here's what she said: "I'm so proud of you—just the way I was always proud of you when you were in school. I'm proud because you told the truth; as hard as it was for you,

you told the truth." What a mother!

11:30 p.m. I just watched a report about the trial on the 11:00 news. The story is *very* big—big enough for CBS to preempt its normal programming to show my testimony live, coming straight out of the courtroom camera to the entire nation. And since it's such a big deal and the DA's think I need protection, two police officers are sleeping in the adjoining room. We're at a hotel in the city so I can be at the courthouse bright and early tomorrow morning.

Friday, December 2nd—I actually felt a moment of sadness for Joel today as I watched him looking scared and helpless, frantically shuffling papers around while the jury was studying the phrases he'd made me write repeatedly: I will care about Joel's hair; I will care about Joel's teeth; I will acknowledge Joel positively and affirmatively; arguing is destructive, not constructive.

I watched the jurors faces as they read those programming, brainwashing assignments. Wow! You could see them thinking, "*Oh, my God!*"

And when I think about it today, I realize that what he did was *sick*! And he *should* feel terrible; he deserves to feel miserable—for making me write that stuff and for Lisa...dear, dear Lisa.

Monday, December 5th—Another trial day down. Joel's attorneys made a surprise move today. They requested adding an insanity *defense*—not an insanity *guilty plea*. DeLuzio (one of Joel's lawyers) said Joel didn't want it (Of course not! He'd never admit to insanity!), but DeLuzio said if what I've said is true, we're both clearly "nuts." Joel, he said, was offended by that term (tee hee). Anyway, the judge turned down the motion, saying they could offer it again with proper supporting documentation.

Also, this morning, the judge asked the panel if they'd heard what Mayor Koch said or had seen it in the papers. Apparently yesterday Koch said Joel is a "monster," and he would like to dip him many, many times in boiling oil. It's amazing that he would say such a thing. However, I love it, regardless of whether or not it's proper.

I wasn't on the stand at all in the morning, with all that going on. I was on for less than two hours total today—less than an hour to finish direct, and about an hour of cross. Sam, whom I spoke to on the phone twice, said I did fantastically well and drove Ira London (Joel's other attorney) crazy. I didn't let Ira get away with a thing. As Peter said yesterday, I'm smarter than both Ira and DeLuzio. Among other things, I made London clarify many of his imprecise questions that, if answered, would have been left open to interpretation.

One thing that wasn't so good today was that I had to talk about doing nothing after I saw Joel abuse Lisa. I actually cried on the stand, saying I don't know why I didn't act. This was one of the most painful moments of the trial for me so far.

Sam dealt with that very subject—why I didn't do more to help Lisa—in the latest *Newsweek*. That's what people have the most difficulty understanding. And so do I! Anyway, he says, "It's like what happens to someone in a concentration camp. They are reduced by virtue of physical torture, to a mere existence level. They shut off normal human emotions."

I'm also on the cover of *Newsweek*, and inside is a very good story about me and one about family violence. But I can't stand looking at the picture inside of the little white coffin being carried down the stairs. I remember sitting in bed in Elmhurst Hospital, alone, watching that on TV, seeing that little white coffin with my little girl in it. I cried and cried, all alone. I'm crying now. My little girl, my Lisa. My god, Joel is crazy. Lisa's dead… Lisa's dead.

Wednesday, December 7th—No trial today, and am I

glad! I was so exhausted all day yesterday. I'd slept only three hours Monday night. Then I was on the stand all day and feeling like everyone who heard me must have been thinking I was very crazy—Joel too—and that I was supporting his insanity defense.

Poor Michele Launders—hearing about imaginary cults, sexual abuse, drugs. I also felt horrid for admitting I'd thought Lisa was sexually abused and yet did nothing. How could Michele understand? She started to cry when she heard me say I took no action but left it to Joel's wisdom. I feel so bad for her. She looks like a frail, sad Lisa. She looks so much like Lisa, I cried. But I never saw her smile. Lisa was almost always smiling.

When I got back to Four Winds, there was a lot of supportive mail for me as well as three baskets of flowers—all from strangers. Every one of them said they think I'm very courageous. But I'm not, and I'm undeserving of their support because of what I talked about today—that I did nothing when Lisa was sexually abused. I was feeling totally unworthy and lay down with my teddy bear, cried a bit, dozed off, and dreamed a horrid dream. In it, "they" said "they" wanted to bring Lisa's body into the courtroom, but they weren't sure of Joel's sensitivities. I was awakened then because Sam had called. I got up and went to the phone, not sure if I'd been dreaming or if it was real. I think I sounded like a sleepy little girl, crying and asking him if it was true that they wanted to bring Lisa's body into the courtroom. He wants to discuss why I'd have such a dream.

Thursday, December 8th—Another day of testimony. At one or two points, when I sat on the side and looked at Joel, he gave me these "Poor me" looks. It's *his* fault, all of it, so I why should I have sympathy for him?

You know, Ira London's questions today conceded that Joel beat me! Of course, he wants to show that the battered became the batterer—that I was jealous of Joel's taking Lisa out to dinners and such, and that I was the one who killed her—that's the Defense's current strategy. The jury won't buy it—I think, I hope. But I'm still amazed that London admitted that Joel beat me. I'm even more amazed that Joel has admitted it. But I guess my testimony's scared the shit out of him, and he'll admit to that as long as he doesn't have to admit killing Lisa.

Wednesday, December 14th—I finished my testimony yesterday (Phew!) and then was too tired to write. I feel that most of Ira London's cross and especially his recross was feeble. He spent most of the time going over various hospital records, taking things out of context. He kept trying to twist meanings. It was pretty low.

According to the *Daily News*, Joel kept squirming all day nervously. At one point, they said, he stared at Barry and then mouthed, "You happy? You happy?"

Barry told a reporter, almost proudly, "He hates me. He blames me for turning Hedda against him." I loved the story and laughed and laughed. Seriously, however, Joel couldn't possibly understand all the factors that had caused my eyes to open so that I was no longer imprisoned by his brainwashing. So, of course, he'd blame Barry—or Sam or the DA's.

As I left the courtroom, I looked long at Joel. He looked back. I'd describe it as both of us looking without expression, but the *News* said he glared at me, and maybe it *was* a glare.

Beginning to Fulfill My Destiny

Whenever I now see video clips of my testimony, I'm flabbergasted by my appearance. I seem, as one of the jurors later described me, like "a mere shell of a woman." I thought I'd grown and changed enormously by the time I testified, yet I sounded so flat, so empty; there still seemed to be very little of me. It's hard for me to imagine what I must have been like in November of 1987. Joel had drained me of life. However, I would be able to regain it; Lisa wouldn't have that chance.

In spite of my hollowness, my testimony seemed to help many abused women all across the country. Because of the extreme publicity and the live TV coverage, they were finally able to hear what had always been kept hush-hush: a tale of abuse similar to theirs. The attention the press gave the story, although often painful to me and to Mommy, Daddy, and Judy, actually was a blessing to our society. It brought domestic violence out of the closet and into every American's living room. Thousands of women, I've since learned, sat mesmerized in front of their TV screens, identifying with my words as I testified. For years afterwards, in New York City and the suburbs surrounding it, women would approach me in supermarkets, at bus stops, and on the street, telling me of their fascination with my testimony and how they were similarly abused. Their stories would invariably move me; whenever a woman told me that because of my testimony she was inspired to leave her abusive husband, I knew I was fulfilling my promise to Lisa.

During the trial and beyond, I received about 200 letters containing messages like the following:

"Thank you Hedda from the depth of my soul for telling your story."

"You were the ultimate victim and you have spoken for so many of us."

"You have helped so many people you will never know. I wish you the very best and want you to know I completely understand."

"Your testimony brought your child back to life inside the hearts and minds of everybody listening."

"I wish someday I could meet you and just hug you for what you are going through."

"Please realize that a lot of people really *love* you and *care* about you."

"You're an inspiration to me."

At one point, I decided to answer every single letter—individually—and I did, giving rise to many a friendship, some of which exist to this day.

Personal Anguish

After I finished testifying, the trial still absorbed all my attention, even though it was now via reading newspapers—as many as I could get my hands on—and some magazines like *Time* and *Newsweek*. Also, once again, I was watching the TV news reports. Sometimes a letter to the editor or maybe a newspaper column would denounce me, and I'd feel deeply dejected. I didn't deserve such hate! Joel did, but not me. But I also felt undeserving of any praise I got from friends and relatives. It was a time of strong emotions and heavy stress.

A day post-testimony, Barry informed me over the phone, "There are a lot of people out there who hate you." Then he told me the following story: The previous day he'd called a car service to pick me up at the courthouse. When asked who the car was for, he gave my name, and the operator said something like, "She should only drown!" This sure made me feel like the pits. Too many people just didn't understand, especially when the press kept distorting the truth for a more dynamic story. Example: I testify one day that I lied to the police about Lisa's injuries in order to protect Joel. That night, CNN reports, "Hedda lied to cover her live-in lover." CBS says, "Hedda Nussbaum reveals why she lied." So then the general public, who doesn't learn all the details, thinks of me as a liar.

And then comes the defense case. London and DeLuzio's strategy was to denounce me, make me seem to have a motive for killing Lisa, and thereby

455

place reasonable doubt in the minds of the jury. It was agony—especially when a former client of Joel's got on the stand and lied, saying she'd seen me hit Lisa. I was outraged. *How dare she lie like that! I'd NEVER hit Lisa.* Here's what I wrote in my journal on January 4th.

> If you think things have been going badly, wait'll you hear this! Marilyn Walton was interviewed on TV tonight...She said she's going to testify that she saw me physically abuse Lisa—much worse than a spanking, she said. I was infuriated...She liked Joel a lot. She was jealous of me.

In light of Walton's feelings toward Joel, I pondered her motives. What had Joel promised her in exchange for her false testimony? And it certainly was false; here's what she said on the stand: she'd seen me whack Lisa on the side of her head and fling her across the room, and that she, Walton, almost came to blows with me over it—all absolute lies. *Did Joel promise that if she got him off, he'd marry her?* I wondered. After all, Peter Casolaro told me that Walton had visited Joel nine times at Rikers. Such a deal would've given them a lot to discuss.

Another aggravation was Susan Brownmiller and her book, *Waverly Place*. The novel was supposed to be based on Joel's and my story, but wasn't except for superficials, and it really showed zero understanding of domestic violence. Amazingly, the book was published even before the trial was over—in the hopes of making big money, of course. At that point, Brownmiller began making talk show appearances and giving newspaper interviews to promote the book—and denounce me. "I think Hedda Nussbaum was an accomplice," is one example of her infuriating words. The newspapers were full of the controversy Brownmiller inspired. Fortunately, the book was so poorly done that it never sold many copies. But in the meantime, it caused me much anguish.

The Trial Continues

Just as I'd predicted, Joel's lawyers did not introduce a formal insanity defense. Ira London said it would allow the prosecution to use it "to poison the jury's mind about Joel." But I was sure then and am still certain that Joel would *never* have agreed to such a defense. What? Him, insane? Ha! How could Joel Steinberg ever agree to *that*!? He was always the one referring other people to psychiatrists, but never once did he think that *he* might need such help. The only therapy he ever went to was Ed Eichel's group, which I know he considered different from all the rest; you could be perfectly normal and totally sane and still make good use of it.

Then the DA's asked the judge to allow a psychiatrist of their choosing to examine Joel, and Rothwax approved it. But although Joel met with the doctor, Mr. Steinberg didn't cooperate at all, which didn't surprise me one bit. And since Judge Rothwax said the results of the examination could be used by the prosecution if and only if Joel's lawyers introduced an insanity defense, nothing ever came of this exam.

The defense summation came on January 20, 1989. It was a direct attack on me: I murdered Lisa out of jealousy, they said; I blamed Joel and then faked mental illness to avoid being prosecuted for murder. Adrian DeLuzio said I was a poor excuse for a woman and a mother. Reading that, I broke down and cried. The press, however, didn't react to the defense summations in such an emotional way. One columnist said they were so boring that after

457

the lunch break most of the press left the courtroom to watch the trial on TV. But since I was feeling fervent about them, I called Peter Casolaro and told him, "Give 'em hell for me!" His summation was next.

And he did good. He said that the strongest witness was Lisa talking from her grave, delivering enough evidence to convict Joel of murder. He had beaten her to death, said Peter, because as she grew older, she began rebelling, and Joel was no longer able to control her.

"This isn't just depraved indifference to human life," he told the jury, "this is monumental indifference to human life."

"Let Lisa rest and punish her murderer."

The Verdict

So the trial was over all except for the jury's deliberations, and I had no idea that they would take eight full days to make their decision. The wait was agonizing for me. Pure torture, and I didn't stop eating the entire time.

The jury had to decide amongst four charges against Joel:

- Criminally negligent homicide: Causing death by negligence. Sentence: 1 1/3 - 4 years.
- Second-degree manslaughter: Recklessly causing serious injury. No need to prove intent. Sentence: 5 - 15 years.
- First-degree manslaughter: Intentionally causing serious injury. Sentence: 8 1/3 - 25 years.
- Second-degree murder: Showing depraved indifference to life, creating a grave risk of death. No need to prove intent. Sentence: 25 - life.

<><><><><>

Monday, January 30, 1989. The jury has finally come back! The verdict is guilty of first-degree manslaughter. Barry says it was obviously a compromise verdict. In any case, it shows that they

459

didn't consider me guilty at all. They said Joel had intent—which he didn't. I know he never intended to kill or seriously hurt Lisa. But I'm relieved that it's over and that they found *me* not guilty. I think 8 1/3 -25 years maximum sentence is appropriate and that Rothwax will give him the max. Sentencing is in four weeks.

<><><><><><>

Five members of the jury were interviewed immediately after the verdict was given, but the rest slipped away. The foreman told the press the jury's conclusion: that since I "was anemic and malnourished," I could not have struck the blows that killed Lisa. Ever since deliberations began, he went on, many jurors believed that the force of Joel's attack indicated intent to cause Lisa serious physical harm. But others felt differently and in the end voted for first-degree manslaughter to avoid a deadlock.

Sentence and Parole

On March 23, 1989, as I'd predicted, Joel Steinberg was given the maximum sentence for first degree manslaughter (childslaughter?): eight-and-a-third to twenty-five years. Judge Rothwax recommended that he serve the full term, without parole. But that didn't cause him to admit the truth or move him to remorse. As of this writing, Joel still continues to deny that he abused me or killed Lisa, still, as always, manufacturing his own truth.

In all he came up for parole five times, and helped by my efforts that generated many hundreds of letters and petitions, his application was rejected each time. I would think that after parole was denied once or twice, he'd have gotten the picture: that he should have admitted the truth and showed contrition. But Joel Steinberg never did that. Instead, I think he did what he'd done many times in the past—begin to believe his own lies. So today, I don't even know if Joel's mind understands what he did to the child he loved. But there's no doubt about it in my mind, and I won't forget, and I can't forgive.

In any case, with 8 1/3 years off for good behavior—he supposedly was a model prisoner—Joel's conditional release date was scheduled for June 30, 2004, which means at the time of release, he'd have served 17 years and 7 months. As I told a reporter after the fifth denial of Joel's application for parole (Yes, I'm still asked to give newspaper and TV interviews), I don't care what Joel does when he gets out of prison, as long as he stays far away from me.

461

Postscript

Like the blurb rolled across the screen at the end of a TV movie based on real people, I'll now tell you what's happened since 1989 to the major characters of this book. I'll concentrate on just three—Joel, Mitchell, and myself, since the fourth lies still where she was buried in Gate of Heaven Cemetery in Hawthorne, New York, where I visit often. I'm sure, however, that Lisa's soul has had much to do since that time and now probably inhabits another body—or else floats above us with the other angels.

However, on this earth, another Lisa Steinberg was being created as I was writing this chapter—a Lisa made of wood—a life-size silhouette of her, one of many images made by the Silent Witness Initiative, all of which represent victims of domestic violence. Across the chest of Lisa's Witness is a shield with these words:

Elisabeth "Lisa" Steinberg
Age 6
November 5, 1987

Lisa was in first grade with big blue eyes and strawberry blonde hair. She was bright, loved to roller skate, sing, draw and dance ballet. Lisa was loved by everyone and exuded love and kindness. She died of brain injuries after being struck with great force by her father, a lawyer in New York City. He was convicted of her murder and is currently serving time in prison.

This "Lisa," like all the silent witness images, will appear at events that highlight the need to end domestic violence.

< > < > < > < > < >

Mitchell Barnet Steinberg is now Travis Christian Smigiel Micoli since his mother, Nicole Smigiel, married John Micoli. Travis still lives in the same town where his mother lived when she was his age, 18. He has a brother and a sister. It is my fervent dream to one day meet and become friends with this young man.

For about three or four years after I left Four Winds Hospital to live on my own, Travis, whom I still think of as Mitchell, became my obsession. I had fantasies of disguising myself and becoming his nanny or of stealing away with him to South America. Whenever I'd hear a love song—an *I want you, I need you, I love you* kind of song—I'd weep, thinking of my little boy. Because Lisa was dead and buried, I had to accept her loss, but Mitchell was out there somewhere growing up, and I couldn't see him because his family did not wish for me to have any contact at all with him. My heart ached. I'd drive along in my car with a singer crooning a love song on the tape deck, and tears would stream down my eyes.

After several years of this, I decided one May to give myself a Mother's Day gift—to let go of my fixation. And I did it, so that although I never lost my love for Mitch, I did lose the obsession.

< > < > < > < > < >

I've not been privy to what's happened to Joel since 1989—other than that he was moved from Riker's Island Correctional Facility in New York City to Clinton Prison, somewhere in upstate New York and then to Southport Correctional Facility in Elmira, New York. Rumor has it that he was attacked and beaten so often at Clinton that he was moved to Southport where he's pretty much isolated from the general population. Yes, rumors have been my main source of information about him. I heard that while still at Rikers he'd been beaten so many times (prisoners are known to hate anyone who harms a child) that he had no teeth left. My reaction? Good! Let him know what it feels like to be a victim.

Joel appealed his verdict to the Appellate Division; it was denied. He then appealed it to the highest court in New York State, the Court of Appeals. It was denied. So Joel would have to live out his sentence and pray that he'd make parole. But after five tries, each parole hearing had the same result—release denied. Since Joel Steinberg does not accept responsibility for the crime he committed—no less show any remorse for it—how could a parole board possibly give him early release? I'm certain that the hundreds and maybe thousands of letters and petitions generated through my efforts each time Joel came up for parole helped the New York State Parole Board see that he was a danger to society and better off left in prison until his conditional release date, which was June 30, 2004.

On that date, he was released from Southport Correctional Facility accompanied by a feeding frenzy of reporters and is now living in New York City. What lies ahead for Joel depends on whether he complies with the conditions of his release. Among those is this: he may not have any contact with me, and of that I am truly glad.

< >< >< >< >< >

Obviously I know quite a bit more about my own life since 1989 and could write an entire book about it. But I'll be brief.

I left Four Winds Hospital on April 21, 1989, the same day that Daddy passed away. At first, neither Judy nor Mommy wanted to tell me, but they did, and I was strong enough to endure the news. He's buried, as is my mother, who died in November 2000, in the Jewish cemetery right next door to the Catholic one where their granddaughter lies.

I moved to a small rented cottage surrounded by grass, trees, and flowers somewhere not too far from my psychiatrist, Sam Klagsbrun, whom I continued to see for quite some time. I had no money and no job prospects. My name was anathema to many, and most of those who understood and sympathized with my situation were too cowardly to hire me. Certainly, editing juvenile books was out of the question.

I qualified to be retrained by New York State and learned word processing. But, in spite of unwavering efforts on my part, no job offers ensued. So I set up my own writing, editing, and word processing business, again with the state's help. But clients were quite few and far between. Fortunately, my family was able to help me somewhat financially, but mostly I had to live on the only money I had—my IRA. Yes, the penalties were high, and I wasn't able to stop withdrawing IRA funds until it was down to a mere $3,000. But I survived.

Since my years with Joel bestowed upon me a love of the law, I went back to school and became a paralegal. Ads for paralegal training said that it was the fastest growing new profession, but no one mentioned that in the area where I lived, you need at least two years experience to get a paralegal job. Catch 22: Where do you get the experience? I tried volunteering my services at a Legal Services center for six months. Still no paralegal job offers, finally leaving me with no option but to accept a job as a legal secretary with a good-hearted labor lawyer named Ralph P. Katz, now deceased.

For a short time after that, I had a job as an editor again, (Oh, happy day!) which, Judy tells me, infused in me new confidence and pride. In spite of that, the circumstances of the job were, shall I say, not in my best interest, so I left and took a job as a paralegal with the Legal Center of My Sisters' Place, Inc., which represents abused women in their family court matters—another way to keep my promise to Lisa. When I finally got *that* job, I quit running the weekly support group for battered women I'd been co-facilitating (as a volunteer) for about eight years.

So that's the story of my work life, but a woman cannot live by bread alone. She needs love and support, especially when she's still healing from intense trauma. And I got plenty of both from my family, old friends who returned, new friends who sympathized, my psychiatrist Sam Klagsbrun, who continued to see me gratis, and the members of a support group for battered women (the same one I later co-facilitated). Without the affection and comfort of all these champions, I couldn't have continued to grow into the person I am today.

These days I'm living far from New York State. I moved shortly before Joel was released from prison, but not just to avoid him. Instead of running *from*, I was traveling *to* a new and wonderful life adventure.

Much has also happened in the legal arena. From the time of Joel's trial, both he and I were being sued by both children's birth mothers. Nicole Smigiel dropped all her suits, even the one against Joel—I assume to take Travis out of the spotlight and give him a normal upbringing. But Michele Launders continued her wrongful death suit, which went on for years. Finally, in October 1999, there was a settlement. She'd get $985,000 from New York City, and I agreed donate $500 to a charity that would help abused children. Joel, who's considered liable for Lisa's death because of his conviction, may still have to pay a money judgment to Ms. Launders—if he ever shows that he has assets. Currently, he claims to have none—a specious contention, if I've ever heard one.

Because of Joel's claim to indigence, even though I won the right to sue him in civil court for my many injuries, I've not pursued the case. I was satisfied, as was my attorney, Betty Levinson, to have won a precedent for other battered women to toll (picture a dropping of a toll gate that stops the counting of time going by) the statute of limitations if the women are proven unable to function in society for up to ten years after the abuse. We had a hearing on this matter in the fall of 1994, much of which was televised on Court TV; we did not get a decision on it until March 1997. The decision allowed the tolling of the one-year civil statute of limitations in New York for assault in the circumstances described above. So I *could* sue Joel for the entire nine years that he abused me, but I didn't because of his poverty claim. But if we ever learn that he's dug up that stash I'm sure he has somewhere, he won't have it for long.

From the time I'd sued Joel in 1988 and during the entire three-and-a-half year wait for the decision on that hearing, Betty Levinson, being a cautious attorney, didn't want me doing any public speaking. I might say something that would go on record and hurt the case. To me, this was agony. I had an intense desire to fulfill my promise to Lisa and give public talks and also one to get a positive decision for other battered women. Finally, Betty and I reached a compromise, and I began giving talks about domestic violence in general, but not about my own case. However, after the favorable decision in *Nussbaum v. Steinberg*, I was able to talk about my own situation. Since that time, I've given well over 50 lectures at colleges, universities, women's groups, synagogues, and other gatherings. These give me great satisfaction, especially when women come up to me at the end and tell me how the information I've given them has opened their eyes. And sometimes a woman has informed me that hearing my testimony at Joel's trial motivated her to leave her abusive husband or to change the focus of her job as a social worker. Then I know I'm fulfilling not only my promise to Lisa, but my destiny in this life.

Epilogue

What I've Learned since Joel

Before I met Joel Steinberg, I knew nothing about abusive relationships. They were something that happened to other people—not *me*. In the family in which I grew up, I was considered the baby and was coddled and overprotected. Neither of my parents was ever abusive in any way. I was never hit or spanked—not even once—by either of them. In fact, I had a childhood that, except for a few weird relatives, was so normal, it's quite boring. With this kind of upbringing, I was very trusting. Why would anyone who loves me ever hurt me in any way? Abuse was a concept that never even entered my brain. But I learned—the hard way.

In order to spare others that fate, I've given numerous talks around the country, mostly to college students and domestic violence organizations. One of the most popular aspects of those lectures is my list of warning signs.

Warning Signs of an Abusive Partner

1. He's pushing the relationship too far, too fast. Is planning your future together from the moment you meet.
2. He hates his mother and is nasty to her. Chances are he'll treat you the same way.

3. He wants your undivided attention at all times.

4. You feel controlled because he must always "be in charge."

5. He's very competitive and always has to win.

6. He breaks promises all the time.

7. He can't take criticism and always justifies his actions.

8. He blames someone else for anything that goes wrong—often that someone is you.

9. He's jealous of your close friends and family members.

10. He's jealous of any man you talk to, always asks you where you went, whom you saw.

11. He has extreme highs and lows—both unpredictable.

12. He has a nasty temper.

13. He has no respect for your opinion. Always says you don't know what you're talking about.

14. He makes you feel like you're not good enough.

15. He withdraws his love or approval as punishment.

16. He pushes you to do things that make you feel uneasy—like taking the day off from school or work or doing something illegal.

This list isn't, by any means, complete. There are other warning signs, but these are pretty common to abusive men. And let me get this clear right now: 95 percent of all abusers are men, so although some women are also abusive, in the above list, I referred to abusers as "he."

Why do some men act in these ways? Why would anyone want to abuse another person? Research has shown that the main cause of abuse is the desire for power and control over an intimate partner. A man doesn't abuse a woman because of what *she's* done—even though that's the excuse he uses. He does it because of his own need for power and control.

The Domestic Abuse Intervention Project in Duluth, Minnesota, came up with a Power and Control Wheel that has been used around the country and probably around the world for quite a few years now to educate both abused women and those who work with them. Because of the page size, I've eliminated some of the text in the chart (that would have been too small to read) and have included it in the copy that follows.

As you can see, the man will use the following: Coercion and Threats (making and/or carrying out threats to do something to her; threatening to leave her, commit suicide, or report her to welfare; making her drop charges; making her do illegal things); Intimidation (making her afraid by using looks, actions, and gestures; smashing things; destroying her property; abusing pets; displaying weapons); Emotional Abuse (putting her down; making her feel bad about herself; calling her names; making her think she's crazy; playing mind games; humiliating her; making her feel guilty); Isolation (controlling what she does, who she sees and talks to, what she reads, and where she goes; limiting her outside involvement; using jealousy to justify actions); Blaming, Minimizing, and Denying (making light of the abuse and not taking her concerns about it seriously; saying the abuse didn't happen; shifting responsibility for abusive behavior; saying she caused it); Using Children (making her feel guilty about the children; using the children to relay messages; using visitation to harass her; threatening to take the children away); Male Privilege (treating her like a servant; making all the big decisions; acting like the "master of the castle," being the one to define men's and women's roles); and Economic Abuse (preventing her from getting or keeping a job; making her ask for money; giving her an allowance; taking her money; not letting her know about or have access to family income), all as tools of Power and Control. Rotating around those items on the wheel are physical and sexual violence, which happen in addition to all the rest.

At this point in my narrative, the way Joel used each of the spokes in the Power and Control wheel should be obvious. Although his "helping" method of gaining control was somewhat unique, its effect on me was typical of what happens to any woman in an abusive household. Very slowly, without her realizing it, she becomes a victim because he's taken away all her power.

If she could see what's happening (assuming she's a normal, healthy woman—something most abused women are when they begin the relationship), we must suppose she'd find some way to extricate herself from the situation. But in most cases, she's blind to the reality and continues to try and please him. After all, he's convinced her that his abuse is all her fault anyway.

Typically, he's been complaining about how she looks and what she does. She wears her skirts too short, she's too fat, she doesn't keep the house clean enough, or she's a terrible cook. So, since she believes him and thinks all the bad stuff is her fault, she begins wearing her skirts longer, losing weight, keeping the house spotless, or taking cooking classes. But do her efforts satisfy him? Of course not, since the skirt length, the weight, the dirty house, and the bad cooking aren't the real reasons for his complaints. The real reason is to get power and control over her. Once she accedes to his demands, he finds something else to complain about. As long as this pattern continues, the end result will be the same: He gains a little control, she loses a little and ends up feeling more and more frustrated.

"So why doesn't she just leave?" you may ask.

Well, for a battered woman, it's not a matter of "just." There is a host of reasons for her staying, and as I do in my talks, I will here list a few of the most common ones.

- Like me, she loves the guy.
- Like me, she thinks it's her fault and keeps working to make it better.
- Though she necessarily fails every time, she has hope and keeps trying.

- She has no money and no place to go.
- She doesn't want to impose herself upon family members who have no room, especially if she has children with her.
- If she does go, she's often told to go back because, "You made you bed, and now you must lie in it," or if she's left him before and then returned, "You may as well go back now because you'll do it eventually anyway."
- She's scared to leave. And well she should be because at the time a woman leaves or even threatens to leave, statistics show she's in the most danger of being killed by her abuser.

Joel never threatened to kill me, and I never feared that he would. But any abusive man can become a killer—intentionally or not.

One of the most difficult things for me to realize about myself coming out of the extremely traumatic life I'd lived with Joel, is that I had symptoms of what is called by Judith Lewis Herman, MD in her book, *Trauma and Recovery*, complex post-traumatic stress disorder.

Earlier in this book I talked about one such symptom that I definitely manifested: numbing due to endogenous opioids secreted by my brain. Another that I clearly experienced was disempowerment during my years with Joel.

Still yet another symptom, or group of symptoms, of this disorder that I demonstrated is described by Herman as follows:

"Alterations in perception of perpetrator, including
- preoccupation with relationship with perpetrator
- unrealistic attribution of total power to perpetrator
- idealization of paradoxical gratitude
- sense of special or supernatural relationship
- acceptance of belief system or rationalizations of perpetrator"

It's because of such beliefs that in 1987 I was whisked off to a psychiatric hospital. And thank goodness for that. Because there I was able to become empowered again and to create new connections—ones that weren't controlling or abusive, ones I could trust.

Herman says that recovery from extreme long-term trauma evolves in three stages: safety, remembrance and mourning, and reconnection with ordinary life. And looking back, I can see how my experiences at both Neuro

12 and Four Winds provided me with those things, step by step.

So when the time came to go out on my own, I was able to do it—with the help and psychological nourishment of Dr. Klagsbrun, the battered women's support group, loving family, and compassionate friends.

And here I am today, a woman transformed into—to quote my "Muse"—a woman of "strong fibers, tough meat, intense heart" who has overcome the mental and emotional debilitation that was forced upon me by an evil and controlling man.

Afterword

By Samuel C. Klagsbrun, MD

I was totally convinced that Hedda was a deeply pathological masochist when she was first admitted to Four Winds Hospital, having heard her grim story from the press and having seen her deeply scarred features on TV. I took for granted that the reason she had not run away from Joel Steinberg was that she had derived some twisted gratification from the beatings, the abuse, and the brutal torture she endured. In my mind, I knew the answer. I now only needed to verify it and to work with Hedda to tackle the source of her masochism.

Three months later, having failed completely to unearth any inclination toward masochism, having delved into her upbringing in great detail, including interviewing her parents and her sister, and having found no evidence to support that theory, I finally became available to listening to Hedda with an open mind. All my years of training, which taught me what masochism was, had apparently deafened me to hearing her story.

And so the question, " Why did this well brought up woman who had established an identity for herself in part as a children's published author, a children's editor in a major publishing house, an attractive, light-hearted, comfortable woman, succumb to the pathologically evil Joel Steinberg?"

473

Hedda's initial experience with Joel was romantic, exciting, sensuous, and more profound than she had ever experienced with anyone else up to that time. Once Joel felt that he had achieved a powerful influence over her, his need to subjugate her to his control and demonstrate total mastery over her knew no bounds. When Hedda experienced her first slap at his hand, she was stunned. But Joel immediately held her, kissed her and made her feel that it was simply an overreaction on his part. As the beatings and tortures escalated, Hedda had by then fallen so deeply under his control that she actually wondered what she had done to push this wonderful, wonderful man to behave in such an uncharacteristic fashion. It was all her fault.

It's not as if Hedda wasn't aware on occasions that her life had deteriorated into a bizarre pattern. In fact, she had even tried to run away from him on six separate occasion, only to return out of fear, as well as out of an inability by then to exercise her own judgment and rely on her own ego to make decisions and try to fend for herself. Joel had by then successfully isolated her. He had her leave her work, forbidden her family from visiting or calling, and separated her from all her friends. He had in effect taken over total control and forced her to become completely dependent on him.

And so the first answer to the question, "How could she have tolerated the abuse in the relationship?" is that she had gradually become totally dependent on him and felt that in fact there was no way to escape and survive on her own.

The question however remains: "How did she feel about the situation she was in?" The awful answer to that question is that at a certain point there was no such thing as "feeling" anything anymore. Hedda's beatings and tortures were so incessant that her entire focus was on sheer survival and, as much as possible, avoiding pain. Her whole being was aimed at anticipating any behavior which might elicit a torturous beating from Joel. She lived not only from day to day but also literally from moment to moment. Whenever there was a lull in the torture, she was able to simply escape into the absence of pain for that brief moment. There was no capacity to think about the future, to analyze her circumstances, make a decision, and act. There was only the focus on survival and avoidance of pain. That was the goal of every moment. That was survival.

Finally, "How did Hedda come back to health, independence, self-efficiency, and even an ability to develop new relationships?" That's where Hedda became my teacher in a profound and surprising way. In the beginning of our work, the horror of her life, the murder of their child, Lisa, at Joel's hands, and the erasure of her identity were the main foci of our work. The most puzzling, frustrating and, I will admit, irritating aspect of the initial work with Hedda was that at first, she never got as angry at Joel as I was. I inquired about anger, rage, and resentment and got a noncommittal response. I even tried modeling my anger, my own murderous rage at him for her as a way of encouraging that form of expression, all to no avail. I finally thought that what was necessary was to help Hedda become her own unique person again first before being able to confront the image of Joel in her mind.

Quite accidentally it turned out that Hedda expressed an interest in photography. We created a darkroom for her, made a camera available, and she went to town. Her investment in this totally different, new, and safe interest became intense; she spent many hours shooting, developing, and printing some remarkable photographs culminating, in fact, in a photography show open to the public at the hospital. As her identity took shape, as she began feeling the precious joy of recognition from others for the work she was doing, her identity took shape again.

As her personality began to emerge, she was able to go back and begin the work of reconstructing what had happened to her. It became clear in our therapy sessions that part of the hold that Joel had on her was in fact based on her own profound longing for the love she had experienced in the initial stages of the relationship. The intensity of the image of Joel as her mentor, her lover, her security, had swept her up with such intensity that she could almost not bear to see the man as he really was because that would destroy the image she longed to hold on to. The hardest work we had to do, in fact, was to take this incredible, positive early image and put it side by side with the reality of who he now was, her horrible life with him along with the murder of the child, and allow her to take distance from the image, which she longed to hold on to.

Hedda was first able to accept the evil of this man when she read an article in which Joel was quoted as not only denying that he had ever hit her but also even more so denying that he had killed Lisa. It was that denial which ironically became a turning point for Hedda, finally allowing her to begin the process of fighting back and liberating herself from him. It was at that moment that she began a lawsuit, opening the door to the long arduous therapeutic process undoing the brainwashing he had so successfully put her through. One year later, Hedda was emotionally, finally liberated.

As part of her own healing, Hedda was able to take her own experience, take what she learned from it, and use it to counsel other women who are victims of domestic violence. Hedda, my teacher, taught me a tremendous amount about the ability of people to deny, in fact, ignore horrible reality for the sake of holding on to a profound wish and suffering terrible damage as a consequence of that need. Hedda's inner strength of character once she was out of the horrible situation she had been in for so long allowed her, with help, to reemerge, to reconnect to healthy people, and to move forward in her life. It is a statement of incredible strength and courage, and I feel privileged to have been a part of it.

Printed in the United States
48928LVS00004B/47